Korean War era /
Peter A. Soderbergh

WOMEN MARINES

Women Marines

IN THE KOREAN WAR ERA

Peter A. Soderbergh

FOREWORD by
Eleanor M. Wilson

PRAEGER

Westport, Connecticut
London

Library of Congress Cataloging-in-Publication Data

Soderbergh, Peter A.
    Women marines in the Korean War era / Peter A. Soderbergh;
foreword by Colonel Eleanor M. Wilson.
        p.   cm.
    Includes bibliographical references and index.
    ISBN 0-275-94827-7
    1. United States. Marine Corps Women's Reserve—History—Korean
War, 1950–1953. 2. Korean War, 1950–1953—United States.
I. Title.
DS920.5.M37S66   1994
951.904′2—dc20   94-8382

British Library Cataloguing in Publication Data is available.

Library of Congress Catalog Card Number: 94-8382
ISBN: 0-275-94827-7

First published in 1994

Praeger Publishers, 88 Post Road West, Westport, CT 06881
An imprint of Greenwood Publishing Group, Inc.

Printed in the United States of America

The paper used in this book complies with the
Permanent Paper Standard issued by the National
Information Standards Organization (Z39.48-1984).

10 9 8 7 6 5 4 3 2 1

To the thin green line: Those dedicated Women Marines who served Corps and country during the turbulent years that enveloped the "forgotten war" in Korea, . . . and

To the 4,262 U.S. Marines who gave their lives in defense of the Republic of Korea between 1950 and 1953.

Semper Fidelis

Contents

Photographs follow page 67.

Foreword

Since the inception of Women Reservists (WRs) into military service in 1943 and the integration status achieved by Women Marines (WMs) in 1948, and continuing to the present day, Women Marines have maintained a proud tradition of excellence, discipline, and professionalism. They have served their nation and their Corps with dignity, devotion, and patriotic zeal. The uncertain path has not been an easy one as they battled the forces of discrimination, apathy, and threats to their survival as an integral part of the Marine Corps' mission of a force in readiness.

Throughout the years, under the superb leadership of Colonels Streeter, Towle, and Hamblet, and of those who followed, Women Marines have persevered, excelled, and performed their duties as a vital part of the strength and spirit of the Corps. "Once a Marine, Always a Marine" is not only a motto, but also a way of life—an essence instilled in every Marine from his or her training experience until the day the heart beats no longer.

This book is written by a man with firsthand knowledge of combat and its painful effect on human sensibilities. He is driven by a compelling desire to write this social history not only to honor the memories of Women Marines who served the Corps admirably, but also to honor the memory of his comrades-in-arms of the Korean conflict, for whom closure has never been attained. Thus, while this synapse of time encapsulates the years 1948–1955, that is, the seven year period between the signing of the Women's Armed Services Integration Act in June 1948

to the withdrawal of the First Marine Division from Korea in the spring
of 1955, the tradition of *Semper Fidelis* (Always Faithful) is timeless.

Dr. Soderbergh's first fascination with the subject of the military service of Women Marines is contained in his volume *Women Marines:
The World War II Era,* published in 1992. This new venture springs
forth from untapped emotions remaining from the first volume—a "frustration at belonging to a 'lost generation' of Korean War veterans" and
a belief that these feelings are also felt by his female contemporaries.
Only those who served during that period in history can answer that
question. It is apparent from numerous media sources that the frustra-
tions, feelings of rejection by society (of which Dr. Soderbergh gives
examples), and the lack of validation of the police action as it impacted
each service member, is very real. During the Korean War era resolution
of conflict, we, as a nation, failed to bring our troops home as warriors—
to a parade and accolades of praise for a job well done. Only now, forty
years later, will we dedicate a memorial (proposed for Washington,
D.C., July 1995).

As the events of the years 1948–1955 unfold, we are treated not only
to remembrances of the eighty women with whom the author corresponded, but to the intertwining of occurrences in the timeline of history
on the international, national, and local scenes—the pulse of the U.S.
citizens as they go about their daily lives—a nostalgic look at their lei-
sure activities of books, movies, music, and the "who" or "what" was
popular during that period. Dr. Soderbergh sets the stage with historical
facts and statistics, governmental roles and climates as political parties
shuffle power. This extensive research of libraries, research centers, archives, and personal interviews brings forth a thorough depiction of the
struggle Women Marines had for validation of their existence and their
mission, as well as the warm remembrances of years too funny and too
significant to ever forget. He includes his personal reflections during the
Korean conflict and the absence of closure on those events.

The content of the book depicts the earliest WRs as "pioneers" in
uncharted territory and reveals the motivations which prompted them to
join the service. He discusses the critical periods where the need for
Women Marines as members of the active Marine Corps is questioned,
such as during Generals Vandegrift's and Thomas's stewardship; of the
desire of women to serve and the steadfastness with which they proved
their worthiness as an integral part of the Corps' mission. He describes
the events leading up to the National Security Act of July 26, 1947,
which legislated the Marine Corps to the roles of amphibious assault
specialists and force in readiness. Treated with the respect they deserve
are the significant contributions during this sequence of time by Colo-

nels Streeter, Towle, and Hamblet, whose professionalism paved the way for future generations of Women Marines.

The reminiscences of "boot camp" experience will trigger both delight and humorous feelings as women relate their thoughts of bonding, pride, and feelings of accomplishment in learning that "there are no limitations except those we place on ourselves." This is the essence of what every Marine learns from training, be he or she officer or enlisted—it makes no difference—a Marine emerges from the training cycle with the spirit of self-confidence and pride in belonging to a cohesive unit with a proud tradition of service. Whether military service takes the form of one enlistment or one career, the training experience and the pride derived therefrom carry through a lifetime and can be recalled whenever needed.

As the Korean conflict begins, we see the mobilization of enlisted women, and again, discussions arise as to how to employ them. Dr. Soderbergh relates the patterns of attitudes and discussions of acceptance and non-acceptance of Women Marines as an integral part of the Corps. He touches on the sensitive issues of homosexuality and racism as related to him in interviews and during the course of his research, pointing to the fact that the military is a microcosm of society.

A sea of changes was taking place during this period, and as LaVergne Novak so aptly describes the prevalent attitude, "The whole atmosphere surrounding the Korean War was entirely different from the days of World War II. . . . In World War II the whole country was at war. . . . In the Korean War, only the military and naval services were at war. For the rest of the country it was business as usual." The author describes the scant treatment of the war by the print media and television and the minimal coverage of Women Marines' contributions. Again, questions arise in his mind as to the understanding of the conflict, but his descriptions are no more poignant than his recounting of events that took place on Hill 104 and the painful recollections of the devastation in human life that occurred there.

We return with him to Hill 104 as he relives those indelible moments that pierce the pages of the manuscript with utter horror of the events, of the loss of bonded brothers of Company A—too much for his mind to comprehend. He will never forget them, nor will we. The traditions of the Corps dictate that we shall *never* forget those who do not return. As Marines all over the world celebrate the Corps' birthday 10 November of each year, the past, present, and future of the Corps is celebrated. Marines *do* remember; they *do* honor and recognize the contributions of those into whose footprints we step with great honor and respect. But for those of the "Forgotten War," unanswered questions still persist, and each must reach closure in his or her own way. The author has chosen his method of healing and, in so doing, has left us with a social history to be enjoyed by generations to follow.

As the WM story continues, the enormous contributions of Colonels Streeter and Towle and, then, Major Hamblet are presented. Unfortunately, there still existed an attitude of ambivalence toward Women Marines and a lack of knowledge as to the most advantageous means to employ them. To male Marines, women were "intruders." Often, they were forced to leave the Corps simply because of dependent status. Through resilience, tenacity, and courage, Women Marines continued to serve to the best of their abilities. The Armistice in 1953 brought a posturing by North Korea and a view toward reunifying the country (a concept which persists today). But for those combat Marines who served in Korea, there was no finality to the conflict; no conclusion; neither monuments nor recognition.

As the Eisenhower era brought funding cutbacks, the attitudes towards Women Marines and their roles and contributions began to change for the better. Interviewees discuss their unique experiences during this time, some of whom served a short period of time and left the service, while others contributed insight into their military careers. But if one were to look for the common denominator that threads its way through the entire effort placed on this social history, it would be the bonding or the solidarity of the spirit of Marines, be they male or female.

This bonding, which is shared by all Marines, is a trust in fellow man and in the Corps—a leap of faith. It is a sense of "self" tied to a need for connection or attachment to others who serve this worthwhile cause. In their pursuit of excellence, these men and women who served and continue to do so share the experience of belonging to a unique organization. The friendships and loyalties fostered during their service transcend time. The bonding and trust felt by comrades-in-arms in combat situations such as described by Dr. Soderbergh's experiences are so vivid in his mind that he will never forget their sacrifices, while the women about whom he writes feel the fierce loyalties to those with whom they have served—as kindred souls. The contributions of all Marines during the Korean conflict, those who returned and those who did not, remain as a building block in the wall of the history of the legions of the Corps—"Lest We Forget"—that precious something that can only be appreciated by, and entrusted to, those who have earned the honor of wearing the EAGLE, GLOBE, and ANCHOR. Semper Fi, Marines!

Eleanor M. Wilson
Colonel, U.S. Marine Corps Reserve

Acknowledgments

The people who participated in this project will understand if I say that I owe my greatest debt to the former WRs (Women Reservists) and WMs (Women Marines) who provided their memories and memorabilia. Had they not been so forthcoming and so trusting I could not have completed this volume on women who served in the U.S. Marines during the Korean War era (1948–1955).

I wish it had been possible to mention in the text the names of every one of the eighty women who responded to my inquiries, and to have included all the splendid photographs they offered for my consideration. I know the contributors are aware that space limitations and the desirability of literary balance impose constraints upon every writer. I accepted the former *a priori,* and strove to achieve the latter by being selective with the abundance of material I received. In short, I am responsible for whatever sins of omission and commission readers identify as they move through this tribute to a heroic generation of America's womanhood.

I hope it will be obvious that I care very much about the following fellow Marines: Marie E. Anderson, Edrey (Schendel) Anker, Delphine (Biaggi) Baeta, Ethel L. Barker, Gladys (DeKlotz) Beale, Mabel K. Bennett, Bertha (Peters) Billeb, Carol (Kramer) Blair, Betty (Moore) Brich, Doris (Reeves) Brown, Margaret (Zemien) Brown, Virginia (Dupuy) Brown, Ann (Homza) Burke, Grace A. Carle, Edna Mae Cogswell, Joan M. Collins, Dolores C. Cressy, Wilma (Shaw) DeiCas, J. June Dempsey, Mae (Sande) Duge, Anne (Emser) Ferguson, Myrtle (Seavey) Furst, Gladys E. Gaillard, Edna (Stein) Garrett, Joan (Walter) Gerichten, Annie

L. Grimes, Connie (Musumeci) Guaraglia, Lenore (Sandager) Hansen, Fern P. Hauss, Clare (Bullitt) Hokanson, Carol J. Homan, Anna (Orlando) Hopkins, Joan (Kammer) Horton, Mary M. Jamison, Ellen M. Juhre, Ann (Sloan) Kielty, Joyce (Bechtel) Knapp, Barbara J. Lee, Betty (Patterson) Lewis, Evelyn H. Liringis, Jayne (Burgess) Loraine, Mary (Boyd) Lum, Jean (Willett) Martin, Carol R. McCutcheon, Maurene L. Miller, Rosemary (Thompson) Morrison, Maria (Matta) Muniz, La-Vergne R. Novak, Virginia Ruth Painter, Althea M. Partch, Clara (Lapean) Poulsen, Marie A. Proulx, Patricia (Logan) Quilty, Dorothy Mae (Griffin) Rice, Olga (Lanzione) Rogers, Lois (Ernst) Ross, Eleanor (Bach) Russell, Bonita (Carlisle) Salamanca, Patty (Stamper) Schindler, Josie (Pracht) Schueler, Paula (Wiltshire) Sentipal, Pearl (Morris) Shaklee, Dolores Shutt, Dorothy (Bode) Sieben, Gene D. Sims, Dolly (Katzer) Smart, Mary Ann (Bernard) Soderbergh, Theresa (Malone) Sousa, Mary (Vertalino) Stremlow, Barbara Ann (Hollar) Thompson, Josephine (Janco) Tibbetts, Charlene (Enders) Turner, Marilyn (Rehm) Verna, Mary Lou (Clough) Voight, Rosemary (Cardamone) Voorhees, Esther D. Waclawski, Joyce (Pulliam) Wallace, Ada (Hazel) Wells, Ruth (Barakat) Wirstad, and Anne (Youngblood) Zink.

These women's recollections were the foundation of this book. I then turned to individuals whose expertise I felt was indispensable to shaping my raw material into a colorful, accurate study. Foremost among my reinforcements was Colonel Mary V. Stremlow USMCR (Ret.), author of the only official history of Women Marines in the post–World War II period (1946–1977). Not only did I rely heavily upon her monograph (1986), I was granted access to her collection of materials on women in the military. Throughout 1993 she was always generous and patient when I requested assistance, which I did frequently. I have in mind also Colonel Julia E. Hamblet USMC (Ret.), who prepared a foreword for my earlier study, *Women Marines: The World War II Era* (1992). Her career covered both World War II and Korea and she was director of WMs from 1953 to 1959. Colonel Hamblet was kind enough to handle my pesky questions graciously. I am grateful for her insights into what was a difficult period in WM history. The last director of WMs—and the first women general officer in the Corps—Brigadier General Margaret A. Brewer USMC (Ret.) sent me a statement that capsulized her remembrances of the status of WMs in the 1950s and 1960s. I found her comments invaluable, coming as they did from someone who knew what it was like to be at both the bottom and the top of the officer corps.

Naturally, I am extremely grateful to Colonel Eleanor M. Wilson USMCR for supplying the fine foreword to this volume. Colonel Wilson was commissioned in 1968 and promoted to her present rank in 1988.

Her career has been a remarkable blend of military, civic, and educational services. In addition to her B.A. from San Jose State University she holds three master's degrees, one of which is from the College of Naval Warfare in Newport, Rhode Island. Among her numerous board memberships are the Board of Directors of the Marine Corps Aviation Association, the Advisory Board of the MCAS (Marine Corps Air Station) El Toro Historical Foundation, and the National Board of Directors of the Marine Corps Historical Foundation. She has also served on the Marine Corps Reserve Policy Board in Washington, D.C. I am flattered that she found time in her busy professional schedule to prepare an overture to this tribute to her predecessors.

In the course of my research efforts I visited the Marine Corps Historical Center in Washington, D.C. I want to express my appreciation to the center's executive director, Brigadier General Edwin H. Simmons USMC (Ret.), and his colleagues for their cooperation. They directed me to the materials I sought and then left me to my own devices. I felt quite comfortable there. As he did in 1991, Brigadier General Louie C. Reinberg USMC (Ret.) kept me supplied with current issues of the *Marine Corps Gazette* and other periodicals crucial to my comprehension of what is happening in the Corps today. I thank him for that, again. Colonel John Reily Love USMC (Ret.) gave me a photograph of his lovely wife—former WM Lieutenant Beverly Schofield—who passed away in 1993. "Bev" served on active duty from 1953 to 1960. Colonel Love and I felt she would have contributed to this book had she lived a little longer and I am pleased that Colonel Love gave me permission to include her among her contemporaries. May she, and all WMs who have departed this life, rest in perpetual peace.

I am indebted also to: former Marines Mary (Cugini) Necko and Wilma (Shaw) DeiCas for permission to study their letters to relatives covering the period 1945–1946 and 1952–1955, respectively, and Mary Ann (Copp) Murphy and Virginia (Shepherd) Allred of the Women Marines Association (WMA) who rendered meritorious assistance during the formative phases of this project; Dan Eades of the Greenwood Publishing Group, Inc. of Westport, Connecticut, for his faith in my proposals and his flexibility when I had problems along the way; three young women who took my handwritten material and made it worthy of presentation to my publisher, Jennifer Tullier, Nikki Dement, and Kelly York; and to my wife, Kathryn. It has not been an easy year for either of us—but she never complained about playing second fiddle (temporarily) to eighty women she did not know. Her understanding was the key to my remaining civil to those who had the misfortune to be near me in 1993. But then, that is how she is. *Semper Fidelis,* Kat.

Introduction

As I was preparing the initial volume in this series, *Women Marines: The World War II Era* (1992), I grew increasingly impressed with the qualities of the women of the World War II generation. For over a year I corresponded with 146 former Women Reservists (WRs), studied their faces in the precious, faded photographs they had saved for forty-odd years, read the letters they mailed to their families, and savored both the amusing and the tragic experiences they were willing to share with a stranger.

To say that these women, most of whom are septuagenarians now, were (and are) a special breed is an understatement. Gallant is more to the point. They were pioneers who broke new ground in Marine Corps history and in the history of women in America. Of the 300,000 women who served in our nation's armed forces between 1942 and 1945 more than 20,000 wore Marine Corps uniforms. For the most part these "girls" came from small towns, were innocent in the ways of the flesh, enlisted with either little or no support from their parents and boyfriends, traded the security of "home" for the unknown, and plunged headlong into the arcane world of the Corps armed with only youthful exuberance.

Their motives for doing so varied but, overwhelmingly, they joined up for patriotic reasons. Entranced by the ethos that characterized the "good war" they responded to the Corps' request that they "Free a Marine to Fight." The WRs did that, and more. Their presence in the ranks of a previously all-male, elitist organization was the leavening agent that forced a reluctant Marine Corps to modify many of its practices and attitudes. At first the women were met with cool tolerance. In time WRs earned the respect of the Corps' leaders—and captured the hearts of thousands of their male counterparts. These women were competent, courageous, feisty when it was warranted, well-groomed always, and loyal to country and Corps. They were serious about their assignments. They seldom lost sight of the mission they were expected to fulfill. In fact, by 1945 there were sufficient members of WRs to equal a full Marine division.

I discovered also that the passage of nearly five decades had not dimmed their devotion to the Corps. Almost without exception they told me that they treasured their experiences right into the 1990s. Many credited that training with giving them the strength to overcome the personal problems they encountered later in life. Many looked back upon the war years as an interlude unsurpassed in excitement and self-satisfaction; as a phase to be cherished independently from whatever else they accomplished. There is no group of women quite like them. "Semper Fidelis" (Always Faithful) and "Once a Marine, Always a Marine" are not mere slogans. Those words express sentiments each woman holds dear to this day. "Always" is the key word in these mottoes. The term "ex-Marine" has no place in their vocabularies. In the late 1950s, searching for a vehicle through which their ideals might be preserved, a cadre of veterans organized the Women Marines Association (WMA). Its premiere national reunion in Denver in 1960 was attended by 125 women. Today, the WMA is 3,000 members strong. At its biennial conventions hundreds of women gather to honor the past, renew friendships, and celebrate their common military heritage.

On the occasion of the fiftieth anniversary of the activation of the Marine Corps' female component (February 13, 1943), the current Commandant of the Marine Corps, General Carl E. Mundy, Jr., delivered a message to former women Marines via the WMA's newsletter:

> Throughout the past half century, women marines have significantly contributed to the success of the Corps. Whether in the sands of Saudi Arabia or on the homefront, women marines have displayed the undaunting courage, spirit and honor of the Corps. . . . Semper Fidelis, Marines.[1]

This is an appropriate moment to rewind our historical tape to February 13, 1946, the WRs' third birthday, and review what one of General Mundy's predecessors had to say about his female Marines. General Alexander A. Vandegrift, Commandant from January 1, 1944 to December 31, 1947, circulated an open letter to all WRs dated February 13.

He, too, was very complimentary, saying that the women should be proud of the new chapter in the Corps' history they "helped to write." However, Vandegrift made it plain that he did not expect (nor did he really want) to witness another anniversary in 1947. "By the time February 13 comes again," he said, "the [MCWR] will no longer be on active duty." He wished them well "in the years to come" and, privately, struck the MCWR from his long list of immediate concerns. Colonel Katherine A. Towle, director of the MCWR since December 7, 1945, released her statement on February 13 also. In both tone and content her message was much the same as the Commandant's. She acknowledged that her WRs had established a record of "honorable and fruitful service" during the war, and affirmed that in the "not too distant future the [MCWR] will cease to exist."[2]

As far as the Corps' leadership was concerned, the experiment was over. The women had performed admirably, to be sure—but it was time to return to pre-war conditions. As early as October 1945 Brigadier General Gerald C. Thomas, then the head of the Corps' Division of Plans and Policies, expressed his view in a memorandum to General Vandegrift. "The opinion generally held by the Marine Corps," he wrote, "is that women have no proper place or function in the regular service in peace-time." Where did they belong, then? "The American tradition is that a woman's place is in the home," Thomas said, and he was by no means espousing a minority opinion. As Mary V. Stremlow observed in her landmark work, *A History of the Women Marines, 1946–1977* (1986), the majority of both male and female Marines "displayed a marked lack of enthusiasm toward the prospect of women in the postwar Marine Corps" (p. 1).

The magic word during the months following the defeat of Japan in August 1945 was "demobilization." The Marine Corps truly believed its "distaff members" would be discharged and at home no later than September 1, 1946. Obviously, that was a major miscalculation on the Corps' part. Forces had been set in motion which it could not control. When the dust settled in 1948 the WRs were still in uniform, all 167 of them. Within five years there were 2,662 and the Corps was very glad to have them. There were some rocky times ahead for WMs, as we shall see. But the fact that in 1994 nearly 8,000 females are on active duty is a tribute to the women who stepped into the breach in the late 1940s. They are the "thin green line" referred to in this book.

The subtitle of this volume, "The Korean War Era," needs some clarification. I see that "era" as encompassing the years 1948–1955 or, to be more precise, taking as its central focus the seven-year period between the signing of the Women's Armed Services Integration Act into law in June 1948 and the withdrawal of the First Marine Division from Korea to California in the spring of 1955. A start and a finish. In the former case, the beginning of "regular" service for Women Marines; in the latter instance, the end of the Korean episode for the Marine Corps.

Of course, the Korean War is not over. The cease-fire implemented on July 27, 1953, after thirty-seven months of warfare, only stopped the combat operations. Today, there are 36,000 U.S. troops in Korea south of the Demilitarized Zone (DMZ) and our diplomatic relations with the North Korean government vacillate between diffident and hostile. Thirty years ago military historian S.L.A. Marshall, in his *The Military History of the Korean War* (1963), concluded his manuscript with a statement that still applies:

> The war itself never ended. In theory, it is going on today. There is only an armistice in Korea, not a formal peace, for no treaty in final settlement was ever signed. The two sides merely stacked their arms, having grown weary of the struggle . . . Should there occur another aggression out of the North, America would be automatically at war. (p. 86)

Later in this text we will explore where the Korean War resides in the public mind. For the moment it will suffice to say that it dwells in an historical limbo of sorts. To employ a term made familiar by the Korean experience, the 1950–1953 war floats in a DMZ in the national imagination. Few people are sure what it was all about. It is suspended between "the glories of World War II and the agonies of Vietnam," former CBS correspondent George Herman noted, "and we have forgotten it."[3] It neither scarred nor aroused us. We neither won it nor lost it. "Compared with the two great wars that preceded it," James Stokesbury wrote in *A Short History of the Korean War* (1988), "Korea was a half-war, in which some Americans were all too involved and most were not involved at all" (p. 253). Anyone who served in our armed forces during the late and largely unlamented "conflict" on the Korean peninsula risks being associated with the confusions, controversies, and contradictions that surround the war even now. At the least, he or she is unappreciated.

I am one of those who was "all too involved" in that war. I enlisted in the Marine Corps in the hot summer of 1950 because I wanted to be a Marine, not because I understood the Cold War implications of the Korean contest of wills. Five months after I graduated from boot camp at MCRD (Marine Corps Recruit Depot), Parris Island, South Carolina,

I passed through an officer candidate screening course at MCS (Marine Corps Schools), Quantico, Virginia, and received my second lieutenant's commission. In November 1951 I arrived in Korea and was assigned to "A" Company, First Battalion, Seventh Marine Regiment as a platoon commander.

On my return trip to California in 1952 we laid over for a day or so in Hawaii. It was there that I was exposed to the indifference that, in my absence, had spread throughout the country regarding the "police action" in Korea. Several of my fellow officers and I wanted very much to see the Royal Hawaiian Hotel in Honolulu. We knew it was special and thought it unlikely that we would see Hawaii again in our lifetime. Sober, respectful, and properly attired we strolled into the hotel's lobby like the gawking tourists we were. Out of nowhere came a scowling concierge. He stopped us in our tracks. "Yes, gentlemen? May I be of assistance? What is it you want?" (Nothing, really.) "Are you guests in our hotel?" (No. We're just sightseeing, actually.) "Well, I'm afraid I'll have to ask you to leave, then." (Why? Can't we look around for a minute?) "I'm very sorry. We do not allow that here. Unless you wish to register, or have lunch in our dining room?" (Well, no thanks. I mumbled something inane like, "You see, sir, we've just left Korea and we—." He was not impressed). "This way out, gentlemen." *Exeunt* three bewildered lieutenants.

At that time I was not aware of why we had been snubbed. It was puzzling, though. Perhaps Mr. Imperium was having a bad day. Had a trio of Marines torn up the lobby recently? According to all the war films I had seen between 1942 and 1950, men in transit from the battlefield to "the states" were treated like heroes. It never occurred to me that by the summer of 1952 the hotel authorities—indeed, the American people in general—were tired of thinking about the "sour little war" in the Far East. As J. Ronald Oakley observed in his *God's Country: America in the Fifties* (1986), the Korean War "was not a living-room war but a more remote conflict that generated few pacifists or protesters but few ardent supporters either. Most Americans just wanted to get it over with" (p. 94). When it was "over with" the tally was awesome: 54,246 Americans dead, 103,284 wounded, and (still) 8,140 missing in action. It cost the American taxpayer $67 billion for the three years of warfare (and $2.4 billion per year since 1953 to maintain our presence below the thirty-eighth parallel).

Korean War returnees experienced a form of rejection that foreshadowed what would happen to Vietnam veterans twenty years thereafter. They became invisible men—blotted out by the enormity of our successes in World War II, and later, buried beneath the terrible weight of the Vietnam experience. *Chicago Tribune* columnist Mike Royko spoke for many men when he told Studs Terkel:

> I remember coming back from Korea, the hostility, the indifference. I was almost embarrassed being in Korea because we didn't win. We cut a deal. We got a draw. We failed where our older brothers had won.[4]

When I completed my study of our World War II WRs several years ago I thought I was through with the subject. I turned my attention to other projects. None of them developed very far beyond some basic research. My head was "into" those topics, my heart was not. While reflecting on beginnings, F. Scott Fitzgerald acknowledged that "Whether it's something that happened twenty years ago or only yesterday, I must start out with an emotion—one that's close to me and that I can understand."[5] Clearly, I had some emotions left over from the first volume. I see now that my long-standing frustration at belonging to the "lost generation" of Korean War veterans spilled over to include my female contemporaries. Early in 1993 I opened myself up to a confluence of feelings—my devotion to the Corps, my continuing respect for the women who had the courage to become Marines, my deep-seated distress over the disparagement of the Korean War, and some unexpended stirrings from my reservoir of romanticism—and acknowledged that there was a sequel within me yelling for release. Once I admitted that, the questions began to flow and the excitement returned.

I wondered: What happened to the WRs who formed the bridge between World War II and Korea? What about the women who entered the Corps with no previous military experience? Why did they join? How do they feel about their tours as Marines? In the wake of World War II were changes effected in how WMs were trained and assigned? Was the Corps a hospitable place to be? Did the downgrading of the Korean War impact their attitudes? In short, who *were* these women?

There were not very many of them. At no time in the 1950s did their number exceed 2,700. Compared with their 20,000 forebears of World War II they were a virtual skeleton crew, and many fewer than the number of their peers on active duty with the WAC (12,000) and the WAVES (9,000). We know a good deal about their *generation* of military women from a succession of excellent works published since 1986, notably, Mary V. Stremlow's history of the Women Marines cited above; Bettie J. Morden's *The Women's Army Corps, 1945–1978* (1990), which carries forward Mattie E. Treadwell's seminal study *The*

Women's Army Corps (1954); and Jean Ebbert's and Marie-Beth Hall's *Crossed Currents: Navy Women From World War I to Tailhook* (1993). Naturally, the scope of these invaluable works is so vast that the Korean War era is touched upon rather lightly. However, they do illuminate the prevailing "climate of opinion" in which the women performed their duties and, in that sense, they are indispensable.

To uncover something more personal about Women Marines was my intent and my focus. In 1992 the Turner Publishing Company of Paducah, Kentucky, released a biographical compendium under the title *Women Marines Association.* From the 515 profiles of former WMs included therein I extracted the names of those whose years of service matched the chronological brackets I established for this volume. A member of the WMA was kind enough to provide me with a copy of the organization's directory of names and addresses. I then sent a letter of self-introduction and a questionnaire to each veteran. In addition, I placed a note for all Korean War WMs in the summer 1993 issue of the WMA *'Nouncements,* inviting them to participate in my study. Some of the respondents gave me the names of women who might not have been contacted or seen my request in the WMA newsletter. From those persons who expressed interest in this project I solicited vintage photographs, letters, and other memorabilia, which I received in sufficient quantity to enrich this text immeasurably. The women were very forthcoming with their cherished mementos. Given my positive experiences with the earlier volume, I was not surprised. The level of trust among former Marines is quite high.

If I had any lingering doubts about the value of a work such as this, they were dispelled by a letter I received from one of the participants in August 1993. After expressing her basic interest in our book she said, "Sometimes I think that we are the Forgotten Ones. Thank you in advance for doing this for us."

Thank *you,* Sergeant. You are not forgotten.

NOTES

1. General Mundy's message was printed in the Spring 1993 edition of WMA *'Nouncements,* p. 31.

2. The Commandants' and Colonel Towle's statements are taken from the February 13, 1946 issue of *The Word,* a four-page, biweekly newsletter published by Henderson Hall WRs for their own information and amusement. Statements on p. 2. Copies of *The Word* provided by Mary (Cugini) Necko.

3. Herman's remark was broadcast over CNN on Sunday, July 25, 1993.

See also James L. Greenfield's editorial "Not an Anchorman in Sight: War Correspondents Remember Korea," in *The New York Times,* July 29, 1993.

4. Studs Terkel, *"The Good War": An Oral History of World War Two* (New York: Pantheon Books, 1984), p. 138.

5. Fitzgerald's remark is included in Jon Winokur, *Writers on Writing* (Philadelphia: Running Press, 1987), p. 92.

Chapter One

The Girls of Summer

In this, the last decade of the second millennium, the presence of women in the armed forces is a fact of our lives. The familiar old acronyms—WAC, WAVES, WM, SPARS—are no more, but our women are still in uniform. They perform all the duties formerly reserved for males except direct combat with an armed enemy and, by most accounts, are doing a creditable job.

Women comprise about 11 percent of our nation's active duty forces. By the early 1990s, Jeanne Holm tells us in *Women in Military: An Unfinished Revolution* (1992), females "were so integrated into the armed forces that the United States could not have gone to war without them" (p. xiv). In our latest conflict nearly 40,000 women were posted to the Persian Gulf region. Operation Desert Shield/Storm in 1990–1991 witnessed the "largest wartime deployment of American Military women in history," Holm reports (p. xiii). Approximately 1,335 women Marines were in Saudi Arabia during that war. According to one of the Corps' official histories of that campaign, it was the "greatest participation ever of women Marines in a combat operation."[1] The commanding general of I Marine Expeditionary Force, Lieutenant General Walter E. Boomer, informed Marine Commandant General Alfred M. Gray, Jr. that their women "performed superbly."[2]

Among the many books now available that explore American women's military experiences, Molly Moore's *A Woman At War: Storming Kuwait with the U.S. Marines* (1993) is most revealing. Ms. Moore is a sharp-eyed correspondent and she understands the U.S. Marine Corps as well as any civilian can. Whether or not the Corps understands its 8,000 female members is open to question still. Within the Corps and among its dedicated alumni the debate regarding women in combat swells and subsides periodically, and the women themselves are divided on that point. Tensions between Marine women and the defenders of the Corps' burly image persist.[3]

The twentieth-century origins of these issues may be traced to World War I. Late in that war permission to follow the U.S. Navy's lead and take women into the Marines was granted by Secretary of the Navy Josephus Daniels. Recruitment began officially on August 13, 1918. By the November 11 armistice 305 females had been enrolled in the Marine Corps Reserve.[4] Although the women discharged their mainly clerical duties very well, the entire affair was merely a gesture. Neither the leadership nor the rank and file of the Corps was serious about allowing women to wear Marine uniforms on a permanent basis. At that time it was unthinkable that there would be another global war, therefore there was no need to even contemplate going co-ed, as it were. Anyone who predicted that within twenty-five years 20,000 women would be on active duty as WRs would have been dismissed as deranged.

When Pearl Harbor was attacked on December 7, 1941 there were no female "auxiliaries" or reservists in any of the military branches. Six months later the U.S. Congress and President Franklin D. Roosevelt consented to the establishment of a Women's Army Auxiliary Corps (WAAC), and on July 30, 1942 the U.S. Navy was authorized to form a reserve component, the WAVES (Women Accepted for Volunteer Emergency Service). By November 1942 the U.S. Coast Guard had its SPARS (U.S. Coast Guard Women's Reserve) and the Marine Corps its WRs. Between August 1943 and December 1944, 1,074 women served in the WASP (Women Airforce Service Pilot) organization. All told, D'Ann Campbell states in her splendid study, *Women at War with America* (1984), over 275,000 females served in our country's armed forces sometime during the hostilities. In addition, 75,000 Army and Navy nurses served with traditional distinction in every combat zone (p. 258 n. 8).

The Marine Corps, reluctant from the outset to admit women into its ranks, finally succumbed to political, social, and personnel pressures and began taking female candidates on February 13, 1943. What happened to the WRs and the Corps in their shotgun marriage is examined in a number of sources, notably: Ruth Cheney Streeter's unpublished, 448–page final report, "History of the Marine Corps Women's Reserve: A Critical Analysis of Its Development and Operation, 1943–1945"; Pat

Meid's *Marine Corps Women's Reserve in World War II,* published in 1968 by the Historical Branch of Headquarters Marine Corps; and my own *Women Marines: The World War II Era* (1992). This growing body of literature will be enriched in the fall of 1994 by the release of Mary V. Stremlow's *Free a Marine to Fight: Women Marines in World War II,* an official monograph in the Corps' "World War II Commemorative Series."

It appears that, at last, the courageous women who served in the Corps' reserve during the biological mother of all wars are receiving the recognition they deserve. They have even been featured in non-official, commercial publications. For example, in Jim Moran's *U.S. Marine Corps Uniforms and Equipment in World War II* (1992), an entire chapter is devoted to "Beautiful American Marines." There are thirty photographs displaying the various uniforms worn by WRs. (Over the past decade there had been a noticeable increase in "reminiscences" that cut across the World War II women's branches, a signal that the authors wish to leave something tangible to posterity before their generation passes from the scene, I believe.)[5]

If we accept the women's memoirs at face value—deducting just a bit for nostalgia and distance in time—it is plain that World War II was a high-water mark in their lives. And why not? They were young, they were doing something no previous generation had done on such a grand scale, and they were reinforced by a nation aflame with patriotic fervor. It was a rare moment in American history. As entertainer Maxene Andrews recalled in 1993, there was "a sense of national unity, *real* togetherness, a feeling so strong, so exhilarating and so unifying that it did more than help the country survive. It helped us win the war."[6] Women Reservists, if not always treated kindly by servicemen and civilians, had not the slightest doubt that they were making a significant contribution to the war effort.

In the final paragraph of her massive, precedent-setting study, *The Women's Army Corps* (1954), Mattie E. Treadwell expresses an opinion that is apropos to all female veterans of World War II, branch of service notwithstanding:

> In a world where new frontiers had been hard to find, they had found one; in an age where pioneers and their problems were a memory, they had been pioneers. They might . . . shrink from thought of repeating such a passage, but it would be the prized memory of a lifetime. (p. 764)

Suddenly, in August 1945, it was finished. Almost as quickly as our attention turned to war in December 1941, the national mood shifted toward a reconversion to peacetime standards. As Leon Baritz observed, Americans "wanted to concentrate on the intimate details of living rather than on historic events of great consequence, and went in quest of the prosaic—small, domestic, personal events."[7] The postwar "honeymoon" did not last long but the glow of victory warmed our hearts for the better part of a year after V-J Day. It was a mini-era of good feelings, so good "that neither veterans nor anyone else would be able to remember it accurately . . . so good that their children and grandchildren would not believe them that it was ever that way or even could be that way."[8] Between October 1945 and February 1946 over 750,000 persons were separated from the military. By June 1946 approximately thirteen million men and women had been released. Except for the survivors of the 300,000 dead servicemen and women who made the supreme sacrifice, it was a homecoming period of exquisite sweetness.

And what of the females who donned their beloved country's uniforms? Individually, they were justifiably pleased with their accomplishments. However, to their dismay, the general population was not inclined to lavish them with the same volume of praise it afforded their male comrades. Doris Weatherford points out in her excellent survey, *American Women and World War II* (1990), "The war itself was an aberration in American life, and women's role in it an even greater one. It was over now and best forgotten. Few flags flew when Janie came marching home" (p. 111). On this theme Jeanne Holm wrote:

> Unlike the male veterans, who had been welcomed home as heroes, most women had found to their surprise and chagrin that their military service, however patriotically motivated, was not universally applauded by family and friends or the community at large and was in fact divided. Consequently, many women veterans concluded that the less said about their military service the better. (p. 128)

In *Homeward Bound: American Families in the Cold War Era* (1988), Professor Elaine T. May noted that "In the wake of World War II . . . the short-lived affirmation of women's independence gave way to a pervasive endorsement of female subordination and domesticity . . . like their civilian sisters, female veterans were expected to become wives and mothers after the war" (p. 78). In 1942–43 the ultimate outcome of the war was predictable but no one was willing to say how long it might drag on. At best, 1946 looked like the year when the Axis would surrender. The only aspect of the war military personnel were sure of was: they were "in it" for the duration—and perhaps longer. Not until early in 1945 did the "higher ups" give much consideration to the retention of women beyond the end of the war, so our WRs thought about their futures in conventional terms. At the time, there were two, mutually exclusive options, a civilian career as a "single lady" or marriage and family. The latter was the overwhelming preference. Most women wanted that, most males believed that was the choice women ought to make, societal pressures were exerted in that direction—and the Marine Corps had no objection, certainly. Women in reserve units? Possibly. But, as Mary V. Stremlow observed in her *Coping with Sexism in the Military* (1990), the Corps "didn't want anything to do with full-time career women" (p. 17).

Did any of the 18,460 WRs on active duty when Japan capitulated imagine (or wish) that there was an alternative to the "mandatory resignation or discharge of all WRs"? Wish, perhaps. Imagine, probably not. Therefore, as the WR editors of *The Word* said in their December 10, 1945 edition: "Since V-J Day the thoughts of Henderson Hall women have centered in one, big, important subject—civilian life" (p. 1). Corporal Mary Cugini, stationed at the Hall then, wrote her sister, Dena, "Everything is buzzin' here—more discharges, new faces and high hopes of getting out soon." The most symbolic development occurred in December 1945. Colonel Ruth Cheney Streeter, the revered director of WRs since January 1943, resigned her position to return to civilian pursuits. It was no secret that she was opposed to keeping women on active duty in peacetime (an opinion in which the first directors of the WAC, WAVES, and SPARS concurred), and her successor, Colonel Katherine A. Towle, was of like mind.

By February 1946 there were only 7,500 WRs still in uniform. It appeared that the Corps' second great social experiment—the other being the admission of black males in 1942—was destined to be terminated by June. Generals and admirals were having "second thoughts about letting all the women go," but at the lower levels there was no real reason to anticipate a reversal of existing policies. Besides, word was drifting back from the outside world that civilian life was pretty good. There were minor problems, but nothing that could not be overcome. New civilians Marion Barnes and "Peggy" Woodworth sent a note to their former comrades at Henderson Hall that was both cautionary and enticing. In *The Word* for April 8, 1946 they wrote:

> The hardest thing to become accustomed to was to realize that we were once again just ordinary citizens. We missed the uniform, the attention it brought, and the pride felt while wearing it. Getting used to the peace

and quiet of a home, going our own merry way without a liberty card or week-end pass, privacy, and above all, trying to decide what to wear every time we left the house are just a few of the adjustments we had to make. (p. 3)

There were forces at work which would ensure the preservation of the concept of women as Marines. However, for some of the WRs stationed at separation centers in late 1945 and early 1946, waiting their turns, watching their buddies leave the Corps by the hundreds every week, it was a bittersweet experience. Month after month, the numbers of WRs in the passing parade increased, and with them went a unique piece of the mosaic that is American history. Would anyone ever know who these women were? What they did?

Ostensibly, their season in the sun was over. The WRs were going home, forever proud, forever changed. Some had plans to resume their interrupted schooling or begin their studies at institutions such as Columbia, Missouri, Florida State, and California. As one WR wrote to her brother, "Ever since I've been in the service I've realized how important it is to have a good education." The G.I. Bill would help her fulfill her aspirations. As I pointed out in *Women Marines: The World War II Era,* the newly discharged women, in addition to becoming wives and mothers,

became legal, medical, general, military, and executive secretaries. They worked as civil servants in their home states. Some were attracted to nursing. . . . They also became telephone operators, teachers, journalists, social workers, management analysts, insurance agents, tellers, and court reporters. (p. 158)

Into the workplace, and into their personal lives, they took an intense devotion to the Corps. "Among Marines," retired Lieutenant General Victor H. Krulak USMC wrote, "there is a fierce loyalty to the Corps that persists long after the uniform is in mothballs."[9]

And some of the former WRs had fresh visions of their purposes on this planet. "I will do all in my power to keep the world free from war, hate, oppression, and suffering," one of them vowed. "I want my life in the future to be, as has been my Marine Corps life, a continual change for betterment and improvement."

Semper Fidelis, Private First Class Dora Katherine Money—and all the girls of summer.

NOTES

1. Charles J. Quilter, II. *U.S. Marines in the Persian Gulf, 1990–1991: With the I Marine Expeditionary Force in Desert Shield and Desert Storm* (Washington, D.C.: History and Museums Division, Headquarters, U.S. Marine Corps, 1993), p. 72.

2. Robert J. Moskin, *The U.S. Marine Corps Story* (Boston: Little, Brown and Co., 1992 ed.), p. 816.

3. See, for example: Gene A. Deegan, "Women in Combat: A View From the Top," *Marine Corps Gazette,* September, 1992, pp. 42–44; Mackubin T. Owens, "Women in Combat—Equal Opportunity or Military Effectiveness?" *Ibid.*, November 1992, pp. 32–36, and 36–37, 39–40 for additional commentaries; the "Women in Combat" section in *Naval Institute Proceedings,* February 1993, pp. 48–58; and Sherman Baldwin, "Creating the Ultimate Meritocracy," *Ibid.*, June 1993, pp. 33–36. See also, R. R. Keene, "A Blueprint for Success," *Leatherneck,* May 1993, pp. 52–54, in which six women Marines express their views.

4. Linda L. Hewitt, *Women Marines in World War I* (Washington, D.C.: History and Museums Division, Headquarters, U.S. Marine Corps, 1974) is the best reference available on this topic.

5. A list of selected references might include: Nancy Dammann, *A WAC's Story* (Sun City, Ariz.: Social Change Press, 1992); Charity A. Earley, *One Woman's Army: A Black Officer Remembers the WAC* (College Station, Tex.: Texas A&M University Press, 1989); Byrd H. Granger, *On Final Approach: The Women Airforce Service Pilots of World War II* (Scottsdale, Ariz.: Falconer Publishing Co., 1991); Helen C. Gunter, *Navy WAVE: Memoirs of World War II* (Fort Bragg, Calif.: Cypress House Press, 1992); and Dorothy M. Weirick, *WAC Days of WW II* (Laguna Niguel, Calif.: Royal Literary Publications, 1992).

6. Maxene Andrews and Bill Gilbert, *Over Here, Over There: The Andrews Sisters and the USO Stars in World War II* (New York: Kensington Publishing Corp., 1993), p. 4.

7. Loren Baritz, *The Good Life: The Meaning of Success for the American Middle Class* (New York: Alfred A. Knopf, 1989), p. 183.

8. Richard Severo and Lewis Milford, *The Wages of War: When American Soldiers Came Home—From Valley Forge to Vietnam* (New York: Simon and Schuster, 1989), p. 297.

9. Victor H. Krulak, *First to Fight: An Inside View of the U.S. Marine Corps.* (New York: Pocket Books, 1991 ed.), p. 175.

Chapter Two

Goodbye to All That?

The year 1946 was the first full year of peace for the United States since 1940. We were a nation of 140 million people, 10 percent of whom were veterans of World War II. One of the major stories of the year was the rush for higher education by veterans who were eager to take advantage of the Servicemen's Readjustment Act of 1944 (G.I. Bill). Fall semester 1946 matriculations of veterans exceeded one million. Colleges and universities struggled to accommodate the "swollen enrollments." Most institutions had not erected any new facilities since 1941 and were ill-prepared to meet demands for classroom, dormitory, and married student space. As *Life* magazine of October 7, 1946 chose to describe it: "The result [of the influx] was like trying to pack two pounds of rubber bands into a one-pound bag."

The G.I. Bill provisions also covered veterans who wanted to complete their high school studies, start small businesses, and purchase homes. When the benefits for World War II personnel expired in 1956, some 2.2 million men and women had taken the opportunity to enhance their academic and vocational prospects. In terms of effecting substantive alterations in the fabric of American society, the G.I. Bill may be the most important piece of legislation passed in the first half of this century.

There is a paucity of reliable data on how many female veterans used the Bill. In her book *The Home Front and Beyond: American Women in the 1940s* (1982), Susan M. Hartmann estimates that 64,728 women *did* between 1944 and 1956 (p. 106), although that does not tell us what percentage used it for higher education nor how long the women attended college. Elaine T. May points out that "Most of the veteran's benefits were geared toward men, not to formerly enlisted women" (p. 78) and that exhaustive records were not kept on female veterans. Professor May believes we may assume that the postwar generation of women, veterans or not, were "much less likely to complete degrees" than their foremothers (p. 79).

The government discharged its obligations to veterans in other ways as well. Through the Veterans Administration (VA) it provided professional assistance administered by 4,000 physicians. By July 1, 1946, 37,360 veterans were undergoing physical and/or psychological treatment at VA hospitals. Nearly 20,000 of these patients had been hospitalized for "psychiatric reasons." In Fiscal 1946, VA outpatient clinics examined 1.1 million clients.[1] The government also underwrote what was known as the "52–20 Club" for veterans who were unable to find work. Unemployed ex-servicemen and women were allotted twenty dollars a week—a princely sum in an age when the minimum hourly wage was forty cents—for up to fifty-two weeks. When the "club" was closed in 1948 approximately $3.7 billion had been spent on the relief it brought to jobless veterans.[2]

Veterans not only had to find jobs, they also had to procure adequate housing for their young families. In 1946 the U.S. birthrate soared to 3.4 million, 600,000 births higher than in 1945, and the scramble for shelter was frustrating for many Americans. When they did set up housekeeping they found that there was not much money left over for non-essentials. Grocery prices were reasonable and the mortgage (or rental) payments were within reach, but the budget did not allow for many extras (sometimes called "luxuries"). So, pre-TV families relied heavily and happily on the old standbys: records, movies, books, and radios.

Popular records still revolved at 78 rpm and Americans bought 275 million of the fragile scratchy disks in 1946 (and 400 million the following year). On the three million phonographs they played and replayed Eddy Howard's "To Each His Own," Dinah Shore's "The Gypsy," Perry Como's revival of "Prisoner of Love," and, for an uptempo change of pace, "Shoo-Fly Pie and Apple Pan Dowdy" by Stan Kenton. It was a banner year for good movies. Weekly attendance was down to ninety million from a wartime high of 110 million, but for less than a dollar a person could go to the local theater and see *The Best Years of Our Lives, To Each His Own, Gilda, The Killers, The Razor's Edge, Notorious,* and *The Jolson Story,* the surprise hit of the year.

If a new, mass–produced home had any bookshelves one might see thereon John Hersey's *Hiroshima, All the King's Men* by Robert Penn Warren, *The Egg and I* by Betty MacDonald, and the "bible" for new parents, Dr. Benjamin Spock's *The Common Sense Book of Baby and Child Care.* On a coffee table nearby there might be recent issues of *Life, Look, Saturday Evening Post, Redbook,* and *Time* magazines. In the evenings one could put the baby on a blanket on the living room floor and "tune in" to radio programs such as Bing Crosby's The Kraft Music Hall, The Fred Allen Show, Fibber McGee and Molly, Fred Waring and His Pennsylvanians, Duffy's Tavern, Jack Benny, and an assortment of dramatic productions. Most likely, the man of the house garnered some radio time to listen to the National League playoffs between the Brooklyn Dodgers and the St. Louis Cardinals, and then to the Boston Red Sox–Cardinals World Series in October 1946. When we visualize American families this way, William O'Neill's observation rings true: "The war generation's conservatism found its highest expression in domestic affairs. Delayed and disrupted by the war, members of this generation wanted to go back, even beyond their parents, to a time of secure values and traditional practices" (p. 44).

The yearning to "go back" was fueled by disturbing undercurrents at home and abroad. The domestic inflationary spiral was still out of control and 4.6 million workers were out on strike in the meat packing, mining, shipping, and electrical industries. Overseas, hopes for a lasting peace dimmed. The term "cold war" had not yet been coined but "iron curtain" had, by Winston Churchill, and it bore sinister connotations. The Soviet Union's intransigence was not reassuring. A bitter civil war in China showed no signs of coming to an end. Communist leader Mao Zedong was not shy about proclaiming his intention to destroy Chiang Kai-Shek and his Nationalists. In a place we called Indochina the seeds of the Vietnam War of the 1960s and early 1970s were being sown in the vicious struggle for power between the French and Ho Chi Minh's communist forces. There were uprisings against British colonialism in Egypt, India, and Palestine. And, in July 1946, our own country conducted atomic bomb tests at Bikini Atoll in the South Pacific. What did *that* mean, we wondered? There were modest expectations that the United Nations would safeguard global peace and security and smother brushfires before they consumed us. But there was widespread skepticism on that point even as the United Nations chose New York City as its permanent site. The specter of the impotent League of Nations hung over the nascent body, casting a cold shadow across its potential to forestall new wars. "By 1946 hopes for a better world were flickering out," William O'Neill wrote. "The United States, which had just won the greatest war in history, already seemed less secure than before, its interests threatened by aggressive Communism on both sides of the globe" (p. 53).

While these events were transpiring, a shake-up in the U.S. military was occurring which would shape the future of the U.S. Marine Corps and, as a corollary outcome, determine whether or not the idea of females in the Corps was a dead issue. What happened in, and to, the Corps between 1945 and 1947 is a story of survival against powerful forces which sought to reduce the Corps to the level of a sea-going *gendarmerie*. One of the most lively and informed accounts of the Corps' near-demise is Victor H. Krulak's. The full title of his first chapter says it all: "Voyage Toward Oblivion and Back or How the Marines Were Almost Merged Out of Business" (p. 19). The exquisite irony is that in their successful fight to preserve their organization the Corps' leaders—who were not disposed favorably toward females in the Corps—made it possible for there to be Women Marines for another fifty years.

*　*　*

The typical servicemen and women were not privy to "top brass" ruminations, so they were unaware that the issue of "unifying" U.S. armed forces had been discussed on and off since 1943. To Marine Commandant General Alexander Archer Vandegrift, a Marine since 1909 and the holder of both a Navy Cross and the Congressional Medal of Honor, "unification" was a euphemism for an excuse to dismantle the Corps. As he stated in his autobiography, *Once a Marine* (1982 ed.), the unification movement "would have curtailed the role and missions of the Marine Corps to make it little more than an auxiliary police force." In his opinion it "would represent the first steps in the total abolition of the Corps" (p. 302). He was especially concerned about what he perceived to be the U.S. Army's intent to monopolize all of the nation's military operations. A large measure of the U.S. Navy's political "clout" was diminished when President Roosevelt, an "old Navy man" in spirit, died in April 1945. In his place was an "old Army man," President Harry S. Truman, who, Vandegrift felt, "held no particular love for the Marines" (p. 318).

Vandegrift was a junior officer stationed in Haiti during the United States' portion of World War I, but he was well aware of the animosity directed at the Corps by the U.S. Army in 1917–1918. Thomas D. Boettcher believes that the intraservice rivalry began with Belleau Wood in 1918. "There Marines fought a battle that forever changed the role and image of the Corps," he states in *First Call: The Making of the Modern U.S. Military, 1945–1953* (1992). "Marines had always been looked upon as the Navy's soldiers, but after Belleau Wood, the Corps, to the chagrin of the Army, began developing an identity independent of the Navy. . . . Marines became national heroes during the extended battle. Their victory [over German troops] was an occasion for national joy" (p. 80). There was no joy in Army ranks on this subject. It believed that the Corps' achievements in France were blown far out of proportion, overamplified by correspondents (such as Floyd Gibbons), and clearly self-serving. Furthermore, what was the Marine Corps doing behaving like a land army? We already had one fully capable of handling such responsibilities. Besides, "when you got right down to it," the U.S. Army lost nearly 50,000 men killed or dead from wounds—and the Marine Corps? Only 2,456. How could so few people make so much noise? Captain Harry S. Truman of the 129th Field Artillery was in the thick of it during the ferocious battles in the summer and fall of 1918. He never forgot how he felt about the Marines' propensity for self-aggrandizement during (and after) the Great War—and he let it be known thirty-two years later in one of his renowned, intemperate fulminations.

Vandegrift's suspicions about the Army's overarching motives were not entirely unfounded. On Nouméa in 1943 Army Major General J. Lawton "Lightning Joe" Collins passed some comments during a "social hour" that were reported to Vandegrift the next day. Collins, it seems, was expounding on one of his favorite themes, the "postwar reorganization of the military," and pronounced that the Marine Corps "should be eliminated and its duties absorbed by the Army."[3] Vandegrift was probably not surprised when, two years later, the reorganization proposal submitted by the Truman administration to the U.S. Congress was commonly known as the "Collins Plan." By 1949 Collins was Army Chief of Staff.

When Vandegrift became the Corps' eighteenth Commandant on January 1, 1944 he kept a weather eye on the reorganization/unification movement but for the ensuing twenty-two months he was beset by a myriad of concerns that required his attention: the conduct of campaigns in the Pacific (from Kwajalein to Okinawa); budgetary constraints; Washington politics; the deployment of Marines in China; the demobilization of most of his 485,000 Marines and the recruitment of their replacements; the conversion of the best reservists to regular status; the disgorging of "superfluous" high-ranking officers; and the prompt dissolution of the MCWR. In 1945 disbanding the Corps' female component may have been the least of his worries. On December 20 President Truman sent a message to the U.S. Congress regarding unification that has been described as "eloquent," "comprehensive," and as the "most radical military reorganization [plan] in the nation's history."[4] Truman called for the creation of the Joint Chiefs of Staff (JCS), a single department of defense with one person at the helm, sharply reduced functions for the U.S. Navy, and the formation of an autonomous air arm carved from the corpus of the U.S. Army. The absence of any reference to the Marine Corps was viewed by the Commandant as an ominous sign. His testimony before the U.S. Senate's Military Affairs Committee in October, while "forceful" and "forthright" in its challenge to the "Collins Plan," evidently had no deterrent effect on the White House's determination to proceed. After he testified, Vandegrift told his predecessor, General Thomas Holcomb, that the Army was "back on the job in full-force trying to absorb the Navy and with it the Marine Corps."[5]

Professor Allan R. Millett summarized the Corps' dilemma penetratingly in his *Semper Fidelis: The History of the United States Marine Corps* (1991):

Caught in the complex political currents that characterized the unification of the American armed forces, the Marine Corps found itself pitted against a strong War Department—executive branch—Congressional coalition that wanted to strip the Corps of its wartime amphibious assault mission, transfer Marine aviation to the newly independent Air Force . . . In a sense, the Corps' critics wanted a nineteenth century Marine Corps while the Corps wanted its World War II capabilities and missions written into law. (pp. 456–457)

The next set of hearings opened in late April 1946. Going in, the Corps had little cause for optimism. The very popular Army Chief of Staff, General Dwight D. Eisenhower, was known to think that a large Marine Corps was an unnecessary duplication of the Army's role and that the size of the Corps ought not to surpass 60,000. U.S. Army Air Force General Carl A. Spaatz (who would be the new U.S. Air Force's first Chief of Staff in 1947) was said to have asked: "Why should we have a Navy at all?" so confident was he that air power would be the sole weapon required to win future wars. Of course, if the Navy went, so would the Corps. In April, Senator Ebert Thomas (D.-Utah) gave the press a copy of his working group's legislation, which included most of what President Truman wanted. It left the status of the Marine Corps unspecified, a worrisome fact.

To oversimplify the lineup as the hearings began—this time before the Senate Naval Affairs Committee chaired by Senator David I. Walsh (D.-Mass), a "down-the-line Navy man"—it was: President Truman, the Army, the Army Air Force (to a lesser degree), and the Thomas Bill (S.2044) *versus* the U.S. Navy and the Marine Corps. Secretary of the Navy James V. Forrestal was first to come before the committee on May 1, 1946. In Forrestal, the Corps had a cautious ally. A Princeton graduate in the class of 1915, he flirted with the idea of being a Marine in 1917 but decided the U.S. Navy was a more gentlemanly environment in which to serve his country. As Secretary of the Navy in 1944 and 1945 Forrestal revealed his "glowing admiration for the bravery and tenacity of the Marines" in palpable ways.[6] He went ashore at Iwo Jima four days after the Marines landed (February 19, 1945), well before the island was secured, so he could experience first-hand what combat was like for "his" men. Iwo was the ideal place to find out. Nearly 6,000 Marines died wresting the six-mile-long fortress from 22,000 Japanese troops, and another 17,000 Marines were wounded. After Iwo, war was no longer an abstraction for Forrestal. He could appreciate fully what one of his admirals wrote on March 16: "Among the Americans who served on Iwo island, uncommon valor was a common virtue." Signed, Chester W. Nimitz, Commander of the Pacific Fleet.

At considerable risk to himself politically, Forrestal diplomatically and firmly stood opposed to the "Army proposal." Forty-eight hours later Admiral Nimitz expressed his unequivocal rejection of the unification plan. On May 6 General Vandegrift took his turn before the Senators—and electrified the largely partisan audience. In true Marine style he was candid, economical in his choice of words, and fervent in his delivery. In contemporary parlance, he "called it as he saw it." Following his review of the formation and contributions of the Corps, Vandegrift posited that the passage of the merger bill "would undoubtedly sterilize the Marine Corps" and concluded his remarks with a moving 133-word paragraph that has earned a special niche in the annals of the Corps. He said, in part:

We have pride in ourselves and in our past but we do not rest our case on any presumed ground of gratitude owing [sic] us from our nation. The bended knee is not a tradition of our Corps. If the Marine as a fighting man has not made a case for himself after 170 years of service, he must go. But I think you will agree with me that he has earned the right to depart with dignity and honor, not by subjugation to the status of uselessness and servility planned for him by the War Department. (p. 318)

Jaw set, the Commandant sat back in his chair, ready for whatever was to come. "After a second of total silence, shouts and applause burst forth," Thomas Boettcher noted. "Sustained bedlam rocked the room, Marines all around, shaking hands and wearing big smiles. [Vandegrift] had stopped Army plans cold" (p. 87). The Corps had won a delaying action but not the political war. There was still no legislation defining— therefore, protecting—the mission and functions of the Marine Corps, which Vandegrift's brain trust believed was the only way to guarantee the Corps' future. Nor did the parties to the debate relax, relent, or recess. If anything, feelings ran higher as 1946 waned and no closure had been attained. Every once in a while someone would squirt verbal lighter fluid on the simmering charcoals and arouse one side or the other. For example, late in 1946 Brigadier General Frank A. Armstrong of the Army Air Force was quoted as saying that the Corps was "a small bitched-up Army talking Navy lingo. We're going to put those Marines in the Regular Army and make efficient soldiers out of them," a remark hardly calculated to facilitate "unification."[7]

It took fourteen months of hearings and negotiations before the Corps finally got what it wanted. On July 26, 1947 President Truman signed the National Security Act into law. It gave the Corps "legislative sanction for its role as both amphibious assault specialist and force in readiness." The President realized the majority of his original goals and the Marine Corps was left alone to refine what it had learned during World War II. Mr. Truman harbored some resentment toward Commandant Vandegrift for resisting the first reorganization schema and, in 1950, demonstrated publicly that he "had not developed tolerance for the Marines' elitist attitude." By then, however, another interruption forced him to grant the Corps a further opportunity to cover itself with glory: Korea.

*   *   *

While General Vandegrift was between hearings, an issue not very dear to his heart came to the fore, viz., the retention of women on active service. On February 6, 1946 General Eisenhower directed his subordinates to prepare plans "to establish a Women's Army Corps in the Regular Army with concurrent reserve status."[8] Both he and General George C. Marshall were very impressed with the WAC's contribution to our war effort and saw the practicality in having women readily available as replacements for men headed for combat assignments.

About the same time the U.S. Navy was having similar thoughts. Why not keep WAVES on duty? They could aid in demobilizing naval personnel and "continue some of the peacetime programs" initiated since V-J Day. In March 1946 Secretary of the Navy Forrestal asked Representative Carl Vinson (D.-Ga.)—Chair of the House Naval Affairs Committee since 1931—to sponsor a bill (H.R. 5915) that would allow females to enroll in Navy and Marine Corps reserve units and remain on active duty in limited numbers. (The SPARS were disbanded on June 30, 1946 and did not resurface until 1974). Vice Admiral Louis E. Denfeld, Chief of the Bureau of Personnel and future Chief of Naval Operations, wrote Vandegrift in February to inform him that the Navy planned to keep a WAVES component in the Naval Reserve. In her *Lady in the Navy: A Personal Reminiscence* (1984 ed.), Joy Bright Hancock (who was to become WAVES director on July 26) quotes Denfeld as adding, "Further, if Congress approves, we will ask to retain on active duty reasonable numbers of WAVES who wish to do so and who may be needed in certain specialties" (p. 216).

By the Ides of March, then, General Vandegrift knew from official sources that both the Army and the Navy were determined to do what he did not want the Corps to do: make a permanent place for women in the ranks. These developments must have been exasperating for the beleaguered Commandant. Here he and his aides were, trying to save the Corps from virtual extinction, and along comes this intrusive issue which he hoped was already settled by internal fiat. Worse still, the idea of incorporating women in the military had a dimension of inevitability that rankled. Was the Corps going to be swept into a decision it did not wish to make by the sheer momentum of someone else's preferences? The answer to that question was: yes, it was—and there did not appear to be any way to deflect it.

The remainder of 1946 was marked by a series of compromises, rearguard actions, repealed directives, and policy revisions—all of which made it a rather befuddling year for the WRs. As Mary V. Stremlow characterized this period, it was a "Time of Uncertainty" for the women (p. 3). To use the vernacular, they literally did not know whether they were staying or going. In a true sense, they were in, but not of, the Corps. No one seemed to know what "the score" was. The closing down of the office of the wartime MCWR on June 15 was a technicality that meant very little, actually. It left the remaining WRs without a director for nearly ninety days, but a small band of WRs were still at Henderson Hall tidying up administrative details. The apocalypse was scheduled for September 1. By that date *all* WRs were to be discharged. Practical matters, such as the need for competent personnel to assist with the demobilization, perform vital clerical tasks, and fill positions for which qualified males could not be found, decreased the likelihood that such a strict deadline could be met.

Consequently, on August 7—the fourth anniversary of the landing on Guadalcanal he led as commanding general of the First Marine Division (Reinforced)—Vandegrift authorized the retention of 100 WRs at Headquarters Marine Corps (HQMC) until April 1947 at least. The next day he approved the keeping of 200 more until the end of the fiscal year. Eight days later, WR Company E, First Headquarters Battalion was formed. By the end of August, 298 WRs were on active duty at HQMC. The September cut-off came—and went—and WRs were still in uniform.

Was there to be a postwar organization of some sort for women who wished to sustain a connection with the U.S. Marine Corps? General Vandegrift had no objection to the notion of a cost-free inactive reserve as insurance in case of war, which neither he nor anyone else believed would occur in the near future. Someone would have to assume the responsibility for the establishment of a "postwar Women's Reserve." Colonel Towle departed the military life on June 15 to assume her administrative duties at the University of California at Berkeley. Before she went West, she suggested that General Vandegrift invite former WR Major Julia E. Hamblet to lead the amorphous organization. In retrospect, that was one of Towle's most perspicuous recommendations. What she did not know was that her nominee would forge a link between the past and the future that would ensure a place for women in the Corps for the next half-century.

On September 6, 1946 Hamblet was invested as director of the incipient, postwar MCWR. A Vassar graduate, she joined the MCWR early in 1943 and was commissioned a first lieutenant in May. During the war she served at Hunter College, Camps Lejeune and Pendleton, MCS Quantico, and MCAS Cherry Point in positions which burnished her natural leadership skills. From December 1945 until her discharge in April 1946 she was Colonel Towle's assistant at HQMC. In the summer of 1946 Commandant Vandegrift asked her to return to the fold. If anyone ever "started from scratch," Hamblet certainly did. But for herself and two able assistants, the MCWR was people-less. It was a paper organization, a theory, a dream, a risk, and, in the opinion of many male Marines, a total waste of time and energy. It was Hamblet's job to make something out of nothing, to mobilize a cadre of women to whom she could not offer incentives such as pay, promotion, travel, or legal standing, to keep an idea alive that nearly everyone thought was moribund.

Quietly assertive, always gracious, and determined to resuscitate the MCWR's *esprit de corps,* Hamblet took the reins and made decisions that resonate to this day.

I will leave Major Hamblet at that point, for the time being. The occurrences of the ensuing twenty-four months are chronicled in detail and with finesse by Mary V. Stremlow and need not be repeated here.[9] If, in addition to the MCWR's birth year (1943), there is another increment of time that may be seen as a watershed in the history of women in the Marine Corps, it is the last six months of 1948. The Corps had a new commandant, General Clifton B. Cates, who inherited from General Vandegrift a number of unresolved issues, not the least of which was the fate of his WRs. Actually, it was out of his hands. Congressional legislation that would permit—Cates might say "force"—the Corps to make room for females was moving inexorably toward closure. In June 1948 President Truman signed the Women's Armed Services Integration Act into law (P.L. 625). It "authorized the enlistment and appointment of women in the Regular Navy and the Regular Marine Corps" and in their reserve components. By June 1950 the Marine Corps was allowed to have 1,110 women "regulars" in uniform, if it wished.

October and November 1948 witnessed a series of events that had a consolidating effect on the Corps' emerging component. Katherine Towle consented to return to HQMC to direct the organization as of October 18. On November 8, she, Major Hamblet, and First Lieutenant Mary J. Hale were sworn in as regular officers by Commandant Cates. Two days later (the Corps' 173rd birthday) he did the honors for eight enlisted women. A memorandum dated November 16 was promulgated saying, in effect, that the designation WR was to be retired after nearly six years. Henceforth, the proper description would be WM, Women Marines. It was more than a semantic adjustment. To the women it signified legitimacy, recognition, security, and the promise of a future in the Corps, if that was their goal. While this blizzard of exciting events was at its height, Colonel Towle was thinking ahead. She wondered: When we open enlistments to non-veterans, where are the recruits going to take their basic training? Was there a site within the Corps' network of bases, stations, and depots that was topographically and atmospherically suitable for indoctrinating "boots" into the "Marine Corps way"? On or about November 29, 1948 she began to explore the feasibility of using a facility well known to all for its ability to transform boys into Marines: MCRD, Parris Island, South Carolina. Could it convert girls into Women Marines? As we shall see, it could—and it did.

NOTES

1. John M. Blum, *V Was for Victory: Politics and American Culture During World War II* (New York: Harcourt Brace Jovanovich, 1976), p. 335.

2. Richard Severo and Lewis Milford. *The Wages of War: When American Soldiers Came Home—From Valley Forge to Vietnam* (New York: Simon and Schuster, 1989), p. 289.

3. Thomas D. Boettcher, *First Call: The Making of the Modern U.S. Military, 1945–1953* (Boston: Little, Brown and Company, 1992), p. 57.

4. Townsend Hoopes and Douglas Brinkley, *Driven Patriot: The Life and Times of James Forrestal* (New York: Alfred A. Knopf, 1992), p. 327.

5. A. A. Vandegrift, *Once a Marine* (New York: Ballantine Books Inc., 1982 ed.), p. 306. Also see Gordon W. Keiser, *The U.S. Marine Corps and Defense Unification 1944–47: The Politics of Survival* (Washington, D.C.: National Defense University Press, 1982).

6. Hoopes and Brinkley, p. 34.

7. Allan R. Millett, *Semper Fidelis: The History of the U.S. Marine Corps* (New York: The Free Press, 1991 ed.), p. 461.

8. Bettie J. Morden, *The Women's Army Corps, 1945–1978* (Washington, D.C.: Center of Military History, 1990), p. 33.

9. Mary V. Stremlow, *A History of the Women Marines, 1946–1977* (Washington, D.C.: History and Museums Divison. Headquarters, U.S. Marine Corps, 1986), Chapters 1–3.

Chapter Three

The Thin Green Line

Before we turn to the women taken into the Corps in 1949–1950 it is important to pause to recall what a difference six years had made. When the WRs entered the Corps in 1943 our country was deep into a war that permeated everyone's life. The many facets of World War II were omnipresent. It burst upon our homes, markets, schools, workplaces, newspapers, magazines, movie theaters, and radio programs early in 1942 and remained pervasive until the fall of 1945. For nearly four years Americans were bombarded with war-related directives, requests, and bulletins, and, overall, they responded with genuine enthusiasm to what we might describe as constructive propaganda.

Maxene Andrews said it well: "There was something . . . about those years—a sense of national togetherness that Americans haven't felt for a long time since. Those who call it America's 'last popular war' have good reason. Public support for our part in it was almost unanimous" (p.3). The 20,000 women who joined the MCWR then did so for patriotic reasons, in the main. It was their way of contributing to the "inevitable triumph" over our fascist enemies. By the late 1940's the heady atmospherics of World War II had dissipated. As Katherine Towle pointed out some years later, between 1948 and 1953 there was no such "sense of commitment" as prevailed during World War II. There was no "national crisis" and, she thought, one did not "join the services primarily for patriotic reasons."[1]

Another difference was that in 1942–1943 joining the military was perceived as a questionable decision for an American woman to make.

Public memories of the few females who served with the Navy and the Marine Corps in 1918 had all but evaporated. That was too long ago, too brief, and too late in the war to impress us indelibly. By 1949, with women still in uniform, the concept of females in the military had not been banished to a historical graveyard. It was not so stunning a phenomenon anymore. Even if it violated some peoples' sense of propriety, our general sensibilities had become accustomed to the idea that female soldiers, sailors, and Marines were here to stay.

A third distinction worth remembering concerns racial policies. The WAC and the WAVES allowed black women to enroll during World War II. The Marine Corps did not, and would not until it lost its arm-wrestling match with the government in 1949. Even then, Henry Shaw tells us, "It was readily apparent that the leaders of the Marine Corps were not going to be in the forefront of the integration battle" (p. 49). In the other corner, again, was President Truman. On July 26, 1948 he issued Executive Order 9981, which directed the U.S. military to eliminate all manifestations of discrimination in its several branches. Two months before his upset victory in the November 1948 Presidential election, Truman established the Committee on Equality of Treatment and Opportunity in the Armed Services and appointed Judge Charles Fahy, a liberal Democrat from Georgia, as chairman. At that particular junction the Marine Corps had approximately 1,500 black male Marines on active duty, had no black females, was training black recruits in segregated circumstances at Montford Point, North Carolina, and was not eager to effect any changes in its policies or practices.

On January 13, 1949 the Fahy Committee began to hold hearings to ascertain what the military was doing, if anything, to address President Truman's initiatives. In his insightful work, *Desegregation of the U.S. Armed Forces: Fighting on Two Fronts, 1939–1953* (1975 ed.), Richard M. Dalfiume gives this account of the Corps' presentation:

> The Marine Corps . . . had a difficult time explaining why it had failed to follow the Navy's integration policy. The Marine representative told the committee that [the Corps'] policy of segregation had been adapted as the best, following an investigation of all the records of the Army on the subject. Questioning by the committee's members revealed that the Marine Corps had only one Negro officer among eighty-two hundred, and that no thought had been given to changing the policy of segregation. When asked what he thought of integration, the Marine representative replied, "I think you'd be making a problem instead of solving one." (p. 180)

On this issue, strange to say, the Marine Corps and its adversary, the U.S. Army, were bedfellows. Both took a rigid stance against the integration of their units. The Army held out longer primarily because it was its own boss. The Corps' parent body, the U.S. Navy, was committed to a policy of integration (as was the U.S. Air Force) and the Corps was in no position to alienate the Navy beyond a certain point. (The Navy had some work to do too. It had only five black male officers in its group of 45,000 on active service and but six black WAVES out of 2,130 personnel.) The proverbial handwriting was on the bulkhead, however. On July 1, 1949 Commandant Cates "ordered that Negroes be trained with the rest of the recruits at Parris Island, but in separate platoons."[2] By September his position was no longer tenable and on the twenty-second Cates "approved the integration of recruit training." Earlier in the month Montford Point was shut down, bringing to a close "an era in the history of Negroes in the Marine Corps." Was this a concession to Executive Order 9981? Had the Corps had a change of heart? Probably not. Once a black Marine graduated from boot camp and was assigned to a duty station within the Corps, he usually found himself in a "colored unit" somewhere, segregated again. It took another war to cure the Corps of that habit.

September 1949 may have been the end of an era for black males in the Corps, but it was the beginning of an era for black females. On the tenth of the month two black recruits, Ann E. Lamb of New York City and Annie E. Graham of Detroit, began boot camp at Parris Island and completed the rigorous program without incident. A third black woman, Annie Laurie Grimes, arrived at Parris Island in February, 1951. Why did she join up? "I was attracted to the Marines by an advertisement in a magazine which promised to train women for administrative duties, while offering opportunities for travel, adventure and education," she remembers. Her family was "a little surprised" that she chose the Corps rather that the WAVES or the WAF (Women in the Air Force) but they gave their blessings and wished her well. In 1968 Annie was promoted to chief warrant officer 2. When she retired on September 30, 1970 she could take pride in the knowledge that she was the first black WM to serve twenty years in the Corps. "Looking back," she wrote in 1993, "I thoroughly enjoyed my career . . . I made many lifelong friends. The positive experiences completely overshadowed the negative ones." What were the negative ones? "Oh, nothing really terrible," she says. "Just little things, like happen in regular life to black people every day."

Jean A. Willett recalls that she was the eleventh black woman to enter the Corps (and the first from Kentucky). She chose the Marines "because of their high standards," and she met them, head on. She was discharged as a sergeant on September 10, 1955 after a three-year tour. What are her thoughts about the decision she made to enlist when she was twenty-two? She reports: "I am happy to be a WM veteran. It was a position of respect . . . The Marine Corps opened up a whole new world for me . . . I am grateful I joined." Were there any "negatives" for her? "I didn't do a lot of fraternizing for fear of being labeled," Jean says, "but I was always treated with respect."

Another factor that differentiated WRs from WMs had to do with their basic training. During World War II enlisted WRs were indoctrinated at two locations, Hunter College in the Bronx, New York, from March 26 to July 10, 1943, and at Camp Lejeune in North Carolina until the war was over. Early in 1949 Parris Island was selected as the new training site for enlisted recruits. That was front page news in the January 15, 1949 issue of the depot's paper the *Boot:* "Women Marines Recruiting Begins Today; Will Train at Parris Island." The February 5 edition told its readership: "P.I. Recruit Depot to Be Co-Educational Soon." The education of future WM officers was transplanted from Lejeune to MCS Quantico, Virginia, in time to receive the first candidates on June 20, 1949. This may be the appropriate moment to look at both Parris Island and Quantico as places where neophyte WMs encountered the Corps for the first time.

Parris Island lies within Beaufort County, South Carolina. It is four miles long, three miles wide, and encompasses 8,000 acres. Known for its "insects, humidity and heat"—and for snakes, alligators, and renegade offshore sharks—it was designated a Marine Corps training base prior to the United States' entry into World War I. During that conflict 46,000 boots were processed there. Until 1929 personnel could move to and from the island only by boat.[3] In the 1990s "P.I." is an accessible, attractive, well-managed depot that hosts not only recruits but also hundreds of former Marines who want to revisit the place where they began to grow up, their portal to maturity. Today, they laugh at the hardships they endured there. When they were boots it was not so funny.

Over the past seventy-nine years Parris Island has accumulated a reputation which, like barnacles, clings to the depot despite serious attempts to scrape it clean. With successive generations of Marines who passed through "Alcatraz East," the lore surrounding the training grew in quantity, if not in quality, to the point where it was difficult to distinguish fact from fiction. Layer upon layer of tales about "how tough it was at P.I." took on a life of their own. Just the mention of the letters "P.I." drew knowing smiles from Marine veterans, and sheepish grins from boots who were on their way there. Horror stories abounded within and outside the Corps about what really went on at P.I. Some of them were true, most of them were boastful embellishments. Regrettably, it took several fatal incidents to induce the Corps to expunge the gratuitous maltreatment levied upon recruits in the name of "making Marines out of boys."[4] Still, the mythology of Parris Island—that "semper fi bastion of five-star machismo"—persists. "For some," a *New York Times* reporter wrote on September 2, 1993, "Parris Island will always be a hell-hole. About 17 percent of men and 25 percent of women drop out before boot camp ends."[5] Professor Eugene Alvarez speaks for many alumni of the Island in his book *Where It All Begins* (1992), when he says:

> all Marines who have known the depot have never forgotten that Parris Island was a milestone in their life, and a place where the innocence of youth was lost. But most important, the depot was the place that they earned the honored right to be addressed as a Parris Island and a United States Marine. (p. 40)

One of the kinder descriptions of Parris Island might be, "a steamy island of moss-draped live oaks and palmettos, mosquitoes, and diamondback rattlers," not to mention its pesky, gluttonous sand fleas. By contrast, the area occupied by MCS Quantico receives a more genteel portrayal. For example, Quantico "comprises just under one hundred square miles of quiet, lush, green hickory, oak, and pine forests, laced by innumerable streams and wetlands." Located on the Potomac River about thirty-five miles south of Washington, Quantico was designated a Marine Corps Base on May 22, 1917, six weeks after the United States declared war on Germany. As many as 30,000 Marines embarked for Europe from the base during the war. The practice of training officers at Quantico began in July 1917 and has been carried forward into the present decade.

Between the wars Quantico evolved along multiple lines. It became the Corps' "university," a departure area for intervention into Caribbean affairs, an air station, a rehearsal zone for amphibious landings, the location of the Platoon Leaders Class (PLC) program, the home of the Federal Bureau of Investigation academy, and a residence for many of the Corps' best planners and experimenters. The Corps' first newspaper, *The Quantico Sentry,* was founded there in May 1935. During World War II, 20,000 Marine officers were trained on the base and its woodsy environs. On November 10, 1943 the first contingent of WRs arrived for duty at Quantico. Their number rose to 1,000 prior to VJ-Day.[6]

The WOTC (Women Officers Training Class) launched its inaugural course in June 1949. The *Sentry* for June 23 made note of it thus: "Women representatives of every section of the country are attending. . . . Women students from Duke University, Smith College, Texas University, Penn State, and many other colleges . . . are forming in ranks and answering roll call." On September 14, thirty-four "Lady Marines" graduated from the "initial post-war class." Seven received regular commissions, twelve were assigned to the reserve, and the remnant were to make second lieutenant "at a later date." Their training was not intended to duplicate boot camp but it came perilously close. Carol Kramer, who rose to the rank of captain, remembers it this way: "It was good fun, but lots of work, and being treated as less than dirt. . . . I wouldn't want to do it again." How did it feel, being an officer in the Marines at last? Eleanor Magruder Bach, one of the original seven in 1949, describes it as "absolute elation." "Being sworn in by General Shepherd [Commandant at MCS Quantico], walking across the stage to get my commission, and putting on my gold bars—it was wonderful." It was a sign of those simpler times that Lieutenant Bach and her friends celebrated the occasion by going into the town of Quantico, having coffee at the Anchor Room, and attending a movie at the MCS theater.

At the enlisted level a few women avoided the privilege of spending their first six weeks in the Corps at Parris Island. Former WRs were not required to repeat the experience, although there were "refresher courses" given to bring them up to par. Shortly after the Korean War broke out Marine reserve units were summoned to active duty. WMs who had perfect attendance records, outstanding evaluations from their superiors, and critical specialties were often exempted from being shipped to Parris Island. A small number of those "once-a-week warriors" actually were sent to the island and then given a reprieve after a day or two because the Corps needed them elsewhere immediately. Everyone else went to South Carolina and stayed, if they could "handle" the program.

For a while these wartime exigencies fractured the solidarity that boot camp graduates share for the rest of their lives. Boot camp is an adhesive that binds Marines together in a fraternity of formerly lost souls whom the Corps rescued from a wimpish existence. Forty-odd years after she was authorized to sidestep Parris Island, Gladys Gaillard said, "I feel I missed out on something by never having gone to boot camp." She did very well without it, rising to master sergeant before she retired in 1970, but most Marines know exactly what she meant. When one is a lowly boot, he/she would rather be somewhere—anywhere—else. Once completed, the experience takes on a wholly new significance. To quote Ellen Juhre, "The first few weeks? Pure *Hell!* After that—the camaraderie, teamwork, pride, discipline, challenges, and esprit de corps can be understood only by a Marine."

* * *

Pursuant to the passage of P.L. 625 in 1948 the armed forces' female leaders and their supporters hoped for a healthy response from young women. The anticipated tidal wave of enlistments did not materialize, however, despite the inducement of regular status. As of June 1950 the WAC had only 7,000 women in its ranks, the WAVES 3,200, and the WM strength was under 600, a veritable trickle compared to the numbers projected. The Marine Corps was not unhappy that its WMs represented less than one percent of its total personnel on active duty. That was an affordable, comfortable fraction, a mere ripple on waters that were beginning to calm after four years of gusty winds. If trouble came the Corps would rely on its reserve units to supply all the WMs it needed.

As unpalatable as it was to entertain, "trouble" was on the way—although it arrived from a part of the world we were not attending to very effectively. The "Cold War," a term attributed to presidential advisor Bernard Baruch, was encroaching upon the public consciousness. The Americans and the British defied the Soviet attempt to strangle Berlin by flying more than 1.5 million tons of goods to the city in 1948–1949 but it left a residue of suspicion and fear. The month the airlift ended President Truman announced that the Soviets had somehow developed a nuclear capability. Less than a week later, on October 1, the People's Republic of China was declared established by its Communist leaders. Chiang Kai Shek and his followers retreated to Formosa, shook their fists at Mao Zedong from a distance of 110 miles, and vowed to retake the mainland (with our help). On January 31, 1950 Truman directed the Atomic Energy Commission to proceed with the development of a hydrogen bomb. Two weeks thereafter, Red China and the Soviets signed a mutual defense pact. The Cold War, so the saying went, was "heating up" at an alarming rate. In his work, *God's Country: America in the Fifties* (1986), J. Ronald Oakley made the cogent observation that:

To many Americans at the beginning of 1950 the world appeared to have turned upside down. World War II had not brought the permanent peace that so many had sacrificed so much for but had instead merged into another life-and-death conflict. . . . Americans entered 1950, then, under the shadow of the Cold War and the atomic bomb. (pp. 5–6)

Although developments in Europe and Asia were disconcerting, domestic affairs were sufficiently buoyant to distract us from portentous emanations from overseas. The U.S. population was approaching 150 million and, for the most part, prospering. On the average, a two-bedroom house could be had for $10,000, and that Ford or Chevrolet in the carport cost about $1,400. Car sales were nearing six million a year and new home purchases hovered at the one million mark. Five million homes had television sets (for about $250 a piece) and eighty million radios were bringing in music, news, and dramas from 2,800 stations across the country. In 1949–1950 phonograph record aficionados had three speeds to choose from (78, 45, and 33-1/3 rpm) and they listened to Russ Morgan, Vaughn Monroe, Patti Page, and Frankie Laine, among others. If a couple strolled to the nearest market to check the prices they might see a window poster that read: "This week at *Your* A&P: Doz. eggs 75¢ * Bread 15¢ loaf * Butter 60¢ lb. * Milk 21¢ qt. * Coffee 55¢ lb. * Oranges 52¢ doz. * Cigarettes 21¢ pk. * Rib veal chops only 69¢ lb." It helped a little that the minimum wage had nearly doubled to seventy-five cents an hour.

Going to movies was still an inexpensive way to take a break, and the Bijou was showing *All the King's Men, The Heiress, Champion, White Heat,* and *The Third Man.* A war veteran might have noticed the resurgence of combat films such as *Battleground, Twelve O'Clock High,* and, if he or she was a former Marine, *The Sands of Iwo Jima* with John Wayne (which premiered in San Francisco in December 1949). At the local Sears Roebuck there was not an item of clothing from socks to suits priced higher than twenty-five dollars. The sensation of the fashion world for women was still the "New Look," whose lengths and silhouettes were created by French couturier Christian Dior in 1947. By 1949 the "look" was firmly in command, protests from women's groups notwithstanding. The rallying cry of one such club in San Antonio—"The Alamo fell, but our hemlines will not!"—went unheeded by female shoppers.

During this period of relative prosperity, unmarried WMs-to-be were involved in the usual range of activities. At base, they were trying to "make ends meet" while awaiting what the future held for them. Some were clerking in children's stores, optical outlets, drugstores, railroad company offices, and "five-and-tens." Others had secretarial responsibilities in insurance agencies and trucking companies. Among them were beauticians, elevator operators, hospital workers, civil servants, veterinarians' assistants, teachers, cashiers, and telephone company employees. There were others who were attending college, operating a motel, hostessing on commercial aircraft, and serving customers at a Yosemite Park cafeteria. They were at work all across the country, never suspecting that they would be brought together under the Globe and Anchor because of a war in a place most of them had not heard of before 1950.

It is logical to wonder: Why did they join the Marine Corps? There were three other women's branches. What impelled them to choose the Corps?

It is always interesting when people defy convention and refuse to conform to extant norms. Even though by the early 1950s women in uniform were no longer the novelty they had been during World War II, many Americans still had reservations about their daughters entering the military. It could be argued that if a young woman was determined to enlist, a three- or four-year "hitch" in the Marines would be the last option her parents wanted her to exercise. Why not the WAVES, WAF, or WAC? The Corps' reputation for toughness might be fine for men, but would it not rob a woman of her femininity? Is not the term "Lady Marine" an oxymoron? What will our friends and neighbors think? What have we done to deserve this? Where did we go wrong? They need not have been so concerned. Their daughters did them proud.

The former WRs who breathed life into this volume were very straightforward about their motives for joining the Marines. Their reasons fall into three major categories as I see it: predetermination, pragmatics, and pot-luck. In one respect their replies to the question—Why?—differ from those of their antecedents, the WRs of World War II. For WRs the transcendent motive was patriotism, an understandable impulse given the heroic nature of that conflict. Between 1942 and 1945 nearly everyone searched for some means of helping her country defeat the Axis Powers. There was a lot at stake and it was not necessary to explain what it was. The United States was not that deeply committed to what was happening in Korea and, furthermore, that grim peninsular war posed no direct threat to the nation's well-being. The women who enlisted after June 1950 were patriots, of course—but in a less intense way because of the passive national mood and the confusing character of the war.

In the niche I call predetermination, I place those young women whose choice of the Corps was shaped by internal influences. For example, in Mary Ann Bernard's home environment the Corps was a traditional medium of patriotic expression. Her father was a Marine in Haiti in 1918 and her sister Florence was a WR in World War II. In a sense she was responding to a family value system when she enlisted in 1950. Mary M. Jamison's father was a thirty-year Marine and she was born in Quantico. Connie Musemeci's brother Andy was a Marine in Korea. She recalls, "I was so proud of him . . . We went through a hard time when we didn't hear from him during the Chosin Reservoir phase in November and December 1950." After being listed as missing for several months Andy turned up, frostbitten but safe. His ordeal was a "major factor" in Connie's decision to be a Marine. Maria Matta was not as fortunate. Her twenty-nine-year-old brother Elmy, an Army lieutenant, was killed in action in Korea. In December 1952 she paid her own way from Puerto Rico to the United States so she could join the Marines. There was some solace for Maria and her family when a grateful government awarded a posthumous Distinguished Service Cross to her brother in recognition of his bravery. Ellen Juhre's father's use of negative psychology backfired. A World War II Marine who was wounded in Okinawa in 1945, he made it clear that he did not believe Ellen could make it through boot camp. That was not the thing to say. "I joined to prove he was wrong," Ellen admits—and she did.

Two of the former WRs traced their decisions to the previous war. Joan Walter was growing up during World War II and developed a "crush" on the Marine Corps. She followed the Corps as it battled its way through the South Pacific. Then the war ended, and so did women's eligibility to enlist. "I was devastated," she remembers. "When women were again able to join, I was ready to make my move" (the Corps was not quite ready for Joan until 1953). When she was twelve, Clare Bullitt was asked by her teacher to write an essay on what she "wanted to do in life." That was in 1944. "I wrote that I wanted to join the Marine Corps," Clare says. "I forgot all about it until the Korean War broke out—then it was time for me to recall, and carry out my forgotten wishes."

Because many of the WMs had pragmatic reasons for joining the Marines does not mean they had no other purpose. It may just have been a matter of priorities in the palmy days prior to going on active duty. Joan Kammer chose the Corps because she wanted "to shoot on its rifle and pistol teams." She knew of the Corps' prowess in that field. She enlisted in December 1953 and did "a lot of shooting and traveling with the teams" over the next three years. Not only did she realize her ambitions, she met her future husband along the way. Naturally, he was a "shooter," too. Except for what she absorbed from "John Wayne movies," Carol McCutcheon knew very little about the Corps. Her mother persuaded her to chat with a local Marine recruiter and she was impressed. "I wanted a job and an education, and the Marines offered both," she states. Another former WM was quite candid about her self-assessment at the time: "I decided to join the military because I perceived my only options to be teacher, nurse, secretary, or the nunnery." The church's loss was the Corps' gain, in that particular instance. Joyce Bechtel was working very hard to put herself through music college by holding down three jobs simultaneously. She wanted to serve her country and continue her education afterwards. G.I. Bill benefits certainly "would make it easier," Joyce thought. In 1952 Patty Stamper was working for an insurance company in Cincinnati and living at a local YWCA. It so happened that all the women recruiters were staying there too. Patty listened to what they were offering and made up her mind. "I learned that I could join the USMC for three years. All the others were four years, and that helped me decide," she recalls—and adds: "Besides, those green uniforms looked good to me."

Many of the former WMs gave reasons such as: "The Marines had the reputation of being the best," "Very elite," "High standards," "Is there another branch of service?" and "I was convinced they were the best." A few were not so sure which one of the armed services was the right one for them, so they went on a reconnaissance mission to find out. A foremost representative of the pot-luck school of enlistment has to be Gene Sims. In the summer of 1952 she went to the (old) post office building in downtown Pittsburgh to join up with "some branch." Each recruiter had a private office. We will let her tell the rest of the story:

> I really went there to enlist in the Army but the WAC recruiter was out to lunch. I went to the next room to try the Air Force. The WAF recruiter wasn't at her desk. So, I tried the next door, the USMC office. I didn't even know there were Women Marines. This charming WM greeted me and told me about the Corps. So I enlisted.

On September 11, 1952 Gene and five other women from the area were on their way to Parris Island.

Many of the recruits left their home towns with fond goodbyes, "Good luck," "Be careful," "Don't forget to write," and "Take care of yourself" echoing in their busy heads. Some parents, relatives, and men friends were very supportive, others were not. The most poignant reminiscences come to us from women who entrained for Parris Island with-

out endorsements from the people they loved. There was comfort in
being with other recruits who were " in the same boat," but false bra-
vado is no substitute for the afterglow of family subvention. As cases in
point, there were two Joans, both moving by rail toward boot camp.
Their reveries may have been quite similar when they looked out of the
train windows, watching (but not really seeing) tiny towns flash by,
barely noticing the flat clang of the railroad crossing alarms, and won-
dering what lay ahead as they sped south through the humid August
darkness. Joan Walter's family objected strenuously to her decision. "I
was told 'No nice girl EVER goes into the military.' " She recalls, "I
had to wait until I was twenty-one since my parents would not 'sign'
for me. Even then they disapproved." Joan Collins's family was also
opposed to her enlistment plans. "My three brothers were in the Army
during World War II," she says, "and my father was in the Army in
World War I." The Marine Corps was "strange" to them. Joan finally
"wore [her] mother down" by 1953 and went on active duty with neither
a fanfare nor a feeling of acceptance.

Mary Lou Clough's folks were not pleased. Not only had their family
always been "Army," but Mary Lou had settled in as a public school
teacher in her Iowa hometown. Why give that up? The local school
board was not happy either. "They said my students needed me more
than the military did." Nevertheless, Mary Lou joined the Corps in 1951
(and rose to the rank of captain). Clare Bullitt's mother was taken aback
when Clare announced her imminent enlistment. Her father's reaction
was difficult to gauge. "He was hesitant," she states. "He seemed indif-
ferent, expressing neither approval nor disapproval—but I was determined to join." Male friends were not always enamored of the idea.
"Most of mine," Dolores Shutt tells us, "did not like it because of the
stigma attached to women in the military." One young man told Barbara
Hollar that she was "crazy" to enlist and that she would be a totally
different person when she came back. He was right. She was—but not
in ways he imagined. At the time she was called to active duty, June
Dempsey was keeping company with a fellow in her hometown. "He
was real unhappy with me joining the Marines," she says. "We broke
up after he visited me in California." June did not mourn too long.
"Then, I went out with another Marine."

Not all of Pearl Morris's relatives took the news as calmly as her
mother Naomi did. Pearl recalls: "I remember my Uncle Joe's comment
to mother, 'Good God, Naomi, what are you trying to do—make tramps
of these girls?' " Pearl's sister was thinking of enlisting, too. Then, as
was usually the case once a young woman refused to be cowed by these

sorts of pressures, Uncle Joe had a change of heart after Pearl was a WM and her sister Phyllis a WAVE. "Right after I enlisted, Uncle Joe was one of our proudest relatives. How he loved to show me off when we visited him . . . and we'd better be in our uniforms!"

*   *   *

For most recruits headed for Parris Island by train after 1949 the terminus was Yemassee, South Carolina. From there the women traveled the last leg of their journey by either bus or "cattle car." Everything was fine during the thirty-mile ride until the women drew close to their destination. They grew more solemn as the facility came within view. Theresa "Sue" Sousa remembers exactly what she was thinking: "My first reaction when we passed through the gate at P.I. was—*What have I done?* I felt the 'gates of hell' close me in." Joan Collins has a few recollections of that occasion:

> When the male Marines came to pick us up at Yemassee they were very nice to us. You know, real gentlemanly and solicitous. They helped us get out luggage aboard the bus. We were treated like real ladies. All that changed abruptly when we got to P.I. All of a sudden it was, "Alright, *ladies*—off the bus, get your own gear, and fall in over there. Come on, move it, move it, *move* it!" That's when I realized we were in for it.

The new recruits were transported from the depot receiving station to the women-only Third Recruit Training Battalion where, *Boot* reported on March 5, 1949, "the process of evolution from the civilian to the military began" (p. 3). (With due respect to the *Boot* staffers, the process is revolutionary. There is nothing gradual about it. Boots do not unfold into becoming Marines, they explode. The gestation period is only a matter of weeks.)

Psychologists have known for nearly a century how important language is in the shaping of attitudes. A large measure of the Marine Corps' success in converting civilians into Marines may be attributed to the manner in which its trainers employ a special vocabulary. When a recruit enters the Corps' sphere of influence she hears words totally foreign to her untutored ears, and she must make those terms a part of her linguistic currency immediately. Doris Brown remembers that "The D.I.s [drill instructors] used it all the time. We wanted to learn it as fast as possible." "It was taught in some of our classes," Joan Walter states, "and, besides, all the women were 'gung ho' and were eager to learn whatever we had to." Mabel Bennett was philosophical about it: "It was just a part of being in the Corps."

The "it," the Corps' particular lingo, was often printed on paper and distributed to boots, with the clear understanding that they were to master the meanings promptly, if not sooner. If we exercise a modicum of literary license, what follows can serve as a not-too-serious sample of the document boots were given in the early 1950s:[7]

Third Recruit Training Battalion
MCRD, Parris Island, South Carolina

September 18, 1950

FROM: Drill Instructors, Platoon 9-A
TO: All recruits, Platoon 9-A
SUBJECT: Vocabulary, Proper Use of

Commencing immediately upon receipt of this notice all recruits in Platoon 9-A will commit the twenty-three terms listed below to memory. Continued usage of civilian terms is hereby prohibited. Appropriate penalties will be awarded to recruits, hereinafter known as "boots," who fail to learn these terms within forty-eight hours of their arrival at the Battalion. Instructors and NCOs have been ordered to be watchful for any and all violations of this directive.

ALL HANDS. Everyone, excepting only the certifiably infirm and the dearly departed.

ASHORE. The world beyond MCRD, Parris Island, a no-woman's land for persons in training.

AS YOU WERE. Also "carry on." Resume what you were doing before a superior interrupted you.

BOONDOCKS. The "field." A swamp or forest primeval where boots get bitten by insects and develop rashes.

BULKHEAD. A wall, against which frustrated boots may pound their empty heads.

BUNK. A bed, a sack, a rack on which boots' aching bodies may rest when given permission.

CHOW. Food, usually consumed quickly by chow hounds who cannot wait to chow down.

COVER. A hat; a military chapeau not available in civilian millinery shoppes.

DECK. Floor; a level surface on which to place sore feet when ordered to "hit the ———."

FALL IN. Assemble at designated areas as fast as your blisters will allow.

FIELD DAY. The sanitization of a living space by hand, mop, and/or toothbrush.

GEAR. All essential military and personal equipment.

G.I. PARTY. A group celebration of the virtues of hygienic living.

HEAD. Bathroom area. Improperly referred to as a "latrine" in the U.S. Army.

JUNK ON THE BUNK. An organized display on one's rack of all gear in one's possession.

LADDER. Stairs, going up or down from wherever a boot happened to be.

POLICE. Spruce up, as in "police the area" around the barracks whether or not it needs it.

REVEILLE. When the USMC wants boots to get out of their bunks before daybreak.

SECURE. Put away, or, stop what you are doing, as in "secure the butts."

SICK BAY. An infirmary or clinic, normally off limits to real Marines who tolerate pain well.

SCIVVIES. Whatever you wear under your uniform that males are never allowed to see in public.

SQUARE AWAY. Bring perfect order to your gear, living space, or thought patterns.

TURN TO. Get moving, begin, get your posterior in motion.

Distribution "A": CMC, CGMCRD, BNCO, DI

The WMs who endured the rigors of boot camp between 1949 and 1955 share a number of things besides Marine Corps jargon. There is a noticeable consistency in their recollections that has nothing to do with *when* they were boots. Over the six-year span under consideration in this volume, changes were effected in the length of basic training, the content of the curriculum, the Third Battalion's facilities, entrance requirements, and the regulations governing behavior, but the women's reactions to the Parris Island experience do not vary much. There appear to be three stages through which they passed: Apprehension, Consolidation, and Jubilation.

Apprehension may be too mild a term to apply to what our female boots felt, especially during the initial phases of their training. Jean Willett acknowledges, "It was a cultural shock," which it must have been for a black woman. The only word that captured the experience for Virginia Dupuy was: "Rough." Mary Ann Bernard admits that she felt very intimidated: "I wasn't sure I'd make it through the first week." For most boots (this writer included) the first few nights on Parris Island are the memorable ones. Wilma Shaw sat on one of Barracks 903's thirty-eight double-decker bunks and wrote her mother: "I'd better close now because we've got to write a 500–word autobiography, memorize a bunch of laws, learn definitions, write my name on my clothes, and get ready for bed." Joan Walter remembers the first week as "scary." Doris Reeves thought, "What a different kind of life!" Mary Boyd recalls "a lot of crying by everyone for the first two weeks." Lying stiffly in her bunk, eyes shut tightly, Gladys deKlotz was "homesick and scared to death." She continues: "The first night there, lights out, and somewhere off in the distance, 'Taps' was being played. I could not help but think, what have I done?"

Most new boots were so exhausted that they slept the sleep of the drugged. But from day one the Corps showed that it believed in a full day's work for a half-day's pay. Reveille for boots "went" at 0545, military time for 5:45 a.m. Whatever system one uses, that is exceedingly early for ex-civilians. Lights were flicked on by a duty NCO (non-commissioned officer) and even the groggiest boot could not block out the announcement: "Alright, ladies—rise and shine. Hit the deck! Another grand and glorious day in your beloved Corps. Move!" Pearl Morris has not forgotten. "I think I hated reveille most of all," she reports. "What a horrid time to have to get up. We were constantly reminded that 'the Corps didn't ask for us, we asked for the Corps,' so we'd better get a move on or out we'd go."

Being expelled from the Corps so soon was an embarrassment the majority of boots preferred to avoid. After all, they went through a gauntlet of either high praise or heavy criticism to get to Parris Island. Pearl Morris remembers saying to her inner self, "If I don't make it I'll never be able to go home. I'd be ashamed of having failed." What would Uncle Joe think? The women wondered what they might hear: "I told you so"; "Well? What went wrong, dear?"; "Too tough for you, cupcake?"; or, worse yet, abject silence and disappointed looks. Annie Laurie Grimes, the Corps' third black recruit, had an extra reason to complete boot camp. She "had to make it" both for her own sake and for all the African-Americans who came after her.

The Marine Corps knew from experience that boots who are kept busy are less prone to dwell on why they are so miserable. As Clare Bullitt put it, "Boot camp was stressful, with constant attention to enforced priorities, and jobs that had to be accomplished in a certain amount of time"—all under the x-ray eyes of veteran WMs poised to unleash a barrage of rebukes upon those dimwits who did not produce. Consequently, within a week or so the consolidation process began. Before the boots were conscious of the transition, they shifted from the high drama of the initial collision with the Corps to a level of stabilization within "the system." This was accomplished by faithful adherence to daily routines. For example, let us assume we are scanning a platoon's bulletin board while the boots are away from their barracks. We might see this notice, among others:[8]

Daily Routine

Reveille 0545

Morning chow and policing squadbay...0615–0700

Inspection..0700

Classroom instruction 0730–1120

Noon chow..1200–1245

Classroom instruction 1300–1620

Evening chow 1645–1730

Police the barracks area 1730–1800

Study hour..1800–1900

Personal time 1900–2130

Police the squadbay..2130–2145

Lights out..2145

Former WMs will say: "Wait a minute. There's something missing. What about 'drill'?" They would be correct, of course. Learning how to march in unison always has been one of the Corps' methods of encouraging uniformity, stressing coordination of mind and body, and harassing boots into distinguishing between their rights and their lefts. The first class each day was usually devoted to close order drill practice, under the tutelage of male DIs who had to "dry clean their vocabularies" when working with female boots. Some of the DIs were not ecstatic about their assignments to the Third Battalion. "Our DI did not like training women," Dolores Shutt says. "He said he'd rather be in Korea."

We know that some boots mastered the science of close order drill rapidly and others did not. To hear the *Leatherneck* tell it, females were naturals when it came to marching. In a good-natured, patronizing article in its August 1949 issue entitled "High Heeled Boots," written by a male sergeant, it was stated that "girls really shine" at close order. "Drilling is a cinch for women—it's like dancing," the author noted. "They can pick up an intricate maneuver the first time it is explained."

Now and then a DI felt obliged to give a boot a "short inspirational talk" when she fouled up. As for the women's physical condition, readers were assured that the boots were "in good shape—no matter how you look at it." The male swimming instructor thought they looked "very nice in their bathing suits," even if they could not swim too well. Forty-five years later we can be understanding about such condescension. The staff writer was given the task of speaking about the first contingent of female boots to establish a beachhead at Parris Island in its thirty-four-year history. He was doing his valiant best to put a cheerful "spin" on a subject alien to everyone at the depot.

In the evenings between 1800 and 2100 the boots did some consolidating of a more personal kind. It was in the squadbay that they got to know each other. They talked, wrote home, read their mail, spit shined their shoes, talked, washed clothes (nearby), ironed their fatigues, talked, and prepared to face another day in the "Garden Spot of the South." It was a perfect occasion to complain about the program, gossip about boyfriends (or the lack thereof), and tend to aches and pains. "My biggest problem was leg cramps," Edna Cogswell recalls. Her biggest surprise was "how many young women didn't know how to iron." Joan Collins's problem was not unusual for female boots. "The hardest part was living with sixty-two other women," she says. "I was very shy, and getting dressed and undressed in front of others really bothered me." The loss of privacy was bothersome to many boots, particularly when they were required to take showers unprotected from the glances of other women. This was not false modesty. They had been raised in conservative homes where what went on in the bathroom was no one's business but their own. Eventually, the women took such things in stride.

About three-quarters of the way along, say, in the sixth week of an eight-week program, the elation factor came into play. The boots were marching smartly, feeling better psychologically, passing their tests, and beginning to believe that they were actually going to make it. The fun memories were outnumbering the painful ones and the women had learned when to be serious and when to relax. In other words, they were developing a certain *savoir faire* about their circumstances, and with that came an increase in confidence and self-esteem. Together—and that is the key word—they had taken courses in Marine Corps history, customs, and regulations; first aid; administration; interior guard duty, and personal hygiene. They took calisthenics and went on field trips. They went everywhere—together. When I read their reminiscences, so sharp and fresh even after four decades, I can almost feel their emerging homogeneity of skills and purpose. They are becoming a unit, a body of women who are discovering who they really are, a group of bright individuals who are willing to adjust their egos to fit a higher cause, a company of near-Marines who sense that they are about to be inducted into the ranks of "The Best."

Parris Island was not all that bad—or was it? It was safer to believe it was until one was out of there. The time to put it in perspective was *after* graduation. Instructors looked with disfavor upon women who got too "salty" too prematurely. And the permanent personnel never tired of regaling boots with stories about the noxious side of P.I. Two weeks before she graduated Wilma Shaw went for her final check-up at the Navy dentist's office. It was probably no comfort for her mother to get Wilma's letter about that visit: "They said one of the male recruits went A.W.O.L. and got trapped in the swamps. When they found him he was so badly eaten by crabs that the only way they could identify him was from his teeth. Guess maybe I won't desert after all."

Graduation! That wonderful word that meant so much. We will turn this part of the story over to Pearl Morris, who was so nervous she ran into a little trouble:

> Boot camp graduation was the day we all looked forward to. All through training our platoon leader drilled us on the different questions the inspecting general might ask us. We spent our evening hours drilling each other on our general orders and other military subjects so we could answer any question without hesitation. We were really sharp! Graduation day finally arrived. . . . You should have seen us on the drill field. Gosh, we were sharp.

Then came inspection by the visiting general officer . . .

> Let me tell you he was the biggest man I'd ever seen in my life. As he came closer to me my palms were sweaty and my knees were shaking. I was terrified. There he was in front of me. My eyes were straight ahead, looking squarely at a button on his blouse. He said, "What is *your* name, Private?" My mind went totally blank. I had no idea what my name was. Why did he ask me such a dumb question? After what seemed an eternity, I finally blurted out, "Ppprivate Mmmmorris, Ssssir!" He smiled and moved on.

When the former WMs who contributed to this chronicle look back on their Parris Island interlude they refer to it as a positive feature in their lives. They say things such as: "I learned to be more organized in my personal habits," "It helped me develop character strength and a foundation for getting along with all kinds of people," and "I loved the drill—and the love for the Corps shown by DIs, officers, and instructors." A statement made by Carol McCutcheon, eloquent in its directness, sums up the experience for herself—and for others as well, I believe:

> Boot camp was hell. It was fun. New friends from all over the world. Marching here and there. Running all the time. We never walked, it seemed. DIs who acted like they hated us. Food that was not like mother used to make. Shots and physicals. Sand fleas that chewed the tender parts of your body. Beautiful uniforms that were not hand-me-downs from an older sister. No one wore them before. All mine. . . . Ironing and pressing our fatigues till the creases could cut butter. It was hard but we made it. I feel sorry for those girls who couldn't tough it out. . . . They have never known their strength and true grit.

On April 12, 1949, the first platoon of WMs to graduate from Parris Island stood final inspection. They were reviewed by Major General Alfred H. Noble, Commanding General, MCRD, and WM director Colonel Katherine A. Towle. At the time the thirty graduates did not know that they were the vanguard of the thousands yet to come over the next forty-five years. All they knew was that they were the first and that they had earned the right to wear the Corps' emblems. "Boot camp had given them a stock of memories and a new way of life," *Leatherneck* reported. "Now they were Marines with an exciting career ahead of them."

NOTES

1. Katherine A. Towle, "Administration and Leadership" (Los Angeles, Calif.: Regional Oral History Office, Bancroft Library, University of California at Los Angeles, 1970), p. 128.

2. Morris J. MacGregor, Jr. *Integration of the Armed Forces, 1940–1965* (Washington, D.C.: Center of Military History, United States Army, 1981), p. 334.

3. Eugene Alvarez, *Where It All Begins: A History of the United States Marine Corps Recruit Depot, Parris Island, South Carolina* (Byron, Ga: Privately printed, 1992 ed.), pp. 7–18.

4. On this theme see Keith Fleming, *The U.S. Marine Corps in Crisis: Ribbon Creek and Recruit Training* (Columbia, S.C.: University of South Carolina Press, 1990).

5. Peter Applebome, "The Few, the Proud, the Loved," in *The New York Times,* September 2, 1993, B1, B4.

6. Charles A. Fleming, *et al. Quantico: Crossroads of the Marine Corps* (Washington, D.C.: History and Museum Division, Headquarters, U.S. Marine Corps, 1978). Until January 1, 1948 the tract was named the Marine Corps Base, Quantico. For the next two decades it was known as Marine Corps Schools. It is now known as the Marine Corps Combat and Development Command.

7. The list of terms is a composite drawn from a number of sources, e.g., the recollections of the WMs who passed through Parris Island between 1948 and 1955; my own experiences as a boot in 1950 and thereafter until 1958; and a modernized version of the Corps' vocabulary displayed in Daniel da Cruz, *Boot* (New York: St. Martin's Press, 1987).

8. The daily routine schedule was altered from time to time. This version is taken from *Leatherneck,* February 1954, 19.

Chapter Four

Storm over Asia

In early 1950 not many Americans knew (or cared) where Korea was, or that it had been divided at the thirty-eighth parallel in September 1945 by mutual agreements between the United States and the Soviet Union. Over the three years following the partition, the 40,000 U.S. troops in the South found themselves suspended in the middle of a volatile political situation. Twenty-one million South Koreans were in a power struggle to determine what faction would be in control of the new Republic of Korea, and the United States was a midwife anxious to get the birth over with so it could extract itself. As Harry G. Summers, Jr. noted, "With a multitude of political parties [in the South] creating not government but bedlam, with a country in economic collapse and with relief expenses skyrocketing, the main thing the United States wanted in Korea was out."[1]

It took nearly three years to extricate ourselves. Following the election of Syngman Rhee to the presidency of the Republic in May 1948 the United States announced that it was withdrawing its remaining troops. The Joint Chiefs of Staff decided that Korea was "of little strategic importance" to the United States and the State Department offered no dissent. By June 1949 only 500 American officers and men were left in the South in what was called the Korean Military Advisory Group (KMAG). Their charge was to assist in the training of a South Korean constabulary of about 50,000 men. In effect, the United States left South Korea to its own devices and turned its attention to European affairs. To quote James L. Stokesbury, in the late 1940's and early 1950s "there seemed to be far more likely trouble spots than Korea, for at that time, the western world had a lot to worry about, most of it more pressing than an out-of-the way country on the edge of Asia." (p. 15).

Meanwhile, above the thirty-eighth parallel the Soviet Union had succeeded in establishing a satellite of impressive proportions in four years. When the Soviets withdrew their forces from North Korea late in 1948 they left behind a puppet regime tightly controlled by prime minister Kim Il Sung, a trained and well-equipped "people's army" of 100,000 regulars, and nine million peasants who were programmed to view the South as anathema to the communist ideology. Guerrilla forays across the border (both ways) were commonplace for at least a year prior to the invasion by North Korean forces. It was no secret that there was bad blood between North and South. Washington fully expected the Soviets to threaten our interests somewhere. "It was simply that the [Truman] administration expected that if war came, it would not come in Korea," Professor Burton I. Kaufman observed in his *The Korean War* (1986, 29).

When the North Korean army streamed across the thirty-eighth parallel at 4:00 a.m. on Sunday, June 25, 1950 it was post–lunchtime Saturday in Washington. It is no exaggeration to say that the incursion was a complete surprise, if not to all the top people in the Truman camp then certainly to the American public when it heard the news.[2] Typical comments from the citizen in the street during the week of June 26–30 ran along the lines of: "What? Where? What's that got to do with us?" "Hey, we just finished one war, let's not start another one," "Korea? I didn't know we were even involved with them," and "It's probably just another Commie feint, like Berlin. It'll blow over." When they saw the headlines in their newspaper on Wednesday, June 28, it began to sink in that the problem was not going to "blow over" so quickly. For example, the *New York Times* front page was emblazoned with the words: "Truman Orders U.S. Air, Navy Units to Fight in Aid of Korea. . . . Our Fliers in Action; Fleet Guards Formosa." General Matthew B. Ridgway remembered it this way, "When war broke out in Korea, we found ourselves . . . plunged headlong into war without even a week's warning and involved half a world away in a struggle our people neither understood nor felt a part of."[3]

Readiness was the immediate problem. Perhaps we were able to conduct warfare in the air and on the seas, but on land? In his volume, *The Pusan Perimeter* (1984), Edwin P. Hoyt stated that "In effect, the military situation in the United States in 1950 was uncomfortably close to the situation that existed on December 7, 1941. Militarily and psychologically, the Americans were totally unprepared for an attack in the Far East" (p. 18). The seeds of demobilization, troop reductions, inter-service rivalries, and severe budget cuts were about to blossom into bitter fruit. Thousands of American troops died from ingesting it during the summer of 1950. The U.S. Eighth Army, stationed in Japan, was woefully undermanned, insufficiently trained, and deficient in the equi-page of combat. As Clay Blair wrote in his massive study, *The Forgot-ten War: America in Korea, 1950–1953* (1987), due to "the rampant turnover, there was no sense of cohesion, esprit, or unit pride" within the Eighth Army (p. 50). Army Chief of Staff General J. Lawton Collins had executive authority for the JCS in the Far East and discovered the hard way that when the war was in its earliest stages "few units of the Eighth Army had reached a satisfactory level of battalion training."[4]

Less than thirty days after U.S. troops were committed to the fighting, the Army had suffered over 6,000 casualties and "were being squeezed into the southeastern corner of Korea around the port of Pusan." For a "police action" the conflict was looking awfully serious. Back home, the American people were supportive of President Truman's decision to commit air, naval, and ground forces to the Korean melee, even if they did not quite comprehend why it was so necessary. "They applauded the resolute stand taken by the United Nations, and were proud of their country for its response," Lynn Montross and Nicholas A. Canzona ob-served. On the other hand, "Never in their wildest imagination had it occurred to them that an Asiatic peasant army might be more than a match for all the United States ground forces in the Far East."[5]

When the Korean War broke out there were 74,270 U.S. Marines on active duty, 580 of whom were women. Those WMs already on active service knew right away what the war meant to them: an indefinite ex-tension of their time in uniform under wartime conditions. The WMs who were in the organized reserve thought they might be called to active duty, and they were right. "Women, as a result of the Korean crisis, and for the first time in American history, were called involuntarily to mili-tary service along with men," Mary V. Stremlow wrote. "Mobilization of reserves, including women veterans, was announced in June 1950" (p. 44).

Delphine Biaggi, a World War II WR (as were her two sisters), reen-listed on February 10, 1949. When she heard the news about the North Korean push into the South she was in San Francisco serving in the Department of the Pacific as a clerk typist. She was "deeply concerned" for her fellow Marines who were being shipped to Korea. She knew from experience that some of them would not return. Another veteran of the 1941–1945 war, Marie Anderson, was managing a motel in St. Augustine, Florida, in June 1950. She "volunteered for active duty immediately." Both Marie and Delphine took their basic training at Hunter College in 1943, as did Ethel Barker, who was at Henderson Hall the week the war broke out. Her reaction was quite common among former WRs: "Here we go again." A variation on that saying was what Rosemary Thompson murmured to herself, "Oh, no, not again." She was in the inactive reserve. "I figured I wouldn't get called up," she says. "Boy, was I wrong." After a brief stint in San Francisco, Rosemary was transferred to Camp Pendleton. "I was the only female baker at the Post Bakery," she recalls. "Just me and 100 male Marines."

Gladys Gaillard joined the Marine Reserves on December 7, 1949, the eighth anniversary of Pearl Harbor. She was an administrative clerk in the U.S. Army record center in St. Louis, Missouri, when she received a call informing her that her unit was being activated on July 27, 1950. The call came in on July 26. It had been a year since Doris Reeves graduated from boot camp. On June 25 Doris, her sister, and their parents were enjoying a Sunday afternoon picnic at the Shenandoah National Park in Virginia. When she returned to Henderson Hall that evening she learned about the Korean situation. The news surprised her, and she remembers being angry at President Truman for calling the Marine Corps "the Navy's police force." Anne Zink was in the reserves in Detroit. She reports:

> Actually, the war broke out the night I went to a reserve meeting. I found all the early arrivals standing around, their jaws agape, looking at a blackboard bearing the message that the 17th Infantry Battalion was being called to active duty. For me—that meant BOOT CAMP! I ran for a phone and called my mother: *"Mom!* We're being called up!" And she replied, "You got yourself into this. You get yourself out of it."

Anne spent Christmas 1950 at Parris Island.

When she got the word about Korea, Barbara "Bobbie" Lee was employed by an oil company in Seattle. Exactly eleven months before the invasion of South Korea she had joined the organized reserve, so she got to a phone to find out what was going to happen. She remembers clearly that:

> I called the office of the Inspector-Instructor and my CO answered the phone. I asked if there was any chance that our unit would be ordered to active duty. There was silence on the other end but I could hear her

leafing through some papers. Soon, she said yes—we were going on August 7th and I was slated to be assigned to the supply depot in San Francisco. I silently yelled, "Hallelujah!" I was ready to leave Seattle. My employer was willing to hold my job open for me until after the war, if I wanted them to.

That was very thoughtful of Texaco, but they would have had to be very patient. "Bobbie" stayed in the Corps for twenty-three years. She was a lieutenant colonel when she was released to civilian life on February 28, 1973.

About 60 percent of the women who contributed to this study had no military experience prior to June 1950. How did they react to the reports of the fighting in the Far East?

Mabel Bennett was living at home in Okmulgee, Oklahoma. She recalls that although she did not understand fully what the Korean crisis was all about—the news did start her thinking:

> The Second World War was still vivid in my memory and the Korean "conflict" did not seem to be a big thing. I was young, naive, and uninformed, I guess. I knew we were fighting again, and that the U.S. was strong and powerful. Being too young to help in the World War II effort, I was now old enough to contribute. I was very patriotic.

Our future WM captain, Carol Kramer, was a sophomore majoring in physical education at Panzer College in East Orange, New Jersey. "I remember being upset that President Truman called it a 'police action' not a war," she says. Joan Collins, only seventeen, was working for the New York Telephone Company. "Having lost a brother in World War II," she states, "we were all still very patriotic. We were concerned about entering another war—but we thought it right to do so." Two of the women who became WMs were involved in similar endeavors in two different states on the day the North Koreans attacked. Patty Stamper, a newly minted graduate of Beattyville (Kentucky) High School, was supervising youngsters at a 4-H camp that Sunday (which happened to be her birthday). When her parents brought their greetings they also told her about the hostilities in Korea. "I could not imagine how that would affect me," she says—and it might not have had she not lived in the Cincinnati YWCA with all those female recruiters. That same Sunday, in Averill Park, New York, Joyce Pulliam was "helping 4-H leaders set up their summer camp." She was also hoping to find a permanent job for the fall. She thought: "If Congress passes a G.I. Bill like the one it passed for World War II veterans, I would join the armed forces. Then I could finish college." She chose the Marines because it was the "better branch of service"—and President Truman obliged her by signing a Korean G.I. Bill into law (P.L. 550) on July 16, 1952.

Jean Willett found the G.I. Bill useful. It enabled her to pursue a career as a court reporter. But, on June 26, 1950 she was working on a patron's hairdo in her mother's beauty salon in Louisville. When she heard about Korea her thoughts turned toward how best she might serve her country. We may assume Jean's sudden distraction did no damage to her customer's coiffure. In York, Pennsylvania, Pearl Morris was a year away from graduation from William Penn Senior High and mulling over what she was going to do after that. Her fate was already sealed, evidently. The news of the war troubled her greatly. She, too, said, "Oh, no, not again." Then, at the local movie theater, "the newsreels started showing what was happening to our men in Korea and my patriotism really flared," she says. Throughout her senior year Pearl and her sister discussed joining the Marines—"I'm sure the World War II movies had something to do with it"—and they began dropping in to see the local male recruiter once a week. "Lord, he was a patient man," she recalls. On July 24, 1951 she enlisted, no doubt to the recruiter's relief. She was on her way to Parris Island and he could relax for the first time in a year.

*   *   *

On February 20, 1952 Warner Brothers released a film entitled *Retreat, Hell!* Made at Camp Pendleton, it was a well-intentioned tribute to the Marines who escaped entrapment in the Chosin Reservoir area of North Korea. The critics were not impressed. Nevertheless, the film opens with a montage of units and individuals being called to active duty in June 1950 and then focuses on one man. Actor Richard Carlson plays a World War II veteran and a captain in a Marine Reserve battalion in Denver. He is not a happy man. He is, in fact, "resentful of being plucked from his peaceful world" and being directed to report to Pendleton in just ten days. "I've forgotten an awful lot about war," he mutters to his long-suffering, lovely, blonde wife. The worst is yet to come. Not only do he and his family have to share a Quonset hut with another couple, the distraught Carlson has the misfortune of having a real Marine for his superior. His battalion commanding officer is a "hard-driving," unsympathetic Lieutenant Colonel (Frank Lovejoy) who does not want to hear any sad stories about Carlson's two children, his expertise in electronics, or his lack of experience above the platoon level. He makes Carlson a company commander and sends him packing to change uniform.

The merits of the movie as cinema aside, its early segments were reasonably faithful to the events of June and July 1950. Being recalled unexpectedly after a five-year moratorium was a shock to many male reservists. They were established family men, a bit sedentary, and invested in earning a living. Attending reserve meetings kept them in touch with Marine Corps affairs but no one was thinking about war. The recall was an abrupt, "unwelcome interruption" in their postwar lives. Retired Brigadier General Edwin H. Simmons, current director of the Marine Corps Historical Center in Washington, D.C., was a major in 1950. He remembers the replacements who flowed into Pendleton in mid-summer:

> Most were World War II veterans. They were experienced combat Marines. . . . That single fact, the quality of the men who were recalled back to active duty and who made up the bulk of the Marine units sent to Korea, had a lot to do with the outstanding performance of the Marines over there. Not to say there wasn't any grousing. Most of them didn't like the idea of being called back in. After World War Two they had stayed in the Reserve really as a kind of social thing, like a fraternal organization. Nobody was expecting that we'd have another war five years later. By late August we were in Japan.[6]

The story of the Corps' military achievement in South and North Korea during the last six months of 1950 is the stuff from which legends are made. As Allan R. Millett observed, "Even stripped of Corps legend and media myth-making, the Korean campaigns of the 1st Marine Division in 1950 retain an epic quality" (p. 482). The staunch support of U.S. Army units in August, the landing at Inchon and the recapture of Seoul in September, and the valiant return from the "frozen Chosin" in November and December have long been a part of the Corps' glorious record. After Chosin, correspondent Marguerite Higgins wrote in *War in Korea* (1951) that the Marines' "reputation as fighting men remained fully secured" (p. 197). These dramatic accomplishments have been examined in numerous sources, most of which are worthy of study by anyone who seeks a definition of the term "courage."[7]

With the notable exception of Mary V. Stremlow's monograph, little has been said about how Women Marines were faring behind the war's center stage. The wildly unrealistic, long-range goal was to have 112,000 women in uniform within three years. The intake up to July

1951 was not terribly encouraging. The WAC strength was 12,000, WAVES 6,300, and Marines 2,065. A year later the total had crawled upward to only 46,000, well below the two percent legal limit authorized by Congress, and would peak at 48,700 in October 1952. The grandiose plan to induce women into the service had fizzled. The number of WMs rose from 580 in 1950 to 2,700 in 1953 (a high unmatched until 1968).

As mentioned earlier, the Marine Corps was satisfied with its ceiling of 3,000 women. When the Korean War began, Company E at Henderson Hall was the only major gathering of WMs. Recruit training at Parris Island was suspended in May 1950 for lack of adequate numbers of boots, and the staff was reassigned. By October the Parris Island battalion was once again functional; there was a WM company at Camp Lejeune, and a nucleus detachment at MCAS El Toro, California. Over the next year and a half, WM units were operational at MCAS Cherry Point, Camp Pendleton, FMF Pac (Fleet Marine Force, Pacific) Hawaii, Norfolk, and MCRD San Diego. A WM company was established at Quantico in May 1953.

Until the influx of new WMs made itself felt in early 1951 most of the wartime billets were filled by regulars and women called to active service with their reserve units. The hasty mobilization evoked some serious questions. Where are WMs needed most? How many are enough for a particular duty station? In what specialization should the women be utilized? And before they are assigned, are there living arrangements that must be made to accommodate females? The Corps' method of dealing with such issues may be illustrated by how it managed the return of WMs to Camp Lejeune in 1950. We might describe the method as the "advance party strategy."

On July 24, 1950 Major Pauline B. Beckley and two enlisted WMs arrived at Lejeune "to open and ready a barracks for occupancy by women Reservists being ordered to active duty." Within a week the initial contingent of WMs stepped from a bus to Lejeune soil, nearly four years after the last WR departed the camp in 1946. The women, proclaimed the Lejeune *Globe,* were "ready and rarin' to go." Myrtle I. Seavey was one of the seven enlisted WMs deposited at the camp bus station. She may have been out of breath, everything happened so quickly. Just a few days earlier she was NCO in charge of recruiting for the Fifth Infantry Battalion, Organized Marine Reserve in Washington, D.C. She remembers that "We were given ten days to square away our personal affairs and report to Lejeune. It was awesome." Perhaps the strains of the Marine Corps band's bon voyage serenade at Union Station lingered in her mind as she went through the process of being logged in at Lejeune. It was a case of *déjà vu* for her and her six comrades. All of them took their boot training there during World War II. Corporal Virginia S. Kegel looked around her and said, "It's like old times—but it's a pleasure not to have to undergo boot camp again."

Soon after the Washington group landed, reserve units from Boston and Philadelphia contributed WMs to the growing pool. On Friday, October 13, 1950, at noon, the CO of Lejeune's Headquarters Battalion, Colonel James M. Ranck, presented Captain Mary J. Fischer with a warrant confirming the formation of a Women Marines Company at Marine Barracks, Camp Lejeune. Eventually the number of WMs reached 400.

What types of jobs were WMs given to do when they filtered into the Corps' circulatory system in the early 1950s? As one might guess, little was left to chance. The classification process employed was implemented in November 1949. Where a WM was sent and what tasks she was assigned depended on her Military Occupational Specialty (MOS) number and the nature of the Corps' needs at its various posts, stations, and bases. The MOS was set for each woman during her recruit training. As Julia E. Hamblet explained in 1951, at Parris Island,

> during the first week of training, the recruit takes the basic classification test battery, which consists of . . . Reading and Vocabulary; Arithmetic Reasoning and Pattern Analysis. Later in the training period, each marine is personally interviewed by a classification specialist. During this interview, information is obtained relative to the marine's schooling, civilian background and experience, hobbies and interests.[8]

This information formed the basis of the MOS a boot received. When she graduated from training, the new WM was sent to her first duty station. Hamblet continues: "Upon arrival . . . a marine is normally assigned to a billet which carries the same MOS as the marine. Thus a matching of job requirements and skills is obtained." Of the 469 MOSs in effect in late 1950 eighty-six were filled by enlisted WMs. A careful examination of the MOS list reveals a pattern that the women knew existed during both wars, i.e., the vast majority of assignments fell into clerical and administrative categories. It bears out Allan Millett's conclusion that for WMs "the war brought an increase of numbers to almost 3,000 but no redefinition of duties" (pp. 508–509).

A number of new WMs were sent to schools for advanced training following boot camp. Among these post–graduate opportunities we find: Personnel Administration at Parris Island; Basic Disbursing, Paymaster,

Motor Transport, Supply, and NCO Leadership at Camp Lejeune; Kodak Institute for budding photographers in Washington, D.C.; Air Controlman School at the Naval Air Station in Ilathe, Kansas; Journalism at the Naval Training Station at Great Lakes, Illinois; Yeoman School in San Diego; Public Information at Fort Slocum, Georgia; and Naval Justice in Newport, Rhode Island. As a rule, completion of these programs led to assignments that were a bit more exotic—although, not always more exciting—than the postings the typical WM was given.

For example, WMs were ordered to recruiting duty in Oklahoma City; Portland, Oregon; Omaha; St. Louis; Denver; and New Orleans. At face value this sounds very enchanting. But it took a WM out of the Corps' mainstream, isolated her from her peers, and, now and then, placed her in a setting in which people looked askance at females in uniform. Dorothy Mae Griffin, a former WR, was in the recruiting service in both wars. She says, "In my city I found Women Marines were not accorded the same friendship and respect I had felt everywhere in World War II. It was a very difficult job for me to convince most parents their daughters could be ladies and Marines, too." Most WM recruiters were successful salespersons who had a product they truly believed in: the U.S. Marine Corps. Omaha recruiter Edna Cogswell was so dedicated she persuaded her brother Leo to enlist.

A handful of WMs were placed in what some people called "glamour" jobs. These might include senior air traffic controller at MCAS Cherry Point; staff member with the Armed Forces Public Information Office in Los Angeles; teletype operator at the Brooklyn Navy Yard in New York; instructor in the Marine Corps Institute correspondence school in Washington, D.C.; official photographer at HQMC; secretarial aide in Naples, Italy, and Frankfurt, Germany; and Jill-of-all-trades on base newspapers such as El Toro's *The Flight Jacket* and San Diego's *Chevron.*

Future WM officers had to be recruited, too. That task was given to commissioned women who were attached to what was then known as Officer Procurement Offices (OPO) in locations such as New Orleans, Columbus, and San Francisco. Captain Edrey S. Schendel's last assignment was as the Woman OPO for the West Coast. She was given a government automobile, a WM sergeant to assist her, and a fairly free rein. She recalls: "We traveled around California, Oregon, Washington, Idaho, and Nevada to colleges to recruit women officer candidates. It was independent duty. We did all our letters, scheduling, and radio, TV, and newspaper publicity." All OPOs had quotas to meet. Edrey met hers.

The largest slice of WM assignments fell into the traditional category: clerical, the khaki collar level, so to say. In most corporate and social institutions it is the workers—the unseen majority that labor in the vineyards—who keep an enterprise afloat. Thousands of WMs did that over the years with little acclaim and for modest pay. Their major compensation was that they could look in their mirrors and say, "I am a U.S. Marine." They were the female counterparts to the Marine "grunt," the infantrymen without whom (even generals had to admit) the Corps would not have been victorious on so many battlefields. They were the women who kept the vital papers moving through the Department of the Pacific and the Depot of Supply in San Francisco; served as clerk-typists at Quantico, Lejeune, and Pendleton; drove and maintained USMC vehicles at Cherry Point and Honolulu; did the routine chores in mailrooms, P.X. offices, and WM clubs; worked for the Special Services unit at El Toro; supervised the preparation of Marine uniforms at the Philadelphia supply depot; and, as DIs, put recruits through their paces on Parris Island. At HQMC, WMs were the caretakers of other people's futures. They monitored allotments, combat pay, mileage, retirements, and personnel records. Clara L. Lapean was stationed at HQMC during the war doing a herculean job of keeping the Corps' "books." Among her duties, she remembers one that was particularly sorrowful: "I was the person who paid for flowers for all deceased Marines whose bodies were sent home."

When WMs reached their destinations and took up their duties, their male colleagues began to notice there was something new in the vicinity: women. Many of the men had never seen a WM up close before. The old hands had, of course, and probably had a rich mixture of comments about the girls in green. Certainly they cautioned the younger Marines against calling a WM a "BAM" (broad-ass Marine) to her face. Yelling it at a safe distance under cover of darkness was tacitly sanctioned, but still risky.

There were so few WMs that they stood out in the crowd. For example, at Cherry Point in 1944 there were 2,000 WRs on the air station and its outlying fields. After a while they simply became a part of the scenery. In 1953 there were 220, hardly enough to make an impression on the lifestyle of the station. How were the women received throughout the Corps? What sorts of attitudes did they face as they fanned out onto the various installations? Did the slanderous climate of the World War II era carry over into the 1950s?[9]

I will answer these questions at two levels. First, I will use *Leatherneck* magazine as an index of the Corps-wide reaction to the presence of WMs. In most ways *Leatherneck* is a valuable barometer of what is on the minds of Marines. It was (and still is) directed at the enlisted ranks. Its contents not only reflected their tastes and interests, it shaped their values to a slight degree, I feel. I have examined all the issues of *Leatherneck* between June 1948 and June 1955, a total of eighty-four editions, in an attempt to identify patterns of attitudes toward WMs. My suspicion was that how they were portrayed in the "Magazine of the Marines" was a fairly reliable clue to how they were viewed within the Corps proper. Second, I measured those findings against the opinions expressed by the former WMs who contributed to this volume in an effort to establish what, if any, discrepancies existed between the two levels. I was surprised at what I discovered.

I admit to allowing myself to be predisposed to a point of view before I studied *Leatherneck.* From one of the former WMs I received a copy of a letter which nearly undermined my objectivity. Dated January 18, 1954, it was addressed to all WMs from Staff Sergeant Betty Leuthold, assistant to the *Leatherneck*'s circulation manager. Essentially, it was a well-written, spritely advertisement for the February 1954 issue of the magazine. "Believe me," Leuthold said, "this is one LEATHERNECK you won't want to miss!" She was not over-selling. It was an uncommon issue insofar as its coverage of WMs was concerned.

What caught my eye was her letter's second paragraph. "I've been on the Magazine for almost three years," she wrote. "The only real gripe I've had . . . is that no one ever seemed to get around to writing about us [WMs]." For a week or so I took that to mean that *Leatherneck* had virtually ignored the existence of WMs up to that point, and probably subsequent to the February 1954 issue as well. My judgment was tainted by what I knew had happened to WRs during World War II. Was the *Leatherneck*'s aloofness a continuation of the cynicism that prevailed in the previous war? Fortunately, I did not bypass the question and rely on my original hypothesis. I visited the Marine Corps Historical Center in Washington, D.C. and pored over seven years of *Leathernecks*. From that exercise I drew several firm conclusions: Betty Leuthold's complaint was unfounded, and my assumption was wrong. Hers was a case of public relations hyperbole intended to sell magazines and quite understandable in that context. Mine was a case of shaky scholarship and less excusable. The facts were, *Leatherneck* was quite generous with space it gave WMs from 1948 to 1955 and the tone of its reportage was positive, if condescending.

Before we turn to *Leatherneck*'s depictions of WMs it might be helpful to comment on what the magazine was like forty years ago. Its length fluctuated between sixty-five and eighty pages per month. Among the standard sections were: commercial ads; letters to the editor ("Sound Off"); Corps-related cartoons; "The Old Gunny Says," a page of advice from the voice of experience; "Mail Call," in which people are trying to locate other people; a piece of fiction; "Posts of the Corps"; "Bulletin Board," late notices of concern to all Marines; "In Reserve"; a "Crazy Caption" contest, and "Gyrene Gyngles." Somewhere in each issue was a full page photograph of the pin-up girl of the month, generally attired in a bathing suit or sportswear (Marilyn Monroe was the staff's choice four times). There were feature articles on a wide variety of topics and many photographs of Marines at work and at play and, commencing in October 1950, ongoing coverage of the Korean War. Nearly all the material was written by male Marines and there was usually a two-month lag between an event and its appearance in the magazine. The overall tone from cover to cover was upbeat, gung ho, and loyal. In short, it was a bargain at three dollars a year.[10]

Leatherneck's attention to WMs began slowly in its September 1948 edition with a "Bulletin Board" notice that women were legally allowed to enter the "regular service." After several more terse bulletins in early 1949 the rate of references to WMs accelerated. In the March 1949 issue an 8 1/4″ x 11″ advertisement was directed at women who might be interested in enlisting. Private First Class Norris Dolin was the uniformed model who looked straight at the reader and stated "There's a Place for You." In April WMs were pictured marching in President Truman's inaugural parade. The quantum leap into the spotlight for WMs came in August 1949. On the cover was a photograph of the first platoon of recruits to go through Parris Island and, inside, the article "High Heeled Boots" mentioned in the previous chapter, an item in "Bulletin Board" concerning promotion tests for WMs, and a photograph of Sergeant Pearl Jackson, the first woman to go to the WOTC program.

Leatherneck finally caught up with the Korean War in October 1950 and rounded out the year on a very sobering note. A long list of Marines killed and missing appeared near the back of the December issue. The deaths numbered in the hundreds. Forty-five of our forty-eight states were represented on that dolorous roster. For the first time the *Leatherneck*'s readership was confronted with the stark reality of the war in the Far East.

Around that roll of sadness there were pieces on the WM reserve unit in Minneapolis; and a notice that Staff Sergeant Anna Peregrim, a New York recruiter, was chosen "Miss Subways" by model builder John Robert Powers earlier that fall, which meant that her smiling face beamed down on millions of passengers from her 10,000 subway cards. An important article concerning WMs was published in the November 1950 issue. On the Corps' 175th birthday *Leatherneck* declared that the women had "earned the right to wear our emblem as true Marines." It was a clear signal that by 1951 WMs were worthy of acceptance.

At that turning point I will halt my exegetical analysis and touch only on certain highlights from 1951 to 1955. There was some mention of WMs in every issue during those five years and numerous pictures of them doing their various duties. Articles on WMs were included in the November 1951, August 1952, October and November 1953, and February 1954 editions. In August 1952 a piece on the 225 WMs stationed at Lejeune quoted the CO of the Headquarters and Service Battalion, Colonel Walker A. Reaves, as saying, "WMs at Lejeune? We couldn't do without them," a widely held view among post commanders. WMs were on the front covers of the November 1952, February 1953, February 1954, and April 1955 issues. In the first three instances they were drawn by commercial illustrators. The 1952 cover shows a WM corporal applying lipstick on a rugged Marine who is in the cast of "Highlights of Marine Corps History." He is stoically enduring the cosmeticizing, she is being quite professional. The point? Only a woman knows how to do a job a man would not be caught dead doing ordinarily. Neither of them thinks it is very funny. She had better not laugh. The 1953 cover had a "comely" WM Private First Class seated at her desk. ("Comely" was a journalistic euphemism for: a great-looking "broad," "gal," or "dame.") She has a shocked look on her pretty face. Standing before her is a tough, blushing top sergeant with a Valentine's Day card in his hand. He is a little embarrassed, she is stunned. Is his thoughtful gesture a peace offering—or a romantic overture? Either way, it signifies that even "old salts" appreciated the attractive WMs who worked beside them every day. The April 1955 cover was a photograph of parishioners leaving the Catholic chapel at Lejeune after Easter services. There were three WMs, two in greens and one in dress blues, in the sedate procession.

It was in the cartoons that *Leatherneck* catered to the sexist, humorous, juvenile side of its male readers. The cartoons ridiculed WMs as poor drivers, waspish senior sergeants, and airheads (à la actress Marie Wilson)—or depicted them as sex objects. In other words the staff was perfectly attuned to the social mores of the 1950s. They knew what the men wanted and they gave it to them.

In the February 1954 issue that Betty Leuthold was promoting there were eleven cartoons involving WMs. One example will suffice. On page forty-one we see an MP in dress blues checking a bosomy WM's identity card and liberty pass. He is leering wolfishly when he says: "Well, well, Pfc. Swellbilt, Lucy J. Ht. 5'3"; Wt. 115; hair, blonde; eyes, blue; date of birth, 3-30-34—your phone number doesn't seem to be here." His buddy is seated in the sentry box, pen in hand, eager to copy down her number, if she divulges it. All the stereotypic elements are present. The MP has one stripe more than she does, he is the law, she is a naive pigeon ripe for caging, and, naturally, she is a blue-eyed blonde with physical properties Marines fantasize about. Otherwise, the magazine was very mature in its treatment of WMs. There were a number of articles about the women, including a four-page story on Boston's Organized Reserve unit, approximately forty photographs, and a page devoted to WM athletes. In a sense, the contents speak to the ambivalence that prevailed at the time. Were the WMs women first, and then Marines? Or just the reverse? How were men expected to treat them? Some males are not sure, yet.

We can acquit *Leatherneck* of the charge that it never "got around to writing about [WMs]." Now we are ready to listen to the other side of the issue. What do former WMs say about their reception by members of the "club"? I am pleased to report that only a few of the eighty WMs who replied to the question "How well, or poorly, were you treated by male Marines?" had serious grievances. If I may generalize from such a small sampling, it is evident that WMs were not subjected to the abuse their predecessors were during World War II. The worst offenses seem to be teasing, a casual "pass," and foul language that slipped into conversations inadvertently—not new experiences for a young female, civilian or military. Let us hear from the women on this point:

I cannot imagine the problems that some of the young women are forced to consider these days. My relationship with male Marines was always the very best. . . . I felt a companionship with them that I have never felt since with any other group of men or women. . . . I had only one problem with a date and the men in my unit took care of the situation. When it was brought to their attention—no more problem. (Doris Reeves)

I used to get kidded a lot about being so short (4'11")—but when they saw my Pfc stripe and hashmark they'd say, "There goes a true Marine." (Rosemary Thompson)

Very often, male Marines were a challenge to what I felt was the right thing to do or say, but I had friends I could trust in case I needed support. For the most part, I was able to stand my own ground. (Clare Bullitt)

I did not hear bad language in my presence until I retired and worked in civilian life. Amazing! (Esther Waclawski)

Sometimes, walking on the base past the men's barracks, we'd hear, "There goes a rabbit—BAM!" But it was said in fun. (Wilma Shaw)

I just ignored any remarks and laughed them off, as all women have done for years. Since I was neither a lesbian nor a whore—which was many people's attitudes toward women in the military—I felt that was the reaction, for me. (Carol Homan)

Face to face, male Marines were polite and respectful, and always apologized if they used vulgar language in front of us. We never encouraged or tolerated the language you hear today. How times have changed! (Joan Walter)

Some men wanted to be accepting but did not know exactly how to be. Instead of coming right out and saying something positive, their egos required that they take an oblique approach. As one WM who was stationed in Hawaii tells it:

I worked for a male Tech Sergeant who didn't really want WMs assigned to his G-3 section. After hearing him turn down numbers of WMs time after time I asked him why *I* was there. He turned to me and said, "Collins, you're different. You're like one of the guys." Coming from him that was supposed to be a compliment. I suppose, at that time, it was. (Joan Collins)

WMs were no slouches when it came to snappy comebacks, when they were called for. And sometimes they were, when the women had enough male remarks to last a lifetime. For example:

It was late in 1953, as I recall. I was engaged in conversation with Colonel B——— and he said, "You know, Sergeant Rogers—it's too bad you aren't a man. You'd have made a heck of a Marine." Well, I shot right back, "Sir, I'm as much of a Marine as you are. We took the same oath." He laughed so hard it made me wonder if he was sober. (Olga Rogers)

By and large, the women say, male Marines were courteous and friendly, although, as Edrey Schendel reminds us, "There were always a few, enlisted and officer, who thought WMs were there for their gratification." And there were some men who never did accept the idea of women in the Corps. "One time when I had Friday night duty," Dorothy Mae Griffin remembers, "the duty officer made me scrub the stairs three times just because he hated Women Marines." "Bobbie" Lee recalls that the "only problem I had with most male Marines was trying to get them to understand that women respond to a different type of leadership than do men. One doesn't need to yell . . . or use objectionable language to get women to do what you want them to do."

At this point it is important to broach two sensitive social problems that were foisted upon Korean War era WMs: racism and homosexuality. There is no need to dwell on either of these delicate, controversial issues, but to pretend they did not exist would be intellectually dishonest. Racism in American society is an open wound that has yet to be cauterized. Since the military is society in microcosm it, too, has had to deal with the corrosions racism evokes. Most social historians agree that the U.S. armed forces, however begrudgingly, contributed to the equalization of human rights by integrating their units well before the American people were prepared to do so in their civilian institutions. As Richard Dalfiume observed, "By the end of 1954, segregation and discrimination were virtually eliminated from the internal organization of the armed forces" (p. 220).

It is no longer inflammatory to say that the Southern states were the last to acknowledge the rectitude of the civil rights cause. Most new WMs—that is, those who were not World War II veterans—were from regions outside the South and had virtually no contact with segregation prior to joining the military. Their initial exposure to overt racism, then, occurred when they were stationed at major Marine Corps installations such as Quantico, Parris Island, Cherry Point, and Lejeune. Joan Collins experienced it on three occasions on her way to boot camp in 1953. First, during a layover in Union Station in Washington, D.C., she saw "white" and "colored" restrooms and drinking fountains, something very surprising to her. Second, on the train heading South an "enormous" conductor stopped by the roomette Joan was sharing with a dark-skinned recruit from Puerto Rico and told Joan's friend that she had to move into a smaller room across the aisle. Joan volunteered to move, and the conductor barked, "I don't care if you are Goddamn Marines, the colored girl will have to room by herself" (which she did). Third, while awaiting transportation to Parris Island at the Yemassee train station, Joan noticed that the restaurant was divided into "white" and "colored" sections, and they were cordoned off by strands of chicken wire. Her Puerto Rican buddy had to sit in the "colored" zone.

Two years earlier Pearl Morris was on her way to Parris Island from her home in Pennsylvania. She says:

I had never been further south than Baltimore, so you can imagine how shocked I was when the train stopped at Quantico, VA . . . and I saw

for the first time in my life waiting rooms marked "white" and "colored."
Segregation was very strong at that time [1951] and the further South we
went, the worse it got.

Wilma Shaw was ordered to Cherry Point in December 1952. She
was nineteen. "Gee, this sure is different from boot camp," she wrote.
"I can't get over how nice the officers are to the enlisted personnel—so
different from Parris Island." Of course, everything and any place are
different from Parris Island. She made friends quickly and one of her
buddies was a black WM. On a warm August day in 1953 Wilma and
her friend

> decided to hop a bus and go into New Bern for a few hours on the one-
> half day a week we had off. Shopping was what we had in mind. We
> went into this store and the saleslady came over and asked me if I was
> *all* white. I was surprised by the question but answered "yes." She asked
> if we were Women Marines. I acknowledged that to be true and she
> replied, "Well, I guess it's different in the service." Obviously, she
> wanted me to know that she didn't approve of the races associating. So
> we left.

In both wars, I found, women in the Marines were rather naive about
the actualities and social significance of segregation until they were sent
to the Corps' cantonments south of the Mason-Dixon line. Since there
were no black WRs in World War II, and since black men were in
segregated units, the women dealt with race relations only vicariously.
During the Korean War period, white WMs had black comrades in their
units, albeit infrequently. Both generations of WMs were shielded from
racial upheavals in the society at large outside the Corps. Black WMs
who contributed to this text do not appear to have been victimized by
racist behavior any more so than in civilian life. "I got along well with
the other [read: white] women," Annie Grimes recalls. "Some were
friendly, others observed me with curiosity at first, but they soon made
me feel accepted as a member of the team." It was a booster shot to
black and white WM relationships that the Corps was integrating its
male components. With every increase in their numbers black Marines
became less of a "curiosity." As Bernard C. Nalty noted, "By June 1953
. . . almost 15,000 blacks were serving in a Marine Corps numbering
about a quarter million, about 6 percent of the total or almost six times
the proportion on active duty when the fighting began."[11] There was
trouble ahead for the Corps on racial issues in the 1960s at Lejeune,

Okinawa, Hawaii, and in Japan but, for the most part, WMs were insulated from those eruptions.

In the military the "race problem" has been supplanted in notoriety by the gay and lesbian controversy. Scores of books and articles have taken "gays in the armed forces" as their main theme.[12] Some of these materials are written by persons who believe that an open door policy is the only constitutional avenue to follow; some argue that the "Don't ask. Don't tell" approach will protect both the homosexual and the military from each other and from endless litigation; and some are unalterably opposed to allowing gays to wear a U.S. uniform under any circumstances. My impression is that the Marine Corps would choose the latter alternative if the issue were not such a hot potato politically. At least, that is what I deduce from contemporary Marine-oriented publications.[13]

Certainly, the debate will not be dissected in these pages, but it is crucial to acknowledge that female homosexuality has been a matter of concern within the Corps since 1943. During the Korean War era it reached a crescendo unsurpassed previously and not experienced again until the 1980s. What was it like in the 1950s for WMs? I guaranteed anonymity to those women who were willing to share what happened to them four decades ago. The samples I chose are, in my view, very representative of the Corps' (and the Navy Department's) reaction to the presence of lesbians in its branch of service. None of the women were practicing homosexuals then (or now). Each one expressed regret that they were even associated with the "problem"—but they were, and they have not forgotten how it felt. Their testimonies are valuable because they constitute primary evidence of what occurred in an age when lesbianism was a dark, distressing fact of life that was repressed by both the women who knew about it and by the authorities who were directed to purge its practitioners from the ranks. The openness with which it is discussed in the 1990s has not substantially lessened the intensity or rigidity that surrounds the issue. The quartet of reminiscences that follow are drawn from the years 1949–1954.

Woman Marine "A":   She was sent to MCRD San Diego after boot camp. During her tour there she was very active in sports such as softball, volleyball, and basketball. One day she was cornered by a trio of male master sergeants who peppered her with questions such as "Know anyone who's a lesbian? Ever been 'approached'? Seen any homosexual conduct? Have any tendencies in that direction yourself?" The WM said "no" to each question. After that they left her alone, but she remembers that those interrogations, of which there were many, created an atmosphere of "apprehension" on the base and inhibited females from being open with each other. She says, "Frankly, I was so naive that I didn't know what, if anything, was going on."

Women Marine "B":   At San Diego there was a big investigation and I was scooped up in it for some reason. I had to take a lie detector test (which I passed). Talk about intimidation. During one of the interrogations there were two gigantic guys scowling at me the whole time. Of course, I had encountered all this before. In boot camp some of the lesbian recruits would string up a blanket over in a far corner to protect their privacy. At Lejeune . . . there were five WMs in Motor Transport. I was the only one interested in boys and driving. The other girls made no bones about their preferences for each other. Many girls who weren't lesbians at San Diego were harassed by the authorities—and some who confessed voluntarily that they were homosexuals in an overt attempt to get a discharge, they didn't release. It was crazy.

Woman Marine "C":   I was a buck sergeant at P.I. I got on somebody's list of suspects, probably because I played on the softball team. Anyone who was into athletics was a candidate for the inquisition, I guess. Anyway, one day I was told that I was going to be driven to Mainside by some people so I went outside of the 3rd Battalion administration building and there was a car with two men in civilian clothes waiting for me. I got in— and we didn't go anywhere. I just sat there between those men for a half hour while they grilled me. They asked a lot of questions—about me, about other women, about what was going on with other WMs. I told them the truth: I had never been approached by any other women and I had no facts to offer them. They let me out and I never told anyone what happened. I want to say that our WM officers didn't do anything, as far as I could tell, about the situation. Maybe they were scared to get involved. Maybe some of them were afraid of being exposed. Whatever, I remember clearly the atmosphere of unrest the investigations caused at P.I. A pall fell over everything. I recall that some of the WMs who were under house arrest were called somewhere—and disappeared. We never found out what happened to them, and we didn't ask.

Woman Marine "D":   She enlisted in the Corps in 1950 and was stationed at Parris Island, HQMC, and Quantico prior to her discharge in June 1953. About three weeks after her release, two Naval Investigative Service (NIS) operatives came to the small apartment where she and her husband, a Marine officer, had set up housekeeping. The agents were particularly interested in two WMs she had worked with in the photo lab at HQMC. They asked: Was she aware that her two friends had a "relationship"? Did she ever witness them indulging in "compromising" conduct? Did she think they were security risks, given their handling of highly sensitive photographs? She said no to the first two questions, and refused to respond to the third. "After about twenty minutes they left and never contacted me again," she says. "I did learn from one of my good WM friends later on that one of the two girls being investigated had killed herself by leaping from a D.C. bridge."

In mid-1951 the public mood concerning the Korean War began to shift toward Omar Bradley's opinion that it was "the wrong war, in the wrong place, at the wrong time, with the wrong enemy." Initially, as I mentioned above, the American people were very supportive of President Truman's decision to lead the United Nations into battle against the North Koreans. The United States and fifteen other nations contributed resources to the struggle to maintain South Korea's sovereignty. Americans were pleased, if not astonished, to witness such a homogeneity of purpose among disparate nations. Our allies (from some of whom we are estranged) were: Australia, Belgium, Canada, Colombia, Ethiopia, France, Greece, Luxembourg, Netherlands, New Zealand, Philippines, South Africa, Thailand, Turkey, and the United Kingdom—who, collectively, took 3,457 battle deaths. American citizens were not too clear on why the United States was so committed to the preservation of South Korea's independence but there was comfort in having so much reinforcement. Matthew B. Ridgway, Commanding General of the Eighth Army, had no doubts about why we were there. In his memoir, *The Korean War* (1967), his manifesto was included as an appendix. In January 1951 he told his troops:

> The real issues are whether the power of Western Civilization, as God has permitted it to flower in our own beloved lands, shall defy and defeat Communism; whether the rule of men who shoot their prisoners, enslave their citizens and deride the dignity of man, shall displace the rules of those to whom the individual and his individual rights are sacred; whether we are to survive with God's hand to guide and lead us, or to perish in the dead existence of a Godless world. (pp. 264–265)

That was in January. By November a succession of events evoked a serious dip in public interest and confidence that turned to apathy for the remaining nineteen months of the war. For example, still reeling from the licking we took in the late fall of 1950, Americans were confronted with: the loss of Seoul and Inchon to the Chinese Communist Forces (CCF) in January; the dismissal of General Douglas MacArthur in April; a new spring offensive by the CCF in April and May; the extension of the draft in June; the initiation of truce talks in July, which broke down; a resumption of bitter fighting in August and September; mounting casualties; and the renewal of cease fire negotiations in October. As columnist James Brady described the denouement in *The Coldest War: A Memoir of Korea* (1990):

> By November 1951 there was no more oratory. The line had stabilized, partly from exhaustion and cold, partly because the truce talks occasionally flickered into promise. The Chinese, a million of them, and what was left of the North Koreans, dug in. And we dug in, six American divisions and our UN allies. Two armies stood and faced each other in the hills with another damned winter coming out of Siberia. (p. 2)

From that point on the entire conflict resembled World War I, with "heavy usage of trenches, bunkers, and tunnels, with frequent night-patrol skirmishes and intense artillery barrages." When James Brady arrived on Thanksgiving Day 1951 the First Marine Division was in eastern South Korea. His battalion was "dug in" on Hill 749, as was mine. Some semblance of what it was like as the war became static may be found in a letter I wrote home on November 17:

> We are in our third day of fog, rain, and cold. You can visualize the mud we have to contend with. . . . The rats are having a field day. We have one in our Platoon CP named Bruno. Bruno reveals himself only at night—and then for the specific purpose of scratching dirt on us from the ceiling of the bunker, with uncanny accuracy I might add. As you know, a zippered-up sleeping bag forces the occupant to sleep on his back most of the time. Bruno is therefore assured a target for each night and seldom fails to hit the opening through which I breathe. My only consolation is that the North Koreans may be more miserable. . . . I have no idea how the big war is going, only my own little one on Hill 749, but although hope for peace runs high now and then, no one is too confident. We are among friends however. The KMCs hold down our left flank and on our right we have the ROK Capital Division. The Army would prefer to think of that arrangement as analogous to a piece of ham between two slices of stale bread, I'm sure. And, oh yes, directly across the valley is a North Korean OP manned by our good friend and supervisor, Luke the Gook. He is no doubt responsible for the incoming mortar and artillery rounds we receive each day. Maybe, one of these days, we'll get him—somehow.

The year 1952 began to the accompaniment of one, great public yawn. The Korean War was no longer news. By then, as Donald Knox states in his *The Korean War: Uncertain Victory* (1991, Volume 2), "To many it was unreal. Ordinary lives were unruffled by the distant echoes of battle—If neither one's friends nor one's family were directly involved, the war could have been taking place on the desert of Mars" (p. 504). By early 1952 the level of the public disapproval was rising steeply. Did the Marines in the trenches sense that? Did they know why they were in Korea? Did they need to know?

Author James A. Michener went to Korea to acquaint himself with what "the average American fighting men on the static war front were thinking." In the process of gathering opinions—and material he would use in his next book, *The Bridges at Toko-Ri* (1953)—Michener spent three days with the men of the First Marine Division. Reportedly, he interviewed 300 men, perhaps not all of them Marines. On February 3, 1952 Michener visited my luxurious quarters, ate with me and a fellow officer, and chatted with us about the war. I believe he already knew that Marines do not insist on knowing *why* they are where they are. The Corps' reasons for sending you to a particular location require neither defending nor explanation. I do not recall his asking what we thought about the plummeting public interest in the war. Evidently, he posed that question to sufficient numbers of men to draw the conclusion that "They know why we are in Korea and don't feel that the nation has let them down."[14]

A year or so later *The Bridges at Toko-Ri* was published. It follows the fortunes of a Naval aviator assigned to a carrier operating off the Korean coast. Lieutenant Harry Brubaker USNR is a World War II "retread" who is resentful of being recalled to risk his life in a conflict he does not understand. In a fit of self-absorption he expresses his feelings to the task force commander, Admiral George Tarrant, who is not enamored of being where he is, either. "Imagine," Tarrant says, "the United States Navy tied down to a few square miles of ocean. The Marines are worse. Dug into permanent trenches. . . . Militarily this war is a tragedy." Brubaker remarks, "It would be easier to take if people back home were helping. But in December nobody even knew there was a war except my wife. Nobody supports this war." Tarrant, after a moment, replies, "All through history men have had to fight the wrong war in the wrong place. But that's the one they're stuck with."

Perhaps Mr. Michener did hear what the Marines were saying, after all.

NOTES

1. Harry G. Summers, Jr. *Korean War Almanac* (New York: Facts on File, 1990), p. 12.

2. For interpretations of the causes and ignitions of the war that differ from the "accepted" views, see I.F. Stone, *The Hidden History of the Korean War, 1950–1951* (Boston: Little, Brown and Co., 1988. Original ed. 1952); Bruce Cumings, *The Origins of the Korean War* (Princeton, N.J.: Princeton University Press, 1990), Volume II: "The Roaring of the Cataract, 1947–1950"; and Jon Halliday and Bruce Cumings, *Korea: The Unknown War* (New York: Pantheon Books, 1988).

3. Matthew B. Ridgway, *The Korean War* (New York: DaCapo Press, 1967), p. v.

4. J. Lawton Collins, *War in Peacetime: The History and Lessons of Korea* (Boston: Houghton Mifflin Co., 1969), p. 66.

5. Lynn Montross, and Nicholas A. Canzona. *The Pusan Perimeter* (Washington, D.C.: Historical Branch, G-3, Headquarters, U.S. Marine Corps, 1992, Reprinted. Original ed. 1954), p. 39.

6. Simmons quotation from Rudy Tomedi. *No Bugles, No Drums: An Oral History of the Korean War* (New York: John Wiley and Sons, Inc., 1993), p. 31.

7. A selected list of books might include: Montross and Canzona, *supra;* Robert D. Heinl, Jr., *Victory at High Tide: The Inchon-Seoul Campaign* (Annapolis, Md.: The Nautical and Aviation Publishing Company of America, 1979); Eric M. Hamel, *Chosin: Heroic Ordeal of the Korean War* (New York: The Vanguard Press, 1981); Robert Leckie, *The March to Glory* (New York: Bantam Books, 1990. Original ed. 1960); and Jim Wilson, *Retreat, Hell!: We're Just Attacking in a Different Direction* (New York: Pocket Books, 1989).

8. Julia E. Hamblet, "Enlisted Jobs in the Marine Corps Which Can Be Performed by Women in the Event of Mobilization," Unpublished M.S. thesis, The Ohio State University, Columbus, 1951, p. 33.

9. There is no treatment of the trials women endured better than Mattie E. Treadwell, *The Women's Army Corps* (Washington, D.C.: Office of the Chief of Military History, Department of the Army, 1954, Chapter XI, "The 'Slander Campaign,' '' pp. 191–218.

10. For a comprehensive, entertaining review of the magazine's first seventy-five years see "Leatherneck Is 75," *Leatherneck,* November 1992, 18–29.

11. Bernard C. Nalty, *Strength for the Fight: A History of Black Americans in the Military* (New York: The Free Press, 1989. Original ed. 1986), p. 262. See also Henry I. Shaw, Jr. and Ralph W. Donnelly, *Blacks in the Marine Corps* (Washington, D.C.: History and Museums Division, Headquarters, U.S. Marine Corps, 1975).

12. Two recent works are especially useful since they come at the controversy from opposite points. They are: Melissa Wells-Petry, *Exclusion: Homo-*

sexuals and the Right to Serve (Washington, D.C.: Regnery Gateway, 1993), which takes an anti–homosexual (in the military) position, and Randy Shilts, *Conduct Unbecoming: Gays and Lesbians in the U.S. Military* (New York: St. Martin's Press, 1993).

13. For example, William S. Lind, "Homosexuals in the Military," *Marine Corps Gazette,* March 1993, 29–30, and letters to the editor on 30–31; Mark E. Cantrell, "No Place for Homosexuals," *Ibid.,* April 1993, 65–73; and in the June 1993 issue of the *Gazette,* Michael R. Lehnert, "The Homosexual Assault: A Clash of Values," 16–17, and Michael D. Weltsch, "The Homosexual Issue: Back to the Seventies," 17–18. See also Ronald D. Ray, *Military Necessity and Homosexuality* (Louisville, Ky.: First Principles, Inc., 1993). Ray is a colonel in the USMCR.

14. Michener's comment was published in *Leatherneck,* May 1952, 61–62. See also James Michener, "The Forgotten Heroes of the Korean War," *Saturday Evening Post,* May 10, 1952, 19–20, 124, 126, 128, his "special salute" to Navy pilots and the foundation for *Bridges at Toko-Ri.*

CMC Clifton B. Cates (1948–1952) greets LtCol. Julia E. Hamblet at the reception honoring the WR's fifth birthday (February 13, 1948). Standing on Hamblet's left are the WR's first director (1943–1945), Ruth Cheney Streeter, and Maj. Mary Condon. *USMC photo. Courtesy Mary M. Jamison.*

Director of Women Marines (1948–1953) Col. Katherine A. Towle gives dictation to S/Sgt. Dorothea B. Hennan at HQMC in July 1950. *USMC photo. Courtesy Jayne (Burgess) Loraine.*

Women boots prepare their barracks for a forthcoming inspection. They are members of the first platoon of recruits to pass through Parris Island. It is March 1949. *USMC photo. Courtesy Ada (Hazel) Wells.*

It is August 10, 1950 and the WMs from Chicago's 9th Infantry Battalion (Reserve) are packed and ready to depart for San Francisco. S/Sgt. Geraldine Fiorello is reading from the documents that ordered the WMs to active duty. *Reprinted with permission. Chicago Sun-Times © 1994. Courtesy LaVergne Novak.*

All aboard, ladies. New recruits and reservists (in uniform) called to active duty in September 1950 move from the railroad station at Port Royal, S.C., onto a military bus. Destination: MCRD, Parris Island, for boot camp. *USMC photo. Courtesy Jayne (Burgess) Loraine.*

A wartime wedding. Marine officers gather at the MCS Quantico chapel to record forever the marriage of Lts. Virginia Johnson and Warren Sherman on July 30, 1950. *Courtesy Eleanor (Bach) Russell.*

A veteran M/Sgt. introduces women boots to the intricacies of the Browning .30 caliber machine gun during their training in the winter of 1950. *USMC photo. Courtesy Paula (Wiltshire) Sentipal.*

"Henderson Hall buddies" 1952. *Courtesy Olga (Lanzione) Rogers.*

Rosemary Thompson takes a break in a Hobart Mixer at a Camp Pendleton mess hall in 1951. The size-four saddle shoes are authorized. The *Betty Crocker Cookbook* is not. *USMC photo. Courtesy Rosemary (Thompson) Morrison.*

The 1951–1952 WM basketball team from MCAS El Toro. *Courtesy Joyce (Pulliam) Wallace.*

A detachment of WMs from MCAS El Toro step out smartly during a July 4, 1952 parade in Huntington Beach, Calif. *USMC photo. Courtesy Clare (Bullitt) Hokanson.*

Marilyn Monroe (center) in September 1952 serving as Grand Marshal of the Miss America contest in Atlantic City, N.J. She is accompanied by servicewomen chosen to represent the four military branches. *Department of Defense photo. Courtesy Mary M. Jamison.*

Host of the TV show "Musical Jackpot" Paul Bremner is surrounded by WMs in New York on March 29, 1955. Future director of WMs, Lt. Margaret A. Brewer, is seated on Brenner's right. *USMC photo. Courtesy Connie (Musumeci) Guaraglia.*

WMs modeling their new dress blues, summer, and winter uniforms on the U.S. Capitol lawn in February 1953. *USMC photo. Courtesy Gene D. Sims.*

The famous "junk on the bunk" display, in this case the gear of WM Gene D. Sims awaits the sharp eyes of inspecting authorities at MCAS Cherry Point in 1954. *USMC photo. Courtesy Wilma (Shaw) DeiCas.*

Jean Willett

Beverly Schofield

Pearl Morris

Mary Ann Bernard

Betty Moore

Ann Sloan

CORRECTION

Please note that on the last page of the photoessay, the captions for the photographs of LaVergne Novak and Annie Laurie Grimes were reversed. Annie Laurie Grimes appears in the upper right corner, and LaVergne Novak appears at page bottom.

LaVergne Novak

Rosemary Cardamone and her brother Mike

Annie Laurie Grimes

Chapter Five

The Way They Were

WMs who were veterans of World War II were keenly aware that there was something very different about the Korean War years. The élan so characteristic of 1943–1945 was missing. The United States was more business-like in some ways in its pursuit of prosperity and, yet, more prone to hysteria when the threat of Communism was injected into public discourse. The spirit of unity that prevailed during World War II had dissolved into pockets of political, economic, and social self-interest. The new WMs, born in the late 1920s and early 1930s, had no real basis for comparison. For all they knew, the Corps and the country were just fine the way they were and they made the most of what history handed them. A sea change had taken place, however—and former WRs were the first to realize it. LaVergne Novak was on active duty in both wars, so we shall listen to her describe what she saw and felt:

> The whole atmosphere surrounding the Korean War was entirely different from the days of World War II . . . In World War II the whole country was at war, either in military service, in defense plants, in civil defense work, or just in coping with ration coupons and shortages of everything. In the Korean War, only the military and naval services were at war. For the rest of the country it was business as usual. Since it was officially a "police action" in Korea, not a "war," the service people were allowed to wear civilian clothes when not on duty. Therefore, even though a great number of us were on active duty, the public did not see a lot of uniforms to remind them that this police action was, in fact, a war.

The sluggishness of the war, its abstruse rationale, and the absence of obvious "reminders" were contributing factors to the public passivity, no doubt. There were others. For example, World War II was carried to the people via radio with an urgency that drew millions of families to their Atwater Kents at least once a day. Reports from the war zones—one thinks of H.V. Kaltenborn, Edward R. Murrow, and Eric Sevareid—kept listeners involved with how "our boys" were doing in the war's "far-flung fronts." Not so during the Korean War. As David Halberstam wrote, "The nation was not yet wired, and Korea, so distant, the name of its towns so alien, did not lend itself to radio coverage, as did the great war that preceded it" (p. 73). In the 1940s radio also brought us countless shows transmitted from military camps where Bob Hope, Red Skelton, and Kay Kyser were bolstering the morale of men and women in uniform. One searches in vain for comparable instances in the early 1950s. The Korean War was not so newsworthy that the broadcast industry felt obliged to pipe it into our psyches every day.

And what about television? Korea certainly was not the "living-room war" that Vietnam became fifteen years later. "The war in Korea occurred in the early dawn of mass television, but was mostly unseen and therefore unknown," Bruce Cumings pointed out in his 1992 analysis, *War and Television* (p.1). The public's main sources of visual input were pictorial magazines such as *Life,* newspaper stills, and newsreels. On June 25, 1951 photographer David Douglas Duncan, a former Marine, published his classic *This Is War! A Photo-Narrative of the Korean War,* which took the Marines from August through December 1950. Republished in 1990, Duncan's book is without peer, but drops us at Hungnam and leaves the rest of the war to our imaginations. *Collier's, Time, Newsweek,* and *Saturday Evening Post* intermittently included articles about the Marines in Korea. In 1952 two books were released that took the Corps in Korea as their subjects: Andrew Geer's *The New Breed: The Story of the U.S. Marines in Korea* and Pat Frank's *Hold Back the Night.* None of these efforts made much of an impact on the public consciousness. The most dramatic aspect of the war was over by 1951 and the slim literary output reflects the decline in national interest.

How about the movies? Hollywood was World War II's chief propaganda broker, so could we not rely on the "dream factory" to come through when Korea burst into hostilities? We could not. A review of the eighteen films made about the war between 1950 and 1953 confirms Ivan Butler's opinion that "of all the war films that have yet appeared those of the Korean fighting, taken as a whole, make the most dismal viewing."[1] Gilbert Adair described the Korean War movies as "a ragbag of duds" in his *Hollywood's Vietnam* (1989, 18). James R. Parrish thought it a "strong reflection on American culture and political climate that so few significant films were made about 'the country's nastiest little war,'" and said so in *The Great Combat Pictures: Twentieth-Century Warfare on the Screen* (1990, 46).

Of the sixty movies Hollywood produced between 1950 and 1970 which had Korean War themes, seven focused on Marines: *Fixed Bayonets* (1951), *Retreat, Hell!* (1952), *Battle Zone* (1952), *Battle Flame* (1959), *All the Young Men* (1960), *Marines, Let's Go!* (1961), and *The Nun and the Sergeant* (1962). This "mishmash" of offerings told us nothing about the war and little about Marines we did not already know: they are hard-fighting, hard-drinking womanizers whom the country could not do without. Unfortunately, the only movie made about Marines in Korea after 1962 was *Inchon* (1981), a forty million dollar "bomb" financed by Reverend Sun Myung Moon and distributed by MGM/UA. It may have lost more money than any other film in the 1980s. It has been described as one of the great film turkeys of all time and the worst movie ever made. In the 1991 film *For the Boys* there is a segment about Marines in Korea that says more in a few moments than *Inchon* does in two hours and twenty minutes.

During World War II commercial films filled the public's needs to "see" what combat, death, loneliness, and sacrifice looked and felt like. Of the 1,400 movies Hollywood released between 1942 and 1945 approximately 350 had war-related plots. They were intended to inform, uplift, and make money, and they did. Some—such as *Wake Island* (1942), *Gung Ho* (1943), *Guadalcanal Diary* (1943), and *Pride of the Marines* (1945)—were recognized as films of quality and served the Marine Corps well. Hollywood was not confused about its role in the national war effort. The war was "a struggle between good and evil that would be fought until victory was achieved" and the film industry was to do what it did best to help the United States realize that objective. At the outset of the Korean War, Hollywood thought another bonanza had been put in its lap. *Variety* for August 9, 1950 put it this way: "Pix Biz Spurts with War Fever." Other articles that summer read: "Hollywood Scurries to Capitalize on Korean Shooting," and "Hollywood producers are scanning both their picture and story backlogs in an effort to discover some property through which they can cash in on the current war headlines." Things were going so well for filmmakers in general (they thought) that Abel Green of *Variety* said: "The Korean War? What war? Who needs it?"

A year later it was a different story. Hollywood was tacking up the black bunting. Among the developments that sent the industry into a panic attack were: the continuing closings of indoor movie theaters, investigations of suspected "Reds" in the studios, slower responses by banks to requests for funding, hardening government anti-trust policies, the industry's inability to attain intramural unity, unpredictable box office receipts, and the failure of the Korean War to provoke a "boom" in income. Then there was the ultimate rapscallion: television. When Monogram and Republic studios attempted to sell their old films to TV companies in 1951 a shudder went through Hollywood equivalent to a 9.5 on the Richter scale. But the Korean War was still on and Hollywood was not sure what to do with it. As Lawrence H. Suid observed in his excellent study, *Guts and Glory: Great American War Movies* (1978), "If Americans had a difficult time understanding the conflict as the stalemate dragged on, Hollywood had as difficult a time portraying a conflict shaded in gray instead of in the easily defined black and white of World War II" (p. 113).

What Hollywood decided to do was stress a new phenomenon, collaboration with the enemy, in films such as *Prisoner of War* (1954), *The Rack* (1956), and *Time Limit* (1957)—precursors of the masterpiece *The Manchurian Candidate* (1962)—and stay with combat movies that were cast in a Word War II mode but contained increasingly strong anti-Communist messages. And what about the war *qua* war? Among the numerous examples available I have chosen one, *Men of the Fighting Lady,* because it harks back to author James A. Michener and his evolving views on the war. Released on May 8, 1954 the film revolves around Naval aviators who fly from a U.S. carrier off the coast of Korea in 1952. Michener (played by actor Louis Calhern) goes aboard the vessel to get stories about what the air/sea war is all about. The most interesting aspect of the semi-documentary movie is what the players are given to say about the Korean War (which has been "over" for nearly a year). For example, it is a "nuthouse chess game" to one flyer; a "police action" to another; and a mystery to all aviators in terms of why they are there. "We knew what we were fighting for in 1942," one actor says, implying that "we" did *not* know in 1952. The ship's doctor (Walter Pidgeon) administers the *coup de grâce* when he says to Calhern-Michener, "You and your Shakespeare couldn't make this dirty little war romantic." "There are no heroes this time," an aviator states, "and no Ernie Pyle to write about them." The film's wardroom talk is replete with nostalgic references to the earlier, cleaner, successful war. What *was* Korea all about, anyway? Only in combat-oriented movies such as

Bridges at Toko-Ri (1955), *Men in War* (1957), and *Pork Chop Hill* (1959) did Hollywood reveal that it had not lost its touch for battle action. In no film did movie makers display an understanding of the Korean War. But then, who *did* understand it?

Did Hollywood know that there were Women Marines? By my calculations, between 1944 and 1952, WRs/WMs made appearances in at least seven films. They were:

Lake Placid Serenade (1944). This is a silly story about a female Czechoslovakian figure skater (Vera Ralston) who comes to the United States to escape Nazi oppression. Two WRs in greens are lined up behind her during a skating extravaganza. One carries a bugle, the other our national colors.

Here Come the WAVES (1944). Paramount was a little more generous than Republic. Two WAVES on the prowl for males are waiting for Bing Crosby and Sonny Tufts to walk by. They do, but with two WRs who nabbed them first. The WRs sing, "When a beachhead's got to be established/The Marines are first in any fight" and stroll offstage with their captives. After the musical sketch concludes, the WRs may be seen standing in the wings.

Marine Raiders (1944). Two male Marines are at San Diego. They are veterans of Guadalcanal awaiting reassignment. While they are watching a new platoon of boots arrive for training, one Marine wonders aloud, "Well, what will they be taking into the Marine Corps next?" A moment later a platoon of WRs marches through. "We've been outmaneuvered," the sergeant exclaims. There are additional long-range shots of WRs in various formations at Camp Elliot.

You Came Along (1945). If the viewer can keep his or her eyes from watching Robert Cummings and Lizbeth Scott doing a fox trot in a nightclub, he/she might notice a WR and her partner glide by. If one sneezes or coughs one will miss her. That will be it. This film is not on video.

Till the End of Time (1946). In the early segments of this movie about Marine veterans the fleet of eye will catch a glimpse of WRs coming down a stairway at San Diego's separation center. Press the rewind button just to be sure you were not hallucinating.

I'll Get By (1950). Character actress Thelma Ritter works for two braindead songwriters in the period before Pearl Harbor. Several years later the men are privates in the Marine Corps and meet Ritter. She is a WR lieutenant. One of her former bosses asks her what she is doing in uniform. Ritter replies, "I'm an experiment. If I work out, women are in the war." A grizzled male tech sergeant watches the lieutenant walk off arm-in-arm with her tunesmiths and grumbles, "It ain't like the old Marine Corps." Ms. Ritter does not look very svelte in her ill-fitting greens.

Skirts Ahoy! (1952). Made during the Korean War, this is a 105-minute insult to the intelligence of all women in the military. It depicts WAVES recruits as a pretty dippy bunch who turn to swimmer Esther Williams for leadership. Fortunately, WMs are featured as props during a United Service Organizations (USO) gala at the Great Lakes Naval Training Station and are not besmirched by their appearance in the puerile film. MGM should be ashamed. The U.S. Navy should file suit retroactively.

As far as I can determine, WMs have turned up in only five movies over the past forty years. In *Heartbreak Ridge* (1986)—not to be confused with a 1955 French film with the same title—a black WM sergeant pops into an office to deliver a document while "Gunny" Highway (Clint Eastwood) is being read off by a lieutenant colonel. The following year in *Nowhere to Hide,* actress Amy Madigan is cast as a former Marine captain and WMs are included in cafe and experimental laboratory scenes. The 1988 film *Feds* begins with a segment in which a Woman Marine (Rebecca DeMornay) is packing her gear in preparation for her trip to Quantico. She is headed for a recruit class at the F.B.I. academy. Looking very smart in her dress blues she is bade farewell by a group of her Marine friends (all in greens) at the local bus stop. All that is done with style. If one strains and squints, a WM officer may be seen among the jurors in *A Few Good Men* (1992), and in *Bob Roberts* (1992) a WM captain in dress blues is seated among several hundred persons attending a political banquet.

I have excluded films about Army, Navy, and Air Force nurses from the foregoing because they have been treated seriously by the motion picture moguls. Several notable movies were released in 1943 which set a precedent of mature portrayal of our angels of mercy, viz., *So Proudly We Hail* and *Cry Havoc.*

I cannot resist mentioning two Korean War era movies which did nothing to advance that pattern. On May 28, 1953 MGM premiered the aptly-named *Battle Circus,* a formula film that had the support of the Department of Defense and the Army's Office of the Surgeon General. Humphrey Bogart is a doctor with a M.A.S.H. unit and June Allyson joins his outfit as a nurse lieutenant. After the usual shadowboxing they fall in love. The dialogue is routine and the overall presentation is demeaning to the medical service. There is one exchange between the principals, however, that deserves to be repeated. Bogart asks what is probably a rhetorical question, "What do the people back home know about what's going on here?" Allyson replies, "Not much, I guess." And Major Bogie says, "Less than that. Nothing." Republic released *Flight Nurse* on January 30, 1954. An Air Force nurse (Joan Leslie) is torn between her "Grade A, irradiated love" for a helicopter pilot and a career in the military. The rapid, clichéd plot is not rescued by the inclusion of documentary shots of atrocities. The sole positive development in this third-rate soap opera is when Ms. Leslie chooses the military life rather than marriage to either of her suitors.

* * *

The new WMs of the early 1950s were an enthusiastic, sharp, and lively band of women, if somewhat less skilled and suave than their elders. Despite Colonel Katherine A. Towle's objections, in 1950 the requirements for enlistment were altered some because of the demand for additional WMs. The age limit was lowered to eighteen. Candidates had to be single, unburdened of dependents, and present either a secondary school diploma or pass an examination that measured if they had the equivalent of a high school education. For most of the Korean War era there was a comfortable blend of two generations of WMs, a mix of girlishness and womanly maturity that was beneficial to both the women and the Corps. In a manner of speaking, the younger WMs provided a little seasoning for a tried and true recipe.

Wherever the women of the "new breed" were sent it was to be expected that they would want a social life that would offset their military responsibilities. Perhaps because the Korean War was less draining on their energies than World War II was for WRs, I sense that the WMs were more relaxed and carefree in some ways. The simple fact that they could wear civilian clothes under so many different circumstances was a form of relief from the regimentations of life in the military. It preserved their concept of femininity and reduced the conspicuousness of wearing a uniform in public places. Indeed, the only time WMs were required to appear in military dress was when they were at work or on duty in some official capacity. Otherwise, on or off base, civilian attire was permissible. At MCAS Cherry Point, for example, slacks and pedal pushers were sanctioned—but shorts were outlawed in 1954 on the grounds that they were a bit too risqué. For those WMs who wanted to circumvent the regulations that prohibited fraternization with male officers, the liberal dress code made it a lot less dangerous off base. MPs could not tell who was who.

Were WMs a contented bunch? On the whole it appears they were. Naturally, they had some complaints. A survey done in late 1953 and published in the February 1954 *Leatherneck* (p. 24) was interesting, but no revelation to anyone who has served in the armed forces. *Leatherneck* did not say how large the sampling was from which a list of WM "gripes" was drawn. It was composed of seven items:

Gripe #1.   WMs expressed displeasure with their "living conditions." I can only guess that they were referring to the unrefurbished barracks and makeshift quarters to which they were assigned. The Corps was not ready to bring scores of females aboard in the early 1950s, but my impression is that it adjusted its physical facilities to the needs of WMs as quickly as the budget would allow;

Gripe #2.   WMs were not thrilled with the food that was dispensed in their mess halls. Inmates, boarding school pupils, summer campers, and college students often are not satisfied—so why would we expect WMs to be? Institutionalized menus seldom please every palate. Very likely it was a question of quality and variety—and the assembly line delivery—rather than quantity. Many of the women gained a few more pounds than their uniforms could hide. They could always "eat out," if they could afford it—or found an independently affluent male who was eager to "pick up the tab" indefinitely;

Gripe #3.   The poll reveals that WMs felt there was a serious imbalance in the way their waking hours were arranged by the Corps, i.e., there was "too much work and not enough liberty." My survey of WMs does not show that the women felt indentured or deprived in this arena. Perhaps there is never enough free time? Perhaps the passage of time sandpapers away the little things that annoy us when we are young and the former WMs have put all those trivialities to rest;

Gripe #4.   In 1953 WMs said that they did not like the number of inspections and formations imposed upon them. The key word must be "number," since they certainly expected to meet both requirements in any military branch;

Gripe #5.   WMs did not think the promotion system was rapid enough, nor did they believe there were sufficient opportunities for travel. The military has always overstated the prospects for travel to fancy locales, so there may have been some justification for that gripe. As for promotions, the Corps was as generous as it could be. Many WMs went up through the ranks quickly—more so than male Marines in some instances—and others were stuck at a low level with no hope of parole. The main problem was inconsistency within the system, not discriminatory practices, I feel;

Gripe #6.   Inconceivable as it may seem, WMs told *Leatherneck* staffers that "taking orders" was not to their liking. If they imagined that being a Marine was designed to be a Montessorian experience than that was an act of self-deception, not a flaw in Corps policy; and

Gripe #7.   The last objection raised by the WMs was to the "rigid discipline" levied by the Corps upon its larvae. The Corp's reputation for discipline was not a well-kept secret by any means, so even the uninitiated knew it was standard practice. However, it can be argued that until one actually feels it first hand one does not fully comprehend what "discipline" means. Witness how new boots reacted to Parris Island methodologies.

It is prudent not to take all these grumblings to heart. *Leatherneck* was only trying to be what it really was—a casual, informative, titillating in-house outlet. It made no pretense at being scientific. It knew that since 1775 personnel spent a fair share of their time fussing about the mindlessness of the military. As the magazine said, "Regardless of how much the Marine Corps improves . . . it cannot outdistance the beefs. But, to gripe is the serviceman's or woman's prerogative and the Marine Corps considers it a healthy attitude" (p.24). That is good to hear. If we took the survey results too seriously we might deduce that the WMs were a lazy, spoiled, witless, whiny group of malcontents. Some of them were, the vast majority were not.

Leatherneck also asked its interviewees what they thought about the uniforms they wore. For the most part, the responses were positive. Summer dress was nice, but it was the forest green winter service outfits that made them feel like real Marines. A number of former WMs said it was the distinctive greens that caught their eyes originally. What were WMs wearing in the early 1950s? We know that, like it or not, the "New Look" lowered skirts almost to the shins in the late 1940s. What dress regulations were in effect during the period covered in this volume?

One way to describe the uniform requirements is to imagine that a platoon of recently graduated WMs is about to leave Parris Island for their first duty assignments. It is November 14, 1953. The platoon is in a classroom awaiting the arrival of a WM officer, Captain Charlotte B. Smith WO53111, who is scheduled to give them the latest scoop on the uniform situation. I will take a few liberties for the purpose of dramatization, but the content of Captain Smith's remarks are based on fact. For Parris Island it is a relatively chilly day. Some of the WMs are a little cold—but "C.B.," as she is known to her close friends, will warm them up in short order. The back door opens, Captain Smith enters and strides briskly to the lectern at the front of the room. The new WMs snap to attention.

Smith (Congenial but firm) Good morning, Marines.

WMs (In unison) Good morning, Captain Smith.

Smith Seats. (The platoon sits) Today, I am here to speak to you about Marine Corps uniforms regulations as per (She checks a document then looks up) Chapter Four of the Marine Corps Manual, Section 14, pages 104 through 201. This is the only instruction you will receive on this important subject. I want you to pay close attention. Take notes if you wish. There will be no written test on this material. The smoking lamp is not lit. I have allowed a few minutes for questions at the end of my presentation. Save your questions until then. Do you understand?

WMs   (In unison) Yes, M'am.

Smith   Good. Very well. Now, working from the epidermis outward, we come first to the category commonly called "unmentionables." We all know what they are, do we not? (The women nod "yes"). Excellent. Let us move on, then. You may decide what styles of brassieres and underpants you wear but, and I want to stress this, girdles and slips *must* be worn at all times when you are in uniform. Garter belts may *not* be substituted for foundational garments. All hosiery will be beige in hue and full-length. Seamless and mesh stockings are strictly forbidden. Do you understand?

WMs   (Almost in unison) Yes, M'am.

Smith   Very good. Now, cosmetics and hair. You may wear lipstick. However, its shade—and that of your nail polish—must be the same as the red cord on your winter service cover. (She points to her own hat) Rouge and mascara are to be used sparingly, if at all. Women Marines are not show-girls. Save that sort of thing for your next incarnation. Hair? Bleaching, coloring, streaking or otherwise altering the natural color of your hair is prohibited. Your hair color is expected to match that which is specified on your identification card. MPs have been known to check that. Styles must conform to extant regulations and will not cover the collar of your uniforms. (A WM raises her hand)

WM   Captain?

Smith   (A bit annoyed) What is your name, Private?

WM   Private Betty Brown, M'am.

Smith   Brown, you obviously were not listening when I said save your questions, is that right?

WM   (Subdued) Yes, M'am. I mean, no, M'am.

Smith   Well, then, sit down and wait until I am finished. (The woman sits) Alright. Now, next is footwear. You will not wear spike heels, flats, sneakers, wedgies, loafers, or shoes with ankle straps when in uniform, correct? (They all nod) I quote from the Manual, page 158: You will wear "smooth leather oxfords or pumps in dark brown, dark russet, or cordovan color." The heels on your pumps will be one and one-half and two and one-half inches. There will be no rundown heels. I need not remind you that your footwear will be spit shined to a fine gloss at all times, and will be scuff-free. Today, we will omit any reference to your utility and exercise suits and proceed directly to your winter service "A" uniform, normally described as the "greens." As you can see, I am wearing the officer's version of that uniform. The jacket is tailored. The skirt does not flare at the hem line. (She makes one complete turn) Underneath your jacket you will wear a khaki, long-sleeve shirt and a tie to match. If you do not know how to tie a man's-type tie find someone who does and practice. In the Corps we have a saying, "A messy tie means a messy mind," and I have found that to be true during my ten years as a Marine. Next: your purse is no longer a purse—it is a brown handbag. You will place its long strap over your left, I repeat, *left* shoulder. I presume by now you know which shoulder that is. Does anyone know why the *left* shoulder? (A WM raises her hand) Yes? Oh, it is you, Private Brown. Well?

WM M'am, so we are able to salute officers. You see, if we wore our purses—

Smith Handbags, Brown, handbags.

WM Oh, yes, M'am. Switching your handbag to the other shoulder all the time would be very awk—

Smith (Tersely) That is fine, Brown, just fine. We get the point. Sit down, please. (She sits, promptly) Now, listen up for some additional items. First, when you wear an overcoat or a trenchcoat you will wear a red wool muffler. Second, wherever you are sent for duty it will rain. In some places more than others, of course, but it *will* rain. Therefore, you will always have "plain, black galoshes, boots, or rubbers" at your disposal to meet such contingencies. Umbrellas are unmilitary, so do not expect to use them. Third, it goes without saying, your uniforms—winter and summer alike—will *always* look as if you just stepped out of a bandbox. Wrinkles, wayward threads, frayed edges, stains, and bulging pockets are unsightly and will not be tolerated. Remember—you are *Marines*. You may not have cared how you looked when you were civilians but you had better start caring now—unless you want to spend all your time in the barracks on extra police duty. Do you understand? (The women nod) Good. Now, do you have any questions? Make them specific and brief, if you do. (A WM raises her hand, tentatively) Yes? Brown? You again? What is it?

WM (Gingerly) Captain, what if we get runs in our stockings?

Smith (Curt) The Marine Corps does not condone any WM having more than three runs in her hose. Next question? (Brown remains standing)

WM M'am? (Captain Smith acknowledges her) Is that three runs in *each* stocking, or is it three cumulatively? Like, six?

Smith The Manual says three, Private. *Three*. That is all it says. (Brown sits) Anyone else? Yes? What is your name?

WM Private Tillson, M'am. M'am, I've heard rumors that enlisted women can have dress blues. Is that true, M'am?

Smith It's better than a rumor, Tillson. It is fact. They were authorized a year ago. (Tillson sits. Another hand goes up) Yes, what is it, Private? What is *your* name?

WM   Terwilliker, M'am. Private Terwilliker. M'am, what are we supposed to do about handkerchiefs?

Smith   What do you mean *do* about them?

WM   What I mean is, do they have to be any particular fabric or color?

Smith   Excellent question, Ter . . . Terka . . . uh, Private. The answer is: the fabric is up to you. It's your nose. But, be sure you get this, handkerchiefs must *always* be white. The only exception is, you may use khaki ones that match your shirt, if you can find them. And, incidentally, in the Corps we do not refer to these items as "hankies." The proper nomenclature is "USMC Handkerchief, Female, M-2, 1943," never "hankies." Is that clear?

WMs   (In unison) Yes, M'am. (When the WM who is sitting at the front right corner of the first row notices Captain Smith is gathering up her papers, she shouts "ten-shun" and the platoon stands up)

Smith   (On her way up the aisle) Thank you, Marines. It's been a pleasure being w—(She stops in her tracks. She notices that one of the WMs is saluting) Who *is* that? Private Brown? Is that you?

WM   (Meekly) Yes, M'am, it's me.

Smith   It is *I*. Why are you saluting?

WM   (Trembling) Well, M'am, you being a captain and all, I thought—

Smith   (Exasperated) Brown, you never, I repeat, *never* salute indoors unless you are covered *and* under arms. They only do that in the . . . in the WAC. Are you a WAC, Brown?

WM   (Tearing up) No, M'am.

Smith   What *are* you, then?

WM   A Marine, M'am.

Smith   (As she leaves) I hope so. You'd better shape up—or ship out, Brown. (Private Brown collapses in her chair. The other WMs gather around her. Brown reaches into her utility uniform and pulls out a chartreuse "hankie")[2]

As I mentioned above, there were occasions when wearing a uniform was mandatory. When WMs were on duty or involved in public ceremonies they were expected (and wanted) to look their best. WM companies and detachments often were called upon to participate in patriotic observances. For example, Joyce Pulliam and Barbara Hollar were two of the sixty-six WM volunteers flown to New York City to march in the 1954 Armed Forces Day parade. Barbara was delighted to have a chance to fly and to "experience New York." She remembers, "We proudly marched down Fifth Avenue that spring. What a thrill! . . . How proud we were of being in the uniform of the United States Marine Corps." Joyce recalls another aspect of that junket. (Could she have been present at Captain C.B. Smith's briefing?) She states:

> We were billeted in WAC barracks at Fort Hamilton in Brooklyn and our quarters were not up to Marine Corps standards in cleanliness. The WACs who shared our facilities were, compared to us, quite sloppy. They wore barely polished, NOT "spit-shined" loafers. We wore spit-shined oxfords, neat uniforms, stockings all the same shade and the same shade of lipstick. We never left the building without our "covers" and never smoked in uniform outdoors. While we held our daily muster in front of their barracks and were inspected thoroughly by our company "Exec" they watched with open mouths, apparently never having seen this event since their own recruit training. After the inspection the "Exec" gave us a brief drill before dismissal that really impressed all of those watching. I was really proud of the Marine Corps and happy that I was a part of it.

From 1950 onward, women in the military were employed to advertise the "unification" concept. The U.S. Postal Service issued a stamp that featured women from each branch of service (Army, Navy, Air Force, and Marines) standing together in a spirit of unity. Periodically, quartets were formed to represent the branches at special functions. WM Mary M. Jamison was one of the four women selected to mingle with the contestants and be photographed with V.I.P.s at the 1952 Miss America contest in Atlantic City. Mary recalls that

> We met Marilyn Monroe, grand marshall of the pageant, and had our picture taken with her. She had a very revealing dress on and the public information officer [a male Air Force officer dispatched from Washington] who was our chaperon banned the photo. Of course, that did it. In all the newspapers and magazines across the country people read "Military Bans Photo." So, everybody wanted to see it.

What sort of social life a WM had depended on her personal tastes and on where she was stationed. At locations such as Lejeune, Cherry Point, and Parris Island she had to travel fairly far to experience the vibrations of a large city, which most young people have a hankering to do every once in a while.

The Marine Corps went to great lengths to provide on-base activities for its personnel. On each major post there were clubs for both officers and the enlisted ranks, the latter having two levels, the "E" club for all enlisted Marines and a Staff NCO club for staff sergeant and above. WMs had a club of their own on some stations but were welcome at either of the men's facilities, at their own risk. Several of the "E" clubs were modern, well-furnished, and spacious, altogether attractive watering holes where Marines could relax after work. Daly Hall at MCS Quantico, for example, opened in 1948. Named for Sergeant Major Daniel Daly, a two-time Medal of Honor winner, and dedicated to Marines killed in World War II (19,733), the building cost $500,000. On the first of its three "decks" was a new piece of technology that proved to be a main attraction: a large television screen. The second level was suitable for dancing. Daly Hall was a handsome manifestation of the Corp's concern for the lowly enlisted Marine who always seemed to have more time than money.

Now and then, things got out of hand at "E" clubs, as they will when youth, emotion, and alcoholic beverages are mixed disproportionately. At the Cherry Point club on March 17, 1953 the management held a St. Patrick's Day bash. WM Wilma Shaw was there. The club was overcrowded, raucous, and stuffy. Then: "There was a fight," she recalls. "A table was flipped over, beer spilled everywhere, and glasses were broken. The MPs always step in before anyone's killed so it just made the evening more interesting."

There was usually some form of music at the various clubs. As a rule, on weekends it was supplied by flesh and blood musicians. While she was at Cherry Point Private First Class Bonnie Carlisle was the pianist in an all-enlisted combo that played at the officer's club on Friday and Saturday nights. For such a gig, performed in civilian clothes, she received fifteen dollars, a welcome supplement to her monthly paycheck of ninety-six dollars. "And I saved enough to send money home every month," she states.

During the work week, clubs, slopchutes, and lounges used a back-up musical system. Popular, danceable songs of the day were available to Marines via the bulky, bubbling Wurlitzer (or Rock-Ola) jukeboxes. What was in the machine was metamorphosizing during the Korean War period. Although some diehards refused to admit it, the big band era was over, never to return in the manner that enthralled young Americans between 1935 and 1945. It is significant that only a few former WMs refer to any big bands. There were good reasons.

By 1950 the big band movement was defunct. One-night stands were too expensive, amusement taxes were high, television was keeping dancers at home, and the cost of night clubbing was increasingly prohibitive. There were some post-mortem twitches in the band business but the golden goose was dead, slain by that unpredictable monster: public tastes. Big bands simply do not figure in the memories of WMs the way they did during World War II for WRs. There is no group of orchestra leaders in the 1950's who meant as much to the people as Artie Shaw, Tommy Dorsey, Benny Goodman, and Kay Kyser did to the previous generation. There is no collection of songs from the early 1950's that can bring the Korean War to mind the way the "Moonlight Serenade," "I'll Walk Alone," "It's Been a Long, Long Time," and "Sentimental Journey" personified what World War II signified to its participants. Only "China Nights" can do that for some Korean War veterans, and it never made it to American charts.[3]

Imperceptibly at first and then noticeably after 1945 popular tastes in music were changing. Record sales were healthy but what was *on* them was different. As the bands receded—taking their barn burning swing arrangements with them—vocalists moved into the limelight. If the years 1948 to 1954 were to be given a title it would have to be the Era of the Crooners and Canaries. Among the men and women who ranked high with young Americans were: Perry Como, Patti Page, Nat "King" Cole, Frank Sinatra, Rosemary Clooney, Eddie Fisher, Frankie Laine, Jo Stafford, Doris Day, Buddy Clark, Guy Mitchell, Tony Bennett, Kay Starr, Peggy Lee, and Teresa Brewer. The postwar bands of Ray Anthony, Ralph Flanagan, Richard Maltby, Bill May, and Sauter-Finegan were special in their own ways and cut some splendid sides, but they were unable to reverse the public's willingness to allow singers to articulate their deeper feelings. A review of the top songs of 1948–1954 reveals that record buyers were partial to ballads and novelty tunes. There is not a big band instrumental to be found among them.

In 1954 jukeboxes on Marine bases across the nation were stocked with standard fare: "Secret Love," "Answer Me, My Love," "Three Coins in the Fountain," "Hey, There," "Let Me Go, Lover," "Little Things Mean a Lot," "Papa Loves Mambo," "Wanted," and "Mr. Sandman," to name only a few of the disks. There was an agent provocateur lurking among the hundreds of recordings released that year. A ditty called "Sh-Boom" by the Crew Cuts popped up in the top ten in July and remained there through October. It was the herald of an entirely new brand of popular music. Within a year Chuck Berry, The Platters, and Bill Haley and the Comets were turning our heads toward "rock and roll." Waiting in the wings was a teenager from the South, Elvis Presley. "In cultural terms," David Halberstam wrote, "his coming was nothing less than the start of a revolution" (p.456).

Not all WMs had musical talents like WM Bonnie Carlisle, but there were other means of earning "pin money." Once WMs began to arrive at their duty stations, they, and married personnel who had children, had an instinctive meeting of the minds. Why not volunteer to baby-sit? Why not use WMs as baby-sitters? They were trustworthy, readily available, and, above all, inexpensive. It was a natural match—at fifty cents an hour. Mary Ann Bernard baby-sat at Parris Island; Wilma Shaw did the same at Cherry Point, with the offspring of both officers and senior enlisted men. Wilma sat for a lieutenant who lived in a trailer with his wife and two children, a major and his family who kept a "messy house," and a master sergeant whose home was so neat that Wilma had to pocket her orange peels because "there was no other place to put them." (These experiences may have come in handy for Bernard and Shaw. Between them, they eventually had nine children.)

Extra dollars could be had on the base proper in one other way. At Marine Corps installations, movies were shown every evening. Admission was ten cents. WMs discovered they were employable as ticket-takers. The pay was minimal but it was better than nothing and they got to see films such as *Snows of Kilimanjaro, The Crimson* Pirate, and that paean to World War II Marines, *Battle Cry,* free. Working off the base—say, as a car hop at a drive-in—was frowned upon by the authorities. One WM tried it for one night and then quit. "It made me so nervous," she says. "I was afraid of being recognized." Besides, she did not have written permission from the base CO, a requirement at that time. Baby-sitting and ticket-taking were safer, if less lucrative.

For the sports-minded WM there was no lack of opportunities. Softball and basketball were the most popular activities but there were volleyball and bowling teams as well. For women who preferred smaller crowds provisions were made for tennis, bicycling, archery, and swimming fans. When there was sufficient interest WMs were permitted to form "trick" drill teams. Sometimes they were invited to display their silent routines at public functions.

Ever mindful of the relationship between organized activity and morale, the Marine Corps encouraged the WMs' softball and basketball teams to compete, and a number of the groups reached a level of proficiency ("For women," the Old Gunny would murmur) high enough to go to the playoff round. In 1953, for example, the first All-Marine Corps Women's Softball Championship was held in August at Camp Pendleton. When the dust settled, the WMs from FMFPac Hawaii were the victors. They beat El Toro's West Coast team and then Parris Island's East Coast champions. The seventeen women athletes received a special tribute from Commandant Lemuel C. Shepherd, Jr. Grace Amy Earle, who retired in 1976 as the last Sergeant Major of Women Marines, was a member of the club that blew in from the islands to take the trophy. "When we flew back to Hawaii," she tells us, "they held a parade to honor all the players. That was a very big thrill for all of us." Edna Mae Cogswell was on a Parris Island softball team that went to the championship round several years later. They were tripped up by the WMs from Camp Pendleton that time—but all was not lost, as it turned out:

> The Marine Corps probably did not think it was funny, but some of us went to Camp Pendleton for the softball tournament, which we lost—but we stayed there for a month. No real duties, just police the area and go on liberty. Later, we discovered that a WM from our team and a male Marine from MCAS El Toro had "sort of" covered up flights that would have taken us back to P.I. When our Lieutenant found out we were put on the next "flying box-car" out of El Toro.

WMs were no less resourceful in finding ways to entertain themselves than were their WR ancestors. In addition to whatever diversions existed on the base they went on picnics, toured local beaches, took in football games, played bingo, attended church-sponsored socials, and, yes, curled up with a good book now and then. If a WM left her station she might be in for a surprise when she returned. Once in a while WMs were a bit mischievous and frisky, as young people often are. Joan Collins has not forgotten what happened to her.

> I'll never forget the hi-jinks that went on in the barracks. . . . If you went out on liberty you went at your own peril. When you came back. . . . Your bunk might be missing. Or, your dresser drawers might be in backwards—or taped shut—and it's hard to find out what's wrong in the dark. Perhaps you'd been short-sheeted. Maybe there'd be critters in your bunk. One time, a rubber monkey holding a whiskey bottle was placed on my rack *after* I mustered for inspection and the CO found it during her rounds. The comment on the inspection sheet was: "Collins: Gear Adrift."

One of the reasons WMs sought creative ways to amuse themselves was the relative absence of outside shows. It may be unfair to use World War II as a touchstone for so many subsequent developments but in the early 1950s it was the yardstick by which many things were measured. If we do that, then it can be said that military personnel were not viewed as terribly needy by the entertainment industry. The contrast with World War II was sharply evident.

Maxene Andrews and Bill Gilbert point out that by the end of 1945 the USO had given "293,738 performances in 208,178 visits to a combined audience of 161,000,000 service men and women in the United States and overseas." They believe that effort may have been "the biggest production in the history of show business" (p.32). By December 1947 all USO facilities were closed. They reopened for one year in January 1949 and suspended operations again five months before the Korean War began. Caught with its doors shut in June 1950 the USO made a hurried contract with the Department of Defense to "provide much needed social and recreational support" for men and women in uniform. Due to the fluid and inconclusive character of the first six months of the war "camp shows" were slow in setting foot on the Korean peninsula.

One person, Al Jolson, made it to Tokyo and Pusan before any USO troupes. In fact, there was no rush on the part of other entertainers to do what Jolson did—on his own and at his own expense. Exhausted and sicker than he knew, Jolson died shortly after his return from Korea in October 1950. Later, Secretary of Defense George C. Marshall presented Jolson's posthumous Medal of Merit to the singer's son, Asa, Jr. It was generally agreed that Jolson was as much a casualty of the Korean War as any soldier who died on the battlefield. Eventually, the USO put on 5,400 shows for military personnel in Korea and the old reliables—Jack Benny, Danny Kaye, Bob Hope, Frances Langford, and Mickey Rooney—plus some attractive new reliables such as Jan Sterling, Piper Laurie, Debbie Reynolds, and Rory Calhoun made contributions to the troop's morale. By the end of the war there were 113,394 USO volunteers in the United States and nearly 300 USO centers overseas.[4]

Still, operating on downscaled budgets and reduced backing from the U.S. Government, the USO was forced to consolidate its services and cut back on expenditures. Consequently, the number of camp shows were far fewer than during World War II. When Marines see a vacuum they usually strive to fill it. During the Korean War they compensated by producing their own shows. To be specific, I shall cite three examples, one each from Lejeune, MCRD San Diego, and MCS Quantico. WMs were a part of all three productions.

In the summer of 1951 the personnel at Lejeune put together what they called an "All-Marine Variety Show." There were ten acts during which twenty-two Marines, including three WMs, gave their all to provide their audience with an evening's fun. Accompanied by members of the Second Marine Division Band, the show played at sixteen posts and bases on the East Coast and then disbanded.

Perhaps inspired by the Lejeune thespians a group of Marines at San Diego developed an all-Marine one-act musical and called it "Show Daze." Ann Sloan, who was in the "bevy of comely Women Marines" in the show, remembers that it took three months to prepare "Show Daze" and that it played at all bases and stations on the West Coast over a six-week span. *Leatherneck* for February 1952 declared it a hit, saying in a headline: "Marine guys and gals generate gags and glamour to score a success for San Diego." The magazine learned that the cast longed "to play the Korean theater—for the foot-slogging, gravel-crunching men of the First Marine Division" (p.31). It was not to be, much to their disappointment.

The Marines at MCS Quantico outshone all their competitors. They enjoyed a number of advantages their peers at other bases could not match. First, the post–Special Services unit had a pool of talent called The Quantico Players, many of whom had performed in *Roberta* and *The Hasty Heart* before capacity audiences at the MCS theater in 1952. Second, the company did not have to go on the road. Its home was the stately mainside theater, so there were none of the logistical problems that plague traveling shows. Third, there was no need to write original material. The renowned team of Richard Rodgers and Oscar Hammerstein II granted the Quantico group permission to produce the first amateur version of their famous musical *Oklahoma*. Furthermore, they agreed to forego receipt of all royalties and offered to act as consultants, if the need arose. With all this going for them, how could the Quantico people miss? They did not. *Oklahoma* was a smashing success.

Directed by Captain Ernest Frankel and choreographed by Corporal Nick Vanoff, who was a prominent television producer for several decades thereafter, *Oklahoma* opened on March 16, 1953 and played to a packed house for four nights. It took ninety-six people to make it happen: twelve cast members, thirteen dancers, sixteen musicians, twenty-one singers, and thirty-four support personnel. Who were these people who worked so hard to keep faith with the play's creators? Lieutenant Colonel Fraser E. West, head of Special Services, answered that question this way: "The members of the Quantico Players are both officer and enlisted, working side by side on stage and behind the scenes. They come from the offices, from the boondocks, from the air station, from among regulars and reserves." WMs, in their roles as singers, dancers, and stage-hands, were an integral part of this unique effort, and they did it above and beyond their regular duties.

WMs who were assigned to positions removed from the major, self-contained bases may have felt somewhat isolated at times—but they were not too envious if, like Fern P. Hauss, they were stationed in San Francisco. She recalls:

> We went dancing at the Marine Memorial Club, attended free band concerts in Golden Gate Park, and saw musicals at the San Francisco Opera House. Usually, special services got box seats for us. We went on picnics, swam in the Olympic-size pool in Golden Gate Park, and rode the S.F.–Oakland ferry at night to enjoy the lights of the city. We got to know the city by taking a bus or a streetcar all around the area. Since there were no barracks, I lived on subs and quarters in an apartment with two other WMs.

If there was a duty station more desirable than the City by the Bay it may have been Hawaii. WRs were posted there at Pearl Harbor and MCAS Ewa in 1945. By the end of World War II there were 1,000 WRs on the islands. Betty Moore was one of the originals. When she was called back in 1950 she was very excited to be returning to the fold. Her father was a Marine in World War I and her two brothers were in the Corps in the Second World War. Her younger brother, Bill, was still a teenager when he was killed during the First Marine Division's assault on Peleliu in 1944. "The Marines were the best," she asserts. "I had to choose them." In 1951, after several brief stops in San Francisco and Quantico, Betty was ordered across the Pacific again. "Back to Hawaii I went, assigned to the Marine Barracks as a dispatcher. That was great duty and I was thrilled to be there." She noticed that Hawaii "had changed a great deal" in six years. It had, indeed.

Still a U.S. territory, Hawaii was in a growth phase in the 1950s. The population would increase from 500,000 at the beginning of the decade to 632,000 by the 1960 census. The yearly value of sugar production rose from $124,000,000 to $131,000,000 in that period; pineapple products were on the way to $127,000,000 annually from $101,000,000; and diversified agriculture (beef, milk, vegetables, eggs, coffee, and poultry) went to $43,000,000 from $28,000,000. The construction, garment, and oil refining industries were on the upswing. Over 243,000 tourists visited the islands each year at the end of the decade—five times the number of people who made the trip in 1950—and pumped $109,000,000 into the economy. "Hawaii boys," as General J. Lawton Collins chose to call them, distinguished themselves in Korea, losing 426 killed and 926 wounded in action against the enemy. While the second generation of

WMs were there the campaign for statehood was being conducted with vigor and optimism. On August 21, 1959, after fifty-six years of agitation, Hawaii became the fiftieth state in the Union.[5] It was a dynamic time.

Betty Moore's verdict that WMs serving in Hawaii were "pretty happy and content" may be a slight understatement. Given the testimonies of women who were there, the term "euphoric" seems more appropriate. Dolores Shutt reports, "We were always on the go. Many beach parties. Spent our days off at the pool. Went to the other islands. It was great duty." It was so mesmerizing that Dolores did not slow up for long even after she received a "Dear Joan" letter from her Marine fiancé. To ease the pain, she had a boyfriend in Korea and dated Marines—not all that many—in the immediate area. Joan Collins went from one paradise to another. In 1954 she was transferred from San Francisco to FMFPac Pearl Harbor, where she was a top secret control clerk. As she thinks back upon that lucky streak what are her recollections? "A great barracks, beautiful weather, great friends, wonderful things to do," she says, forty years later. Among the "wonderful things" she did were: going with other WMs to a deserted beach on a Saturday afternoon, staying over to the next day, swimming, cooking out, and hiking; learning the hula; and enjoying luaus at the homes of Hawaiian friends. The *pièce de resistance?* Flying with a Marine aviator over an active volcano at night and, later, walking over the same territory after the lava cooled. *Magnifique.* However, news of what was happening to Marines not so fortunate as Betty, Dolores, and Joan kept filtering back to the islands. Dolores remembers, "Being in communications, we received all the armed services casualty reports. We were very much aware of how serious the war in Korea was."

Were there any assignments more glamorous than Hawaii? Mary Boyd and Josephine Janco might reply, "You bet your stripes there were—ours." It would be difficult to argue the point. Mary was ordered to Naples, Italy, and Josephine was sent to Frankfurt, Germany. Mary and two other WMs were attached to NATO's Headquarters Allied Forces Southern Europe, thanks to Assistant Secretary of Defense Anna Rosenberg. When she learned of the plan to send thirty-six women to Naples she insisted that four of the Navy's allotment of eight females be WMs. Mary's two years in Italy were as idyllic as any recruiter could conjure up. As a stenotypist and conference reporter she traveled to both Rome and Paris. She went to the opera, visited Capri and Mt. Vesuvius, "lived on the beach in the summertime," met dozens of officers from NATO countries, and was billeted in a first class hotel for nine months.

When Mary returned to Quantico in November 1954 she found it strange to see only Marines. "I was completely spoiled," she admits.

Josephine was posted to Cherry Point in March 1951. She was working as a clerk in station operations when she heard that of the twenty-two WMs who applied for a rare assignment to Europe she had been selected to go. How did that happen? "I'm not sure," she says. "They told me that they put all the names in a hat and mine was the one they drew. Luck, I guess." In November 1952 Josephine, seven other enlisted WMs, and two WM officers left for Frankfurt by plane. They worked in clerical jobs at European Command (EUCOM) headquarters and roomed together in nearby apartment buildings. Josephine was able to visit London, Liege, Munich, Wiesbaden, Oberammergau, and East Berlin. It was at Nuremberg that she saw an unforgettable vestige of World War II. On the field where Hitler's elite guard, the S.S., was trained she noticed that one could still see "the faint imprint of a huge swastika in the center of the concrete." She returned to the United States on December 24, 1953, took leave, and then was off to recruiter's school at Parris Island. The memories of her year in Europe have not faded. "It was the highlight of my life," she states.

When former WMs rummage through their experiences in the Corps they come up with fragments which illustrate just how sensitive, how fallible, and how innocent they were during the Korean War era. Most of their anecdotes are amusing now, however devastating to her ego, if not her career, the situations seemed at the time. Wherever the WMs went they encountered most of the pluses and minuses of the human condition. Through the haze of four decades their impressions remain remarkably vivid. They have not pretended that it was all "fun and games." There were sorrows, too. Notice the tragic simplicity of Ellen Juhre's statement: "One Marine I dated did not come back from Korea." Is that all there is left of him? Could she possibly remember anything more about one man she dated so briefly? And then he emerges. "His name was Herb. He was a D.I. at Parris Island," she says. Is there more of him? "He was very handsome, and such a good dancer. We corresponded for awhile when he was in Korea." How did she find out he was not coming home? "Someone at Cherry Point told me." And then Herb was gone—until now. And listen to the poignancy of Charlene Ender's resurrection of a girl who has been lost to us since 1954: "At Quantico there was a very pretty eighteen-year-old WM who was very nice and a good worker but she drank too much. One night she did not come home to the barracks and no one could find her. Three days later they found her body in a Potomac River drain. It was a sad time for all of us."

Several of the women remember accidents that robbed their young comrades of the rest of their lives. The Marine Corps' highway fatality record was staggering. In 1952 nearly 200 Marines were killed in automobile crashes while on leave or liberty. That cold statistic decreased to 178 in 1953 but that slight decline did little to ease concern about the carnage on the roads. The passage of time has not obliterated such images from the mind of La Vergne Novak. She recalls:

> Two of the younger women in our Chicago platoon, Mary Sedivy and Helen Sojka, went first to boot camp and were later assigned to San Francisco and became roommates. Mary went home on leave to get her car. She had car trouble on the return trip west and called the day before she was due back, to say she could not make it before her leave expired. The officer of the day informed her that if she was not at work at 0730 she would be considered A.W.O.L. Mary drove all night, fell asleep at the wheel, ran into a tree and killed herself. I have always wondered why the Marine Corps couldn't get along without Mary for a few hours, but could get along without Helen while she escorted her friend's body home.

Is there such a thing as fate? Are there Guardian Angels? Rosemary Cardamone might testify in the affirmative to both of those questions. Late in 1951, on an impulse, four WMs decided to drive from San Diego eastward. They intended to pass through Chicago. That would give Rosemary a chance to visit with her family and a guaranteed return ride to the West Coast. They invited her to "squeeze in." Rosemary was tempted, but said no, thanks. Why did she refuse their offer? Too short notice? Instinct? Whatever the reason, she was eternally grateful. All four girls who bade her farewell died in a car wreck before they reached the Windy City. And one last reminder of how precious and how fragile life can be comes from the memory of Joan Walter:

> During a basketball tournament at MCAS El Toro I met a WM from Pennsylvania and we became friends right away. I had the duty the weekend she married this tall, blue-eyed, blonde Marine corporal but we had leave the following week—so we decided to drive from San Diego to Philadelphia as a part of their honeymoon. Some honeymoon. We drove night and day and got to Philly in 72 hours. Not too bad for a '53 Chevy and NO interstate highways. I put them on a train for upstate Pennsylvania where her family lived. All was well—I thought. Four days later I received a phone call from my friend. She was in tears. Her husband of one week had drowned earlier that day while at a family picnic. I was

speechless. That was one of the saddest days of my life. It was with a heavy heart that I returned to San Diego from my leave.

Lest we become too solemn, it may be time to flip our hearts over to their lighter sides. WMs see their military experiences as a period of satisfaction interspersed with unexpected doses of reality, which may be what the rhythmics of life are all about. They choose, as Johnny Mercer once admonished us, to "accentuate the positive." It is obvious now that they did not allow adversity to smother their innate ebullience, and I am impressed to say that they retain their enthusiasm for life and their devotion to the Corps. A sense of humor is the lubricant that keeps our spirit from rusting as we age. The WMs have that quality in abundance, and it is nowhere more apparent than when they tell stories about what happened to them during the Korean War era. Perhaps that is why they possess an inner equilibrium we do not always associate with the aging process.

Among the many amusing things they recall are some that deserve retelling. I have selected a representative sample that sheds some light on how funny, charming, and vulnerable the WMs were. For example, to begin, in view of how important "wheels" were to young people in the 1950s, two tales involving transportation problems. First, from Wilma Shaw at Cherry Point in 1955, this "when a feller needs a friend" story: She was assigned to the Administration Building motor pool and:

One day I was ordered to drive three high-ranking Navy officers from Cherry Point to the New River air facility in a Chevrolet sedan. We all piled in and took off. On the way back, for some reason, and without warning, the Chevy stalled in the middle of the road. It stopped dead and refused to turn over. Of course, we were blocking traffic. So, my three passengers got out and pushed the car to a spot off to the side of the highway. Rather embarrassing. There I was in the driver's seat being pushed by a Navy Captain, a Commander, and a Lt. Commander—all in uniform. We were near a hamburger place so they nudged the car into a parking space and the four of us had burgers and milk shakes, in the car. I was so nervous about what we were going to do about the car I didn't enjoy my lunch very much. When we were done (they paid for me) I turned the key and—she started right away. I don't know how or why but she was fine for the rest of the trip.

Maurene L. Miller was a staff car driver in Motor Transport at Quantico in 1954. Before her discharge in September 1955 she had an interesting year behind the wheel. With considerable aplomb she reports:

While driving a huge station wagon full of British Royal Marines I skidded on an icy patch and went into a ditch. Being both officers and gentlemen, the Brits got out and helped me get the "Beast" back on the road and we continued on. But I was embarrassed.

It was not over yet. "While driving a laundry truck at Quantico I managed to back into the portico of the barracks and knocked it down."

"Other than those two incidents," Maurene says, "I was considered one of the best drivers in the motor pool"—which does cause one to wonder about the quality of the rest of the staff. As Count Basie said, "one more time." A few months prior to her release from the Corps, Maurene was involved in an off-duty auto accident that put her in the hospital for most of the summer. What did the Corps do with her after all this? She recalls, "I was assigned to a lab where I had to clean stool sample dishes and other 'fun' things." At least she was safe—and so was everyone else.

We will now change venue to Parris Island in 1951. There was a flurry of activity in preparation for a visit to the depot by none other than Field Marshal Bernard Law Montgomery, deputy supreme commander of NATO troops in Europe. Mary Ann Bernard was given the job of shooting pictures of the viscount for public relations purposes. Since she was a novice the office always sent a senior male sergeant with her. "Monty" arrived to the accompaniment of much pomp and circumstance. Mary Ann's impression was that he was rather prissy. She remembers that he smoked perfumed (Turkish?) cigarettes. Anyway, abiding by his preference for profile shots, she took one from the left side (his "best" side) and the sergeant photographed him from the right. When the film was developed, she had not checked out the background. Mary Ann's photo was perfect—except for the P.I. water tower that protruded from the crown of his head like a Fourth of July rocket. Scratch one official USMC photo by Private First Class Bernard.

Now, north to MCAS Cherry Point again. Carol R. McCutcheon was on leave in Jacksonville, Florida, when she heard that a hurricane was heading for the Atlantic Coast. She said goodbye to her mother and made a beeline for Cherry Point. When she got there the station was under siege by one of the worst storms in recent memory. She takes the adventure from there:

The station was closed to incoming or outgoing traffic and they would not let me in as the base was under water. I was ordered to stay outside.

Heck, I didn't have any money to go to a motel and I doubt there was one with vacancies anyway. . . . I had made friends with two Marines on the bus coming back from Florida. I talked them into finding a way onto the base. We followed a fence and found a gate that was locked and unguarded. Two men put me on their shoulders and I attempted to jump over the fence. Either my balance was off or the wind did it, but my trenchcoat got caught on the loops atop the fence as I jumped over and I hung on the fence like a doll. My dress and coat hiked up and exposed my stocking tops and garter belt straps. I was so skinny back then I was no raving beauty or sex symbol but it was embarrassing. We didn't show our underwear back then. The fellows tried to keep their eyes covered as they helped me unhook myself from the fence. About that time, the MPs drove up. They laughed and said they knew of people breaking out of the base, but never Marines breaking in. They gave us a lift to our companies.

Carol's company was holed up in the Administration Building. She found herself in a Catch–22 when she rejoined her unit. Marine Corps regulations stated unequivocally that personnel were to return to their duty stations in times of potential emergencies such as tropical tempests. Carol certainly did that, but her lieutenant "gave [her] hell for coming back in hurricane weather." Nevertheless, everything worked out. "We got sandwiches and coffee brought to the building by boat," she recalls. "It was so exciting. Some people stayed up all night playing cards. I think I was one of them."

Charlene Enders played second base for the WM softball team at Quantico in 1953. Every two weeks or so the women would board a plane (with "bucket seats") at the Quantico air station and fly off to play teams out of state. She remembers one trip in particular:

One time, before flying to an Air Force base, we were given instructions on how to wear and use a parachute. The instructor, a cute enlisted Marine, was very emphatic about our not pulling the ripcord. I thought to myself, "How stupid does he think we are, anyway?" when I accidentally pulled the ripcord. The chute blew up all around me. Everyone began to laugh hysterically—except the instructor. He was very angry, muttered something about my being "a dumb blonde," and gave me another parachute. Needless to say, I was very embarrassed. I think we won the game.

Then there is the story of the Quantico swimming pool maintenance man who got both a surprise and a souvenir. As one former WM relates it:

Sometimes after hours my buddies and I used to sneak into the base swimming pool to take a dip. When the MPs came around we would duck underwater until they left the area. We had to dress and undress in the dark, of course, and my friend Joyce lost track of her underpants. She was almost hysterical on the way back to the barracks. She was sure she was going to be in big trouble because her name was sewn in them. She was a nervous wreck for days, but nothing ever came of it.

Nor did she get a phone call from anyone on the maintenance crew.

* * *

February 1952 was the "last full month in East Korea" for the First Marine Division. As Lynn Montross *et al.* noted in *The East-Central Front* (1962), the fourth volume in a series about U.S. Marine operations in Korea:

After a winter of positional warfare, the Marines could recall with better understanding the tales that their fathers had told them about France in World War I. For history was staging one of its repetitions; and . . . the trenches of Korea in 1951–1952 differed but slightly from the trenches of the Western Front in 1917–1918. (p. 246)

After six months of defensive warfare, in March 1952 the First Marine Division was ordered to move to West Korea by April 1. By March 25 all three of the Division's regiments were in place in the "I" Corps zone of responsibility, about forty miles northwest of Seoul and four miles southeast of the Panmunjom truce talk site. When it arrived in the West the Division's strength was 26,210 officers and men. Opposing it were two Chinese armies composed of 50,000 well-trained troops. The Division's mission was to obstruct and repel Chinese thrusts in the direction of Seoul and the Kimpo Peninsula. Shortly after the Marines took up their positions along the Jamestown Line the Chinese began probing and shelling. During April they dropped over 5,000 artillery shells and nearly 4,000 mortar rounds on the Marine regiments. By May the war of attrition had begun. Referred to as a rule as the "outpost warfare" phase of the war, it was deadlier than most Americans realize. Between April 1952 and the July 1953 cease-fire nearly 40 percent of *all* Marine ground troops killed during the three-year war lost their lives, as did one-third of all Marine aviators who were killed in action. Almost 44 percent of all infantry Marines wounded in the war received their injuries in the final fifteen months.[6]

Perhaps a tribute to those Marines is called for before we move on. My letter home of May 28, 1952 will not do them justice but it may communicate what it was like for them that Wednesday forty-two years ago.

For the previous three weeks the early-morning weather had been ideal. On May 28 the local fog was so thick that no use could be made of Marine air power. The plan of operation called for the First Battalion, Seventh Marines to launch an attack that would prevent the Chinese from controlling several important parcels of territory north of the Main Line of Resistance (MLR). Hill 104 was a main objective. My old out fit, Company A, was designated to lead the attack. H-Hour was set for 3:00 A.M. When the company returned to the MLR at 2:45 P.M. it had lost nine Marines killed, 107 wounded, and earned one Medal of Honor. I watched the awful devastation of my company from an observation post on the MLR and, that night, I told my parents what I saw:

As I sit here tonight and write you, I, and many others, have heavy hearts. Able Company has been dealt a blow by the Chinese which, for all intents and purposes, has cut its effective strength in half. It has been a day I will never forget. . . . The assault on Tumae-Ri is over, and our casualties as of the moment are nine killed and ninety-five wounded. It is painful to review the day, but I feel I must.

The company jumped off on the attack at 0245 (2:45 A.M.) under cover of darkness and by 0430 had reached the vicinity of Hill 104, a suitable base for future operations against the final objective. There, the trouble began. . . . Our troops, in command of 104 by 0800, were powerless to act without air cover. For nearly four hours they had to sit on the hill and take punishment from Chinese artillery and mortars on the high ground beyond. From my vantage point in an OP bunker the entire scene unfolded as if I were watching a panoramic battle staged by a movie company.

Men were cut down by mortars, pinned in the trenches and bunkers on 104 by artillery, flattened by concussions, and struck by shrapnel while trying to evacuate their wounded. But I was not Cecil B. DeMille. There was no call for a lunch break, no retakes, no tongue-lashing for missed cues. And those 'extras' lying on the ground like cast-off dummies wouldn't get up and walk to the pay window today. It was horrible, fascinatingly real. And to widen the terror I felt for them, from my bunker I could see and hear things they could not. I could see puffs of smoke from the Chinese positions—previews of the arrival on 104 of more artillery shells—but I could only watch them slam down on "A" Company. I could see mortars begin to bracket our wounded-laden amphibian tractors as the clumsy vehicles ambled to safety, then zero in, then hit nearby—spilling frightened men onto the hot divot.

I saw thinly-clad South Koreans dash out into the chaos and, miraculously, return unhurt to the lines with the body of a Marine, time and time again. I saw our tanks lumber up in support but give up in desperation for lack of any real targets. And, finally, when the weather allowed our planes to take to the air and Hill 104 grew quiet, I saw the remnants of Able Company stagger back to our lines. Every officer in the company had been wounded. The medical stations were crowded with the survivors, some crumpled-up, exhausted, some on the tables, some standing around dejectedly sucking on cigarettes.

I haven't really grasped it all yet. It's almost too much for the human mind to comprehend. Dead Marines, their lifeless feet protruding from corpse-covering ponchos, waiting to be picked up by Graves Registration—how do you erase that image? A young Latin-American Marine heavily breathing his last in an aid station while a Navy doctor feverishly tries to plug up the hole in the boy's naked chest—how do I forget him? A veteran Sergeant sitting casually on the side of the table, waiting his turn, his shrapnel-pocked back exposed, bruised, and bleeding—how can I help but be proud?

All these pictures—how, and when, do I organize them into some rational order? How do you mix sorrow, bitterness, and pride—and come out with an answer to the question: why? Able Company paid a terrible price today. I only hope it brought us something that will justify the cost.

Semper Fidelis, A-1-7. We have not forgotten.

NOTES

1. Ivan Butler, *The War Film* (Cranbury, N.J.: A.S. Barnes and Co., 1974), p. 87.

2. For the factual data regarding uniform regulations I turned to Mary V. Stremlow, *A History of the Women Marines, 1946–1977* (Washington, D.C.: History and Museums Division, Headquarters, U.S. Marine Corps, 1986), pp. 157–168.

3. Korean War veterans who wish to hear "China Nights" again, sung with feeling and clarity by actress Ann Blyth, need only rent the film *One Minute to Zero* (1952). Originally an RKO Radio Pictures release, on video it is a Turner Home Entertainment product, serial number 6015 (1989). Some veterans may remember the song in its Americanized version, "I ain't got no yo-yo."

4. The foregoing material is drawn largely from Frank Coffey, *Always Home: 50 Years of the USO* (Washington, D.C.: Brassey's (U.S.), Inc., 1991), pp. 51–76.

5. These data are derived from Gerrit P. Judd IV. *Hawaii: An Informal History* (New York: Collier Books, 1961), pp. 178–191.

6. Pat Meid and James M. Yingling, *Operations in West Korea* (Washington, D.C.: Historical Division, Headquarters, U.S. Marine Corps, 1972. Reprint edition 1987), p. 482.

Chapter Six

In the Wake of War

In his detailed history of the Korean cease fire negotiations, William H. Vatcher, Jr. wrote:

> At 1000 hours 27 July 1953, after two years and seventeen days, 575 regular meetings, 18,000,000 words, the Korean Armistice Agreement was signed at Panmunjom. Twelve hours later the guns were silenced along the front lines and the troops began to fall back behind the four-kilometer-wide buffer zone. Thus ended the longest truce talks in world history.[1]

It did not matter that America's least popular war (up to that time) was halted by means of a temporary truce. It was an unpleasant national experience that no one was sorry to see come to an end, however inconclusively. Draft-eligible men were particularly relieved. Author Joseph Goulden recalls that in 1952 he and his Texas high school cronies agreed (after a few beers) that there were two things that they had to avoid: "Korea and gonorrhea."[2]

The price paid in American lives was very high: approximately 34,000 dead on the battlefield and 20,000 killed from other causes. Over 103,000 men were wounded. The Marine Corps' share of that toll was 4,262 killed and 20,000 wounded. Their sacrifices were duly noted and then forgotten by most Americans. Joseph Goulden makes the point that

> For the first time the United States concluded a war in which it could not claim success. There were no celebrations. News of the armistice signing

flickered across the news lights in Times Square; people stopped to read the announcement, shrugged, and walked on; unlike V-E and V-J days, no cheering throngs assembled. (p. 646)

How shall we assess the impact of the Korean War experience upon the Marine Corps? From the standpoint of sheer numbers the war caused a surge of unexpected dimensions. The number of Marines on active duty jumped from 74,279 in 1950 to a peak of 261,343 in September 1953. All told, some 424,000 men and women wore Marine Corps uniforms in that time period. (During those three years the number of WMs rose from 580 to 2,662, and fifteen years would pass before they reached that plane again.)

The lessons learned by Corps leaders were not insignificant. For example, once again, as in World War I in France, Marine ground units were employed as a land army after the amphibious assault at Inchon. The exemplary conduct of Marine regiments in 1951, 1952, and 1953 enhanced the Corps' reputation as a fighting organization certainly, but using Marines as an "army" diverted the Corps from the mission it fought so hard to protect at the close of World War II. The Corps was impaled on the horns of a dilemma: if it prided itself on being the nation's "force in readiness," how could it not take on a land army posture when the country needed it to do so? This issue, first raised in 1918—and again in Korea, Vietnam, and Saudi Arabia—seems not to have been resolved. The mindset, "Send in the Marines," born in the nineteenth century and reinforced so many times in this centennium, still appears to be in conflict with the Corps' legal mandate.

Marine aviation—which lost 436 planes and 258 flyers in Korea—emerged from the war in a somewhat neutral state. World War II demonstrated the value of the concept of close air support of ground troops and for the first three or four months in Korea that tactical formula was employed with considerable success. However, after December 1950 the First Marine Air Wing was tucked up under the control of the Fifth Air Force, which did not value the notion of close air support as highly as did the Corps. Soon, the U.S. Air Force had jurisdiction over what missions Marine Air was given. Of the MAW's nearly 130,000 sorties only one-third were of the combat air support variety. Air-to-air combat between Marine and enemy aircraft was an uncommon occurrence and, Peter B. Mersky tells us in his fine study, *U.S. Marine Corps Aviation: 1912 to the Present* (1990), "kills" by Marine pilots "were, for the most part, registered while flying exchange duty with the Air Force" (p. 141). If the Corps' free-wheeling use of fixed wing aircraft was somewhat blunted by the organizational and strategic character of the Korean War, its discovery of a new capability was a "shot in the arm" that shaped the future of Marine operations for the next four decades: the helicopter. In a sense, the Korean War gave the Corps a legacy that would not only preserve its air potential but would lead to the armed helicopter and evacuation "helos" that so symbolized the war in Vietnam—a bitter-sweet inheritance at best. As early as 1953, Mersky observed, the Corps' leaders knew "the future lay in helicopters." They were more prescient than they knew (p. 193).

Marine authorities also learned that their troops were lacking sufficient training in night operations. The Chinese were far superior in how they exploited darkness to their tactical advantage. They traveled light, were tenacious, did not have to be concerned about U.N. aircraft after dark, were unconcerned about taking casualties, and proved that the "outpost" strategy adopted by the Corps and its allies on the West Coast was both futile and fatal. As J. Robert Moskin pointed out, the Marines discovered that the Chinese "were tough and able opponents" (p. 588). Nearly everyone underestimated the Chinese at the outset of the outpost phase but that soon turned to a begrudging respect.

As the static situation in the West extended into 1953 a philosophical conflict developed between Marine Corps leaders and U.N. "higher headquarters." Marines are taught to be aggressive. They are, from top to bottom, offense-minded men who grow restless when there is no action—one of the handicaps all land armies experience. Ground troops are seldom "in the know" about what the upper echelons are thinking. By late 1952 political considerations weighed heavily on the minds of U.N. commanders. Plenary cease fire talks were recessed in October and would not resume until March 1953. During that interregnum pressures were exerted upon the generals to maintain a military equilibrium along the 140-mile front, keep casualties to a minimum, and be alert to the public relations implications of their decisions. Regimental and battalion commanders were told to restrain themselves. All proposed forays against the Chinese had to be cleared with the military hierarchy. The resultant slowdown chafed the Marine officers at the local level. They, too, were concerned about casualties but the stultifying effect of a non-assertive policy upon the sharpness of their troops worried them just as much. Marines and stalemates do not coexist gracefully, especially when the line troops suspect that politics, not the Chinese, is the real enemy. Strong Chinese attacks in June and July 1953 broke the monotony and inflicted heavy casualties on both sides, making the issue moot.

Overall, what may we say about the long-range effects of the war on the Marine Corps? On that question we shall have two viewpoints. James A. Donovan, a Marine veteran of World War II and Korea, chose to express it this way:

> On the profit side, the war resulted in a rebuilding of Marine Corps strength . . . and saved it from the reductions planned by the Secretary of Defense in 1950. It revitalized the Marine air–ground team, introduced the helicopter to combat operations, and provided a new generation of young Marines with battle experience. (p. 65)

Henry Berry, a Marine in World War II, author of *Semper Fi, Mac* and *Hey, Mac, Where Ya Been?* (1988), an oral history of Marines' experience in Korea, phrased his response a bit differently:

> And what of the United States Marine Corps? . . . Well, one never hears Harry Truman's term "the Navy's police force" any longer. The Marine Commandant is a full member of the Joint Chiefs of Staff. The Corps has three full divisions and a fourth in active reserves. It has 200,000 men on active duty, which, according to its former Commandant, General P.X. Kelly, makes it larger than the British Army. It may have paid a dreadful price, but it is now a vital part of its country's defense, and will remain so for a long, long time. (p. 322)

Current plans call for a reduction in the strength of the Corps to 177,000 by the fall of 1994.[3]

Internationally and domestically, 1953 was a year of the changing of the guard. There was a new tenant at 1600 Pennsylvania Avenue. The inauguration of Dwight D. Eisenhower in January returned a Republican to the White House for the first time in twenty years. Among other things, Eisenhower brought the issue of the Korean War with him into office. During the 1952 campaign that led to the defeat of Adlai Stevenson (whose son was a Marine officer) "Ike" began to talk about the settlement of the war. On that point his audiences were all ears. The more positive the reception to that idea became the more it evolved into an integral part of his platform. In Detroit on October 24, 1952 he vowed to go to Korea to take an ex-soldier's first-hand look at what was really going on there. He told the assembly, "Only in that way could I learn how best to serve the American people in the cause of peace," inferring that, somehow, his reconnaissance would lead to a cessation of hostilities.

Three weeks after his resounding victory at the polls Eisenhower spent three days in Korea, as promised. Whether or not his pre-election

gesture contributed materially to his win on November 4 is difficult to
gauge but, as Burton I. Kaufman noted in his *The Korean War* (1986),
Eisenhower's pledge to fly to the battlefront was a "masterful political
stroke" that capitalized on the public's dissatisfaction with the Demo-
crats' prosecution of the war (p. 294). In Pittsburgh just before the election "Ike" repeated his intention even more dramatically. "So long as a
single American soldier faces enemy fire in Korea," he proclaimed, "the
honorable peace in the world must be the first—the urgent and unshak-
able—purpose of the new administration" (p. 295). How instrumental
the President was in ending the war is a matter of opinion but most
voters, eager to put the unpopular conflict behind them, were willing to
trust him to do that. Even "peace without victory" was preferable to the
alternative. General Mark W. Clark, Commander-in-Chief of U.N.
forces from May 1952 to October 1953, was foremost among those who
made themselves available during Eisenhower's whirlwind visit. Clark
thought "Ike" was a bit preoccupied, as well he may have been, and
Clark was not sure what the outcome of the tour would be. When the
President-elect departed on December 5, 1952 Clark was left with little
but his own thoughts. As he said several years later:

> There was no change in the tempo of the war for months after his visit,
> nor was there any move by either side to resume negotiations for an
> armistice. If anything, indications were that the Reds had dug their heels
> in deeper and were prepared for a long, long wait.[4]

The war dragged on for six months after Eisenhower's occupancy of
the White House but when the armistice was signed he was the President, so the credit was his, deserved or not.

While all these momentous events were in the making, another
change was occurring which did not transfix the American people: the
directorship of the Women Marines was passing from one generation to
another.

For nearly thirty-five years (1943–1977) the Corps' female component
was headed up by a woman "director." Both the Corps and its distaff
members were fortunate in that the caliber of their directors was of the
highest order. Quite simply, they were professionally outstanding and
personally above reproach, role models in whose care the parents of
WMs could place their daughters with confidence. Ruth Cheney Streeter
and Katherine A. Towle served as directors from 1943 to 1946 when
the organization was called the MCWR.

Colonel Towle, a native Californian, took her undergraduate and grad-

uate degrees from the University of California at Berkeley in 1920 and
1935, respectively. By 1941 she was an experienced, respected teacher,
administrator, and editor who had no reason to believe she would spend
her middle years in a non-academic environment. It is unlikely she envi-
sioned what was in store for her in the decades ahead. It all happened
very quickly. In February 1943 she was commissioned as a captain in
the MCWR (without the benefit of any formal training). One year later
she was a major. In September 1944 she began a fifteen-month tour as
Colonel Streeter's deputy at HQMC. On March 15, 1945 she became
Lieutenant Colonel Katherine A. Towle. When Streeter left the MCWR
in December of that year Towle was the logical choice to succeed her.
She held the post of director until June 1946. No doubt she thought that
was the end of the story of women in the Corps. Neither Towle nor
many other Marines reckoned with the skill, devotion, and persistence
of Major Julia E. Hamblet and her tiny squad of assistants who refused
to let the idea die a slow death.

Towle returned to Berkeley in the summer of 1946 and picked up
where she left off. The passage of P.L. 625 two years later resuscitated
the women's program. Major Hamblet suggested that Towle be considered for the director's position. Recalled to HQMC in the fall of 1948
Towle was confirmed director of the revitalized Women Marines organization and proceeded to strengthen and enlarge it—no easy task even
for a person as competent as Katherine Towle. She was director when
the Korean War broke out in June 1950. In the two years prior to that
surprise, the number of WMs had risen from 167 to 580 but, now that
we were at war again, Towle's responsibilities multiplied. Faced with
complex issues of recruitment, screening, training, assignments, and the
aches and pains that accompany instant expansion, Towle did a splendid
job of balancing numerous aspects of conversion to wartime standing:
politics, male intransigence, budget, personnel problems, morale, public
insouciance, uniforms, adequate facilities for her "girls," and—of much
less concern to her but important nonetheless—her own image as the
WMs chief executive.

In the latter category, Towle had a head start. She was a tall, cultured
woman whose beautiful gray hair and patrician features disarmed many
an angry opponent. She was a stateswoman, a keen negotiator, and an
advocate who seldom lost her poise. Her "girls" admired her because
they knew she truly cared about them as people. In February 1953, three
months before she retired, Towle visited Cherry Point and addressed the
200 WMs massed in the station theater. She wished them a happy tenth
birthday, spoke reverently about the past and optimistically about the

future, and urged the WMs to strive for excellence in their work and in their lives. One WM who was in the audience remembers that Towle was "quite attractive and dignified-looking," an apt description. Although they may not have defined it this way, what people saw in Katherine Towle was the subtle light that shone through her composure, the inner brilliance of a lady who believed in and lived by values we have long since ceased to stress. Colonel Towle passed away on March 1, 1986, at age eighty-seven and her ashes were scattered at sea off Point Lobos, California on March 19.

When Colonel Towle retired on May 1, 1953 a grateful Marine Corps honored her with a parade at Marine Barracks, Eighth and I, Washington, D.C. Standing two paces behind Towle was the woman chosen to succeed her, Lieutenant Colonel Julia E. Hamblet. The Corps did not interpret the transition this way but Hamblet was the WM's insurance policy. Her ascension was a guarantee that women would continue to play a role in the Corps and that they would be taken care of in a first class manner.

Hamblet and Towle had much in common. They were taller than the typical WM (who was 5'4") and they were equally striking. To borrow a term from Towle that fits both of them, they had the "looks." Hamblet, too, held an undergraduate degree (in economics) and a master's. During World War II she served in responsible positions at Lejeune, Pendleton, Quantico, Parris Island, and Cherry Point. She knew as little about the Corps when she joined in 1943 as Towle did—she admits she never even *saw* a Marine before then—but once enrolled they were devoted to the Corps. Both were driven by an intense love for their country. Hindsight tells us they were "naturals" in the realms of leadership and organization. Educationally and professionally, then, these two women were very much alike. There, I think, is where the similarities end. Towle was reserved, conservative, and supremely representative of the generation that grew up during the First World War. We might think of her as a ladylike product of America's Edwardian period, when women were dissuaded from being overly demonstrative. To her very close friends she was "Kay." To everyone outside that inner circle it was unthinkable to address her as anyone other than "Colonel Towle"—and it better be pronounced "toll." Even Colonel Hamblet could not bring herself to call her "Kay" until after she (Hamblet) retired in 1965. Towle was neither aloof nor devoid of a sense of humor. It was just that her presence—may we say, her "aura"?—commanded a level of respect that no one wished (or dared?) to violate.

Julia Hamblet possessed all the military qualities Towle had but she was by no means a clone. In the first place, she was eighteen years younger than Towle. When Towle was twenty in 1918 the United States was at war with the Central Powers. At that age Hamblet was at Vassar and the nation was still in the vise-like grip of the Great Depression. Towle was in rural California, Hamblet was in the New York–New Jersey area. While Towle was walking among the groves of academe, Hamblet was working for the U.S. Information Service in Washington, D.C., where the probability of the coming of another war was a subject of much debate. These influences shaped the personalities of two powerful, albeit different, temperaments. Hamblet acknowledges that she was less patient, more impetuous, and somewhat more outgoing than Towle. Only thirty-seven when she became director, Hamblet was sought out by the media. She received consistently favorable press, which she handled adroitly to the Corps' advantage. She was willing to socialize beyond the attendance at formal functions her official standing necessitated. During World War II at the posts to which she was assigned she played tennis, went canoeing, took in movies ("No matter what was playing"), dropped in at the Officers' Club, and dated some. "After all," she says, "there were 40,000 men at Cherry Point and only 1,200 WRs." The incredible demands of the directorship forced her to severely curtail her extracurricular activities.[5]

Eleven weeks before the Korean cease fire, Hamblet was appointed director of WMs and promoted to colonel. At this point it is appropriate to recall how fortunate the Corps was to have Colonels Streeter, Towle, and Hamblet at the helm of its female arm for sixteen years (1943–1959). The four women who followed them were exceptional also but the foundation laid down by the first three directors was the *sine que non* of the continuance of women in the Corps.

Hamblet knew she had her work cut out for her. She was not a novice, and she and Colonel Towle had discussed the problems facing the WM component. The numbers of WMs quadrupled between 1950 and 1953 and then went into a downward spiral until 1957. Size was of less concern to Hamblet than was maintaining a quality organization, whatever its enrollment. WMs in the early 1950s were younger than their predecessors, relatively inexperienced in both living and working, and ignorant of the vagaries of military life. Improved training, adequate supervision, and vocational guidance were high priority goals for the new director. Beyond these basics lay an issue that vexed Colonel Towle and remained unresolved when Hamblet replaced her, i.e., how to get the Corps to expand and deepen its use of WMs. Towle believed that the

Corps' policies covering its women were "unrealistic and shortsighted as well as uneconomical," and she said so in a January 5, 1951 memorandum to the Director, Plans and Policies. She urged her superiors to develop a "systematic long range training [plan] beyond indoctrination for younger enlistees." Furthermore, even if the Corps did what Towle asked, there was the problem of appropriate, forward-looking assignments for WMs.

Whether or not Hamblet's master's thesis grew out of these concerns is less important than the cogent point she made. "My purpose was to demonstrate that the Marine Corps would utilize its women more broadly and effectively than it was doing at that time," she reports. "We were not trying to get the Marine Corps to *invent* jobs for its women— the positions were already available and could be filled by WMs, if only the authorities would take steps to do so." Although there was some movement within the Corps to "increase [WM's] potential effectiveness" nothing substantial was done. Occupational opportunities for WMs remained conventional and limited for both officers and enlisted personnel. Of the 152 WM officers on active duty in March 1953, 122 were toiling in three traditional areas: administration, supply, and disbursing. Enlisted WMs were excluded from being assigned to fields such as infantry, antiaircraft artillery, field artillery, utilities, construction and equipment, tank and amphibian tractors, weapons repair, ammunition and explosive ordnance disposal, supply services, guided missiles, chemical warfare, security, aircraft maintenance and repair, aviation ordnance, and pilot.[6] What WMs should *not* do, rather than what they were capable of, seemed to be the overriding consideration in the minds of the Corps' male leaders.

By way of a summation, it may be said that the Korean War era witnessed a brief, temporary surge of interest in WMs on the Corps' part but it did not result in major, long-term changes in either the women's standing within the Corps or in the duties they were assigned. In the wake of the war their numbers began to decrease, the sense of urgency that surrounded their redux subsided, and WM-related issues were shelved indefinitely. The ambivalence the Corps felt about women in the ranks never really disappeared, even when the war was on and WMs were sorely needed. By 1955 it resurfaced in no less obstructionist form than it took in 1949. Male Marine attitudes were essentially unchanged: women are neat to have around, but not in the Corps. The Marine Corps did not have a monopoly over this syndrome. Women in the other branches were experiencing a similar dwindling of interest on the part of their higher authorities. Jeanne Holm put this diminishment in perspective for us in her *Women in the Military: An Unfinished Revolution* (1992):

> The Korean experience and subsequent events . . . raised serious doubts about the value of women's programs to the peacetime defense forces. Attitudes toward military women in the decade following Korea were influenced by disillusionment stemming from the expansion's failure; the changing military strategy of the Cold War; the continuation of the peacetime all-male draft; societal attitudes toward women's roles; the abnormally high turnover; and the almost total absence of any pressures to use women. Indeed, given this combination of negative factors, it is remarkable that the women's programs survived the Cold War years at all. (pp. 157–158)

*   *   *

On August 15, 1955 Frank Sinatra cut a side for Capitol Records called "Love and Marriage." In less than three months the song rose to number five on the national charts. The lyrics posited that marriage and love were two sides of the same coin, a theory reflective of life in Thornton Wilder's turn-of-the-century village in New Hampshire—but, in the 1950s?[7] Could that still be true? And what has this to do with WMs? A lot.

We know that once the Korean War was brought to a halt, the number of WMs on active duty declined on an average of 250 a year until it leveled off at 1,617 in 1957. But for one year (1959) the WM strength remained below 1,700 until 1966. It is logical to wonder why reenlistments and accessions faltered so (in all the military services). It would be unfair to lay the responsibility for the reduction at the feet of the Marine hierarchy solely. During Colonel Hamblet's tenure as WM director, Generals Lemuel C. Shepherd, Jr. and Randolph McPate were the Corps' commandants. "They were both extremely supportive of WMs," Hamblet recalls. As every chief executive knows—or soon realizes after he takes office—*beaux gestes* from the top do not always result in changes at the lower levels if the middle managers do not enforce the new policies. That may have been—and still may be—the zone of weakness within the Corps. Nearly thirty-five years after the Korean truce the issue of the acceptance and assimilation of women in the Corps were causes of concern for the commandants. For example in 1988 CMC General Alfred M. Gray, Jr. submitted a report to Secretary of the Navy James H. Webb, Jr. that made some revealing statements about the status of the woman Marine. In part, Gray (and his task force members) wrote:

> Attitudes are contagious. . . . Attitude reinforcement comes from the highest levels [of the] Departments of the Navy and the Marine Corps. . . . When Marines see no women anywhere in their chain of command, it sends a message. When Marines see women excluded from "all hands" parade formations or ceremonies because of a personal preference of a regimental, battalion, squadron, or company commander it sends a message. It is certainly no surprise that, when these messages are sent from the highest levels, the result is that women are set apart and regarded as a separate and less-than-equal part of the Corps. . . . There is only one way to counter negative attitudes concerning women. A clear signal must be sent from the SECNAV and the Commandant of the Marine Corps (CMC) that actions which detract from the [Corps'] mission focus will not be tolerated.[8]

The "negative signals" Gray knew were being sent had to do with women being assigned to positions which ignored the specializations for which they had received advanced training; being excluded from parades for no reason other than their gender; being denied opportunities to participate in field exercises; and being forced to seek counseling from "other women outside the chain of command or work area" because male Marines did not feel comfortable with "counseling or chastising females." If such were the problems in the late 1980s then one can imagine what discouragement faced the WMs in the late 1950s. In short, one of the root causes of the decrease in WM enrollments was the perennial problem of the women being made to feel unwelcome. To many Marines they were intruders.

In May 1952 the Attitude Research Branch of the Department of Defense, prodded into action by Assistant Secretary Anna M. Rosenberg, sought to identify "women's reasons for enlisting and reenlisting." In her history of the WAC Bettie J. Morden listed certain findings which no doubt applied to WMs and WAVES as well:

> The most frequent reasons given for not reenlisting were marriage or pending marriage; dissatisfaction with military job, promotion, or pay; desire to obtain more civilian education or training, dissatisfaction with lack of acceptance of women or their perceived reputation. (p. 103)

It is not reasonable to hold the military totally accountable for the loss of enlisted WMs. There were other forces at work in the 1950s that exerted strong influences upon young women—which returns us to Frank Sinatra. The suction that pulled scores of women from the ranks—whether or not they really wanted out—was "Love and Marriage." It was in the air, it seemed, and most WMs were single, eligible, and interested. Not only was that a normal inclination, American society was in the throes of its biggest marriage (and baby) boom in its history. Being in the Marine Corps was an insular experience in many ways, but it did not immunize women from the effects of love bug bites. In fact, it brought the WMs into contact with men who were single, eligible, and interested—*very* interested—too. Since most WMs were not planning to make a career of the military, the milieu in which they found themselves was fraught with promise. Maybe Sergeant or Lieutenant Right was in their midst, somewhere? In most instances, he was.

Despite the panning "The Fifties" has received from some historians, for young Americans it was an exciting decade. The automobile was king. In 1955 car sales reached a record high of 7,000,000 units. Highway construction accelerated to accommodate our increasingly mobile population and the number of motels rose to 30,000 (three times as many as were in operation in 1935). Our cars enabled us to go touring; swing into miniature golf course parking lots; spend a day at Disneyland—which opened on July 17, 1955 in Anaheim, California; scoot down to the local drive-in theater and then pull into a Dairy Queen on the way home; stop at Lovers' Lane for some private canoodling; and visit one of the growing number of campgrounds erected to allow city dwellers to pretend that they were "roughing it." Gasoline was only thirty cents a gallon, and still a bargain because we had a little more money to spend. After all, on August 12, 1955 the minimum hourly wage skyrocketed to one dollar from seventy-five cents. *That* was true prosperity, was it not? And we were becoming a nation of commuters. In the 1950s the suburbs "grew six times faster than cities." During the decade 18,000,000 Americans moved to the suburbs. Surface transportation was not sufficiently advanced to provide rides to and from work for the suburbanites so the prospect of having to finance two family cars arose, one for dad and one for mom and the children. On the weekends and holidays, of course, everyone piled into the Country Squire station wagon, the new symbol of middle class success.

If Americans were troubled about anything during the Eisenhower years it was the issue of atomic conflagration, which would effectively bring all their dreams and hopes to a blinding end. There was not much the average citizen could do, and that sense of helplessness only exacerbated his or her fears that a thermonuclear holocaust—accidental or willful—might turn the planet into a floating cinder. Professor John Lewis Gaddis of Ohio University recaptured that period of "extraordinary perils" in this manner:

> How close we came to not surviving we will probably never know; but few people who lived through the Cold War took survival for granted. . . . The vision of a future filled with smoking, radiated ruins was hardly confined to writers of science fiction and makers of doomsday films; it was a constant presence in the consciousness of several generations after 1945.[9]

It is appropriate to recall that American blacks had more immediate concerns than whether or not the human race "went out with a bang": poverty, lack of educational opportunities, segregated public facilities, discriminatory laws, and high infant mortality rates. But the great social revolution we call the "civil rights movement" was gathering speed. In her comprehensive study, *Born for Liberty: A History of Women in America* (1989), Professor Sara M. Evans noted that while our white middle class was striving to "fulfill a vision of domestic bliss in the expanding suburbs," black Americans in urban areas were beginning "to make their own claims on an American dream they had been denied" (p. 260). The road to black enfranchisement was paved with voter registration drives, protest marches, bus and business boycotts, sit-ins, battles to integrate education, ministerial activism, and violence—always the violence. As William H. Chafe said, "The time for accommodations to gestures and symbols from all-powerful white people had passed. The moment for freedom had come."[10]

It is unlikely that women in the military grasped the full import of that "conflict over the meaning and structure of American society." How many of us did? Until they were discharged into the "real world" WMs were in a cocoon of sorts. But they knew what was going on in general, and they knew what they wanted from life: marriage and a family. That was not so unusual. In the 1950s marriage was a growth industry. Brett Harvey spoke of it this way in her excellent oral history, *The Fifties* (1993): "The institution of marriage had a power and inevitability in the fifties that it has never had since. You simply didn't ask yourself if you wanted marriage and children; the only relevant questions were when and how many?" (p. 69). Between 1940 and 1960 the percent of single persons in the U.S. population dropped from thirty-one to twenty-one. During the 1950s the median age at which women married fell to 20.4 years from 21.5. "By 1959," Harvey states, "a staggering 47 percent of all brides were married before the age of nineteen" (p. 70). Sad to say, Harvey tells us, "There was nothing around to indicate that a single life could be anything other than lonely, empty, and joyless" (p. 87). We know better, now.

When it came to marriage and pregnancy Marine Corps policy in the period covered by this volume was rather self-defeating. Until the early 1970s if a WM was with child (or inherited dependents under eighteen) she was forced to leave the Corps. Between 1948 and 1964, Mary V. Stremlow notes, "a woman Marine could marry, and almost immediately ask for a discharge . . . enlisted WMs could ask for an administrative discharge based solely on marriage." If they had "completed one year of their enlistment beyond basic training, they were discharged for the convenience of the government" (p. 151). WM officers could request a discharge upon completion of two years of active service after being commissioned. Obviously, these regulations contributed to the turnover problem and only prolonged the instability that characterized the presence of females in the Corps.

A large fraction of the WMs who contributed to this book married Marines, as one might expect. Most of the marriages lasted. Some—not as many as do today—ended in divorce, some were terminated by a husband's death. Given the disparity between male and female lifespans in the United States, widowhood is a state women realize may happen to them and, by and large, they deal with it very well. Charlene Enders, for example, lost her husband in 1980. Forty years after discharge from the Corps she is once again "involved with the Marines." She helps plan a Marine Corps birthday ball each November. "We have a color guard, a cake-cutting ceremony, and a video of the Commandant's annual message as a part of the celebration," she reports. " 'Once a Marine always a Marine' sure applies to the men and women in our area [of western Pennsylvania]." And she has "two fine children" (and three grandchildren) to remind her of how it all began. Dorothy Griffin was a sergeant when she met the man she would marry. Since he was a lieutenant aviator at Cherry Point in 1951 they had to be careful about where they "fraternized." They became man and wife in 1952. When he retired in 1974 after thirty years he was a lieutenant colonel. He died of lung cancer in January 1992. Dorothy, the mother of two, carries on. She says, "I still belong to the Marine Corps Air Transport Association and attended their 1993 convention in Nashville." Will she go to the 1994 meeting in Branson, Missouri? "I'm not sure. I found that it wasn't quite as I had hoped."

Perhaps we need not proceed with sorrowful reminiscences beyond this point, but there is one more poignant story I want to relate. Staff Sergeant Patricia Logan was stationed at HQMC when she was introduced to a handsome Marine by mutual friends who—would you not guess?—thought Pat and Sergeant William J. Quilty might "hit it off." Until she met him she was planning to stay in the Marines for thirty years, but the matchmakers' instincts were on target. She and Bill married and she left the service. Three years later Bill died at Bethesda Naval Hospital of a malignant brain tumor and was laid to rest in Arlington National Cemetery. "You know," Pat recalls, "when I was at Henderson Hall some of us WMs would take walks in the Cemetery. It was so impressive, so quiet. I never dreamed then that someday my husband would be buried there, too." In 1971 Pat was stricken with multiple sclerosis. It necessitated that she give up much that most of us take for granted. But there are some things she has not surrendered. Her memories of Bill, and her sense of humor, remain clear and unvanquished by hardship.

We should touch briefly (and anonymously) upon the few marriages—perhaps three percent—that did not withstand the strains and stresses of time, infidelities, personality clashes, and character flaws. One of our WMs, who wanted to make a career in the military, married a Marine in the mid-1950s and had reason to believe it was a union that would last, as they say, "forever and a day." She and her husband had three lovely daughters. Then, after twenty-nine years, her spouse decided to run off and live happily ever after—with another woman. Another WM married a Marine staff sergeant on July 4, 1952 and raised four children. He became a pilot with a commercial airline and, in 1967, came home one day and announced that he was leaving her for—yes— a stewardess. It was a "slap in the face," a total surprise for our former WM. She took it, and the death in 1993 of her third husband, in stride.

The marital breaking point did not always involve the "other woman." Sometimes it was absolute incompatibility, psychic depletion, financial disaster, frustrated ambitions, or external meddling that led to a dissolution of the nuptial contract. And, in some instances, the women admit that they simply made a "big mistake" for reasons that, in retrospect, are difficult to explain. For example, a former WM officer who consented to marry a Marine lieutenant six years her junior did so despite her concerns about his psychological lucidity. Perhaps, at age twenty-eight, she was subconsciously attempting to deflect the onus of spinsterhood that permeated our thinking at that time. She got pregnant, resigned her commission, and was divorced in the spring of 1954. Her casual meeting with that lieutenant at the Quantico swimming pool in 1951 cost her dearly but she had a daughter to raise and a long teaching career ahead of her. She has a grandson she adores. So, in a real sense, her first and only marriage, however ill-advised, bequeathed to her something very precious. Evidently, that compensates for the career in the Corps she forfeited forty-odd years ago.

The remarkable feature of the WMs who outlived their husbands or underwent divorces is their resiliency. Each one has done something constructive with her life. Now in their sixties and seventies, they are active, energetic, and mentally alert. They have strong opinions on most of the controversies of the 1990s, refuse to capitulate to life's "hard knocks," and ascribe a good deal of their tenacity to their Marine Corps training.

The majority of WMs who opted to marry were fortunate in their choices of mates and enjoyed an above average matrimonial experience. From the many durable relationships my survey uncovered I have selected a half-dozen which possess most of the ingredients we associate with successful marriages: fun, mutual respect, intimacy, courage, unwavering commitment, nostalgia, sharing, and a dash of luck. The six marriages cited below took place between November 1951 and June 1954, in locations as diverse as Maryland, Illinois, Texas and California. Five of the WMs married Marines and one married a sailor. Collectively, these couples had fifteen children. Each pair, Lord willing, will celebrate their Golden Anniversary in the next century.

UNION ONE: LONG DISTANCE LOVE

After she graduated from boot camp in 1949 Anna Orlando was sent across the depot to Personnel Administration school and then on to HQMC. For Anna, that was familiar territory. She had worked there as a civilian after World War II. It was there also that she met Paymaster Sergeant Lawrence Hopkins. They went their separate ways and did not see each other for five years. Hopkins returned to the Corps as a warrant officer about the same time that Anna was moving west to Yeoman School at San Diego and the Department of the Pacific in San Francisco. They both ended up at Camp Pendleton and met again—just as Hopkins was shipping out for Korea in 1951. For the next ten months they corresponded and Anna noticed that the tone and contents of (by then) Lieutenant Hopkins's letters "were getting serious." Since Hopkins was a disbursing officer he was required to make trips to Japan periodically. Sometime in the spring of 1952 during a visit to Kobe Hopkins decided enough was enough. From a phone in a USO-like serviceman's center he made a call to Anna's barracks at Pendleton and asked if she would marry him. Anna said yes, she would. "I went up to San Francisco to meet the ships returning from Korea," she recalls, "and we made plans to get married at the Ranch House Chapel at Pendleton." They did so on June 25, 1952—the second anniversary of the outbreak of war in Korea. Did they realize that? "No," Anna says, "it was just a coincidence." Anna was discharged as a staff sergeant two days later and her husband stayed in the Corps until 1969, retiring at the rank of major. Forty-two years, three children, and many phone calls later they are still together—but it was that call from Korea that started it all.

UNION TWO: MOVE OUT! (AGAIN?)

Jayne Burgess had a special reason for enlisting in the Corps in 1950. Her brother Charles was killed on Guadalcanal while serving in the First Marine Division. "My choice of service could be none less," she states. Boot camp was a real challenge for "a young lady [from Boston] who had never washed clothes or had to mend anything," but she did quite well. Jayne was ordered to MCAS El Toro where she was a classification clerk and a court recorder. Then it was back to Parris Island to attend Recruiter's School, from which she emerged the top graduate. While all this was going on, Jacques Loraine was in Korea with the 11th Marine Regiment. Shortly after his return Staff Sergeant Loraine was posted to the Marine Recruiting Office in Dallas, where Staff Sergeant Jayne Burgess was serving as the "head female recruiter." On August 8, 1953 they were married at the Naval Air Station in Dallas. She was discharged on September 30 and began her sixteen year tour as a Marine Corps wife. Jacques retired as a major in 1969. Jayne bore him four children and may never have unpacked completely. "As I remember," she says, "we moved twenty-two times in fifteen years." Perhaps that was, in part, what she meant when she said recently, "I assisted in the development of [my husband's] career." Many former WMs can make a similar claim.

UNION THREE: WHO'S THE BOSS?

Pearl Morris was barely eighteen when she arrived at Parris Island on July 31, 1951. At first, she found the training "scary" and "hectic." "Believe me," she said, "it was harder to stay in the Marine Corps during boot camp than it was to get in." Six weeks earlier she was a high school student in York, Pennsylvania. As she began her senior year, way out west a lad from Kansas was enlisting in the Corps. It was August 1950 and Jim Shaklee was sent to boot camp at MCRD San Diego. In February 1951 he began a one-year tour in Korea with the Fifth Marines. Meanwhile, Pearl was passing through Personnel Classification School at P.I. and receiving orders to report to HQMC. Her sister, Phyllis, was a WAVE stationed two city blocks away from Henderson Hall. Shaklee had been ordered to HQMC also and it was there that he and Pearl met in the spring of 1952. On June 1 they both made sergeant. A year later, on June 6, 1953, Pearl and Jim were married—and so was Phyllis. "Sis and I had a double military wedding at NAS Anacostia," she recalls, "and what a beautiful affair that was." Two months later Pearl was out of the service and Jim was pursuing a career in the Corps that extended to 1974. They moved every thirty months, two children in tow, and Pearl "loved every minute of it." Pearl and Jim still talk about why it took him thirty-four months to make sergeant when she managed it in less than a year. "He was so proud when he was promoted to staff sergeant [in 1955] and finally outranked me," Pearl reports—then adds, "I was Sergeant Major at home, however."

UNION FOUR: TAKE *THAT!* . . . SIR

One of the least favorite assignments WMs were given was: a month's worth of mess duty. In Dolly Katzer's case it was not a waste of time. After boot camp—during which she was "scared stiff" only half the time—she was ordered to Camp Pendleton. That should have been interpreted as a good omen, since she was from Oroville, California. When she checked in at the mess hall, Private First Class Katzer got her first look at the corporal in charge of WMs, Norman Smart, who was chief cook at the time. She remembers, it was February 4, 1953 and that, for her, it was "love at first sight." It must have been. They were married on June 6, 1953 in Yuma, Arizona. Fifty days later Dolly was discharged. Smart stayed in until January 1956. There was a reason why after four years in the Corps he was only a private first class when he was released, a reason most WMs would applaud but the military frowns upon. While Smart was in Korea after the war he and a Marine officer got into a verbal joust over the morals of women in the military. The lieutenant's position was that they were all whores. Sergeant Smart took exception to that, being the husband of a WM, and asked for a retraction. The officer restated his view and Smart put him in the hospital. He was court martialed and reduced to private first class (with accompanying loss in pay). Smart wrote Dolly and explained why she should expect less money in her allotment. Now they were both privates first class and a lot poorer but Dolly was proud—and, one hopes, so were their four children when they grew up and learned about their father's one-punch defense of their mother's honor.

UNION FIVE: HAPPY EASTER, DARLING

The ferocity of the fighting around Bunker Hill (Hill 122) in Korea was costly. Between August 12 and October 7, 1952 five Marines and two corpsmen earned Medals of Honor and nineteen men were awarded a Navy Cross for valor during the struggle for the outpost. Machine Gunner Sherman Thompson, "C" Company, First Battalion, Fifth Marines, was wounded there in October and taken aboard the *USS Consolation* hospital ship to begin a series of recuperative layovers that consumed six months of his life. It was in October a year later that Barbara Hollar enlisted in the Marines at Baltimore. She completed boot camp just before Christmas 1953, was posted to MCS Quantico, and was assigned to the Basic School office as a clerk-typist. It was there that she met Thompson at Easter time 1954. "We would go to the Enlisted Men's Club on Saturday nights . . . and dance the night away," she recalls. "There were also movies, trips to Washington for dinner, USO centers, and roller skating—but mostly dancing at the EM club, if not to a live band, then to a jukebox during the week." The relationship congealed quickly. Thompson proposed to Private First Class Hollar while they were standing outside the WM barracks and she agreed to be his wife. They were married in Barbara's hometown, Severn, Maryland, on June 26, 1954. There was only one problem. Thompson was due for discharge in July but Mrs. Thompson's year of service would not be over until December. In a reversal of the usual pattern—where the woman goes home and waits patiently for her spouse—Thompson returned to Kokomo, Indiana, got a job with General Motors, and stood by for five months until Barbara was released. He only saw her twice during that period but she made it to Kokomo a week before Christmas so all was well. Their two children were (and probably still are, in their hearts) Hoosiers, and each year when Easter rolls around Barbara and Sherman reminisce about how they met and melded forty years ago.

UNION SIX: BELL BOTTOM TROUSERS

It is not uncommon for people who really do not care for each other initially to end up married. A case in point is Marilyn Rehm and Ronald

Verna. Their homes were five miles apart when they were growing up twenty-three miles west of Chicago. Even though they attended different schools they socialized with "the same crowd" and met formally at a roller skating rink when they were in their early 'teens. They dated some when they were high schoolers but, Marilyn says, "I didn't even like him particularly when we were teenagers." Marilyn enlisted in the Marines in October 1950 and Ronald went into the U.S. Navy. She was ordered to MCRD San Diego and then had the distinction of being the first WM to be sent to Journalism School at the Naval Training Station, Great Lakes, Illinois. Since she was the sole WM on the station Marilyn lived in the WAVES' barracks and had "open gate liberty" as a corporal. Verna was retained at Great Lakes after boot camp—and by "happenstance" they found each other. This time she liked him—very much. Their courtship "almost caused an international incident," Marilyn recalls. The men at the Marine Barracks were outraged and tried to pressure her to cease and desist her heretical behavior. "Imagine," she says, "I'm the only WM on the station—and I chose to marry a Navy man!" On November 21, 1951 Marilyn defied convention and married Verna at the Chapel By The Lake. They had eleven dollars between them at that moment (and not as lot more thereafter). Marilyn was ordered back to San Diego in February, 1952, where she was discharged in July, and then returned to Great Lakes. Eventually, she and Ronald were able to enjoy a regularized existence in California. Since 1988 they have lived in Las Vegas where, every Friday morning, Marilyn reports, they conduct "the usual G.I. party" and square away their house for another week. Those eleven dollars went a long way.

A number of former WMs acknowledge that they wish they had not left the service. Of course, they did have a choice. Or did they? Technically, they did—but given the social pressures exerted upon young women in the 1950s (and the power of true love) it is no wonder that so many were willing to trade the military for a marriage. The statements that follow exemplify the sentiments of those WMs who look back and say:

- "It was wonderful. I wished I'd stayed in."
- "My nine years of service [1951–1960] were the best years of my life. I only wish I hadn't quit when I did."
- "I would like to have stayed in longer but after three years of active duty and one in the reserve, and being married, and then pregnant, I had to get out. I could have served longer if they had allowed it."

- "My only regret was not being able to stay in the Marines for thirty years, but I was able to be a part of it through my husband [who was a career Marine]."

- "I would not trade those three years for anything. I went to business college on the G.I. Bill, planning to go back in as an officer and make a career of the Marine Corps [when she opted to get married]."

- "I often wished I could have stayed in the Corps and made a career out of being a Marine. When I got married I got out because my husband declared: 'You either be a Marine—or a wife.' "

- "The saddest thing for me was having to get out of the Marines when I got married. I wanted to stay in but you had to leave."

Although the number of females in the United States who held full- or part-time jobs rose from 16,000,000 to 22,000,000 between 1950 and 1955 the majority of married women were attending to their children (of which, on the average, they had 3.2) and did not reach the workplace until the 1960s and later. When I asked the question of former WMs "What did you do in the years following the Korean War?," I received many "marriage and family" responses, a few rather surprising replies (e.g., "Not a thing!"), reports on the vast range of "regular" jobs, and a short list of out-of-the-ordinary pursuits. They do not mention it very often but it is certain that some of the women were confronted with biases that blocked them from receiving positions they wanted, and for which they were qualified. Lenore Sandager tells us about how she dealt with such obstructionism (in true Marine Corps fashion):

When I recall applying for the Teacher-Work-Coordinator position in Special Education in Rochester, MN—my husband was on the staff of the Mayo Foundation—I am still amused at a comment made during an interview with the Assistant Superintendent: "We really had intended to hire a man for this job." I quickly replied, "I was made an OFFICER and a GENTLEMAN by an ACT OF CONGRESS!" I was hired without further ado.

It is to be anticipated that the jobs taken by former WMs fit the popular perception that constituted "suitable women's work." In the 1950s American females gravitated toward positions either in offices or in the so-called "helping professions." They worked as tax consultants, bookkeepers, insurance and realty salespersons, executive secretaries, bank tellers, head cashiers, assistants to accountants, telephone company employees, beauticians, and bonding agents. A small number served in the legal arena as court reporters. Several made a living working for physicians. A sprinkling of respondents chose to remain within the governmental system and found civilian jobs with the Veterans Administration, the U.S. Air Force, the Social Security Administration, the Marine Corps, and the U.S. Departments of State and Interior, for the most part in clerical rather than managerial capacities. As always, the field of education attracted a substantial number of women veterans. Those who needed to earn a certificate or an advanced degree in order to teach in the lower schools enrolled in institutions such as the University of Washington, Nevada, and San Francisco State on the G.I. Bill. They taught in areas such as elementary education, business education, and special education. On a more exotic level, a few WMs found openings as writers in radio and television, finance company managers, and executives with North American Aviation and the Buick Motorcar Company. It may not qualify as "exotic" but one WM is doing nicely—as any homeowner knows—as a professional plumber in Florida.

Did their Marine Corps experience make any difference when the WMs were catapulted into the world of work? The answer is "affirmative." Indirectly, their time in the military appears to have expanded and refined the personal attributes which lead to success in any given field. For example, since very few people operate in total isolation, the establishing of smooth relationships with co-workers and management is paramount. "Getting along," shy of compromising one's principles, is a useful skill. Many WMs say they learned how to do that when they were thrown together with scores of other men and women. As Edrey Schendel put it "I find it easy to size up people, and I learned that when I ran into thousands of people of all kinds [in the service]." Concomitantly, the women also say their natural compassion and tolerance for persons who are "different" was greatly enhanced. Their newly discovered sense of independence did not insulate them against feeling empathetic toward less fortunate or eccentric individuals.

A word that emerges from nearly all the recollections I gathered is "confidence," sometimes identified as "self-esteem." The Marine Corps is well-known for instilling and cultivating that quality in its members and the WMs believe the Corps did that for them. Mabel Bennett believes: "The experience gave me the foundation I needed (and lacked) . . . The confidence and self-esteem made it possible for me to make good decisions, to set my goals and to go for them, never doubting that I would be successful if I really put forward the effort that I was capable of making." Connie Musumeci phrased it a little differently. There is a charm in her forcefulness: "I learned to be assertive, aggressive, and not to take guff from anyone. I learned discipline and how to be a friend and comrade," she says. Evidently, the women feel they were also taught the value of being neat, loyal, well-organized, respectful, and punctual. For some of the WMs their military service brought direct results vocationally. Listen to the testimony of Gene Sims, who was an air traffic controller at MCAS Cherry Point for two years:

> My WM experience *was* my entire working career. After my discharge in 1955 I was hired by the CAA (later, the FAA) and retired after 24 years as an Air Traffic Control Specialist. In 1971 I was selected as the first female control tower facility chief. What a career—unequaled fulfillment. And to think—in 1953 in boot camp a WM counselor asked: "Pvt. Sims, what would you like to do for the Marine Corps for the next three years?" What does my Marine Corps experience mean to me?— WOW!!

And former Sergeant Carol McCutcheon has no doubt about the dividends she received:

> Those three short years [1951–1954] in the Corps repaid me over and over again. I was chosen to be a Veterans Administration benefits counselor due to my having been in the military. My promotion to the Loan Guaranty Division was, I have a feeling, due to my being a Marine at one time. And I'm convinced that having been a recruit instructor at P.I. helped me later when I had to lecture to real estate people as a part of my VA job.

As I pointed out in a previous chapter, in the 1950s the Marine Corps' female component was a rich blend of World War II veterans and younger women who entered the ranks after 1948. About one-fifth of the WMs who participated in this project belong in the former category. A larger fraction joined the Marines in the period 1949–1954. What these two sub-groupings have in common is: some did not leave the Corps. It would be misleading to imply (which I may have) that nearly all the women who served during the Korean War era had to, or chose to, leave the military. I have sampled the biographies of those who stayed in until the 1970s and I do not wish to overlook their contributions. They were dedicated professionals who understood fully the value of personal and military continuity. Most of these veterans remained single. They had choices other than a career in the Corps and yet they invested a major portion of their futures in the preservation of the idea of women as Marines. They were keepers of the flame. We owe them a great deal more than we have remitted. Only Mary V. Stremlow has attempted to set the record straight, a tremendous effort for which we should be thankful. The women mentioned below served a collective total of 127 years in the Corps either on active duty or in the reserve, or some combination of both.

It is fitting to bracket this acknowledgment between two Sergeant Majors of Women Marines whose honorable careers extended over three wars. Bertha Peters was twenty when she went on active duty in 1943. One of the first WRs to be afforded a regular appointment in 1948, she rose steadily in the ranks and was made the first Sergeant Major of WMs in January, 1961. When she retired she became the first woman Marine to serve for thirty years without interruption. Those were two "firsts" to be proud of. Shall the first be last? Or shall the last be first? Grace Carle, whom we met earlier, conjured up an interesting way of looking at her three decades in the Corps:

I like to think I have the distinction of being *"last."* I was the *last* class (8A) that was trained at Hunter College [in 1943]. . . . My first and *last* duty stations were at Headquarters, USMC. I was the *last* WM 1st Sgt. for the WMs, Camp Butler, Okinawa; the *last* WM Sgt. Major for Women Officers at Quantico, VA; and the sixth and *last* Sgt. Major of Women Marines.

Fern Hauss, Edna Stein, and Delphine Biaggi were WRs during the Second World War, too. Fern retired in 1971 as a master sergeant and moved into the inactive reserve for thirteen more years; Edna was discharged as a master gunnery sergeant in 1975; and Delphine left the Corps in November 1968 as a first sergeant after twenty-two years. Bobbie Lee, Carol Homan, and Gladys Gaillard were among those who signed up in the watershed year of 1949. They each remained in the Corps for over twenty years and attained the rank of lieutenant colonel, master gunnery sergeant, and master sergeant, respectively. Virginia Painter—whose father was in World War I, and whose two brothers and a duo of aunts served in World War II—entered in 1951 and was released twenty years later as a chief warrant officer 2. Joan Walter's anecdote is a near-perfect way to bring this tribute to a close. It is a rare story that requires no embellishment. She enlisted in 1953. When she married a Marine widower with three children in September 1961 she automatically disqualified herself from further service. Her husband retired in the early 1970s. And then, she says:

I reenlisted in the Marine Reserve in 1974 to finish *my* career. The first six or seven years were great, but times were changing. As I aged the staff changed and I became somewhat of an embarrassment to them. Whoever heard of a grandmother in the Marines? Harassment was constant: weight not in line with existing standards (even though my measurements were well within range); couldn't qualify with the rifle (anyone over forty didn't have to qualify if they never fired a rifle); and there were other incidents which I cannot recall. The last few years in the reserves were almost enough to negate all the pleasant memories I had of the "Old Corps" but my husband insisted I persevere, which I did until 1987.

Staff Sergeant Joan fulfilled her "childhood desire to be a Marine"— and then some—and has a retirement check to prove it.

NOTES

1. William H. Vatcher, Jr., *Panmunjom: The Story of the Korean Military Armistice Negotiations* (New York: Frederick A. Praeger, Inc., 1958), p. 1. Of the 159 plenary sessions held, 133 took place at Panmunjom. Between July 10, 1951 and October 25, 1951 talks were conducted in the village of Kaesong, which was in Communist-held territory and was therefore unacceptable to UN representatives.

2. Joseph C. Goulden, *Korea: The Untold Story of the War* (New York: McGraw-Hill Book Company, 1983), XIV.

3. An estimate given orally to this writer by Lieutenant General Robert Johnston USMC, Deputy Chief of Staff for Manpower and Reserve Affairs, on October 24, 1993 at Marine Barracks, Eighth and I, Washington D.C.

4. Mark W. Clark, *From the Danube to the Yalu* (London: George G. Harrap and Co., Ltd., 1954), p. 227.

5. Much of the material concerning Colonels Towle and Hamblet is drawn from my telephone conversations with Colonel Hamblet on October 13, 14, 19, and 22, 1993; and from Mary V. Stremlow, *A History of Women Marines, 1946–1977* (Washington, D.C.: History and Museums Division, U.S. Marine Corps, 1986), pp. 187–190.

6. Stremlow, *A History of Women Marines, 1946–1977,* p. 59.

7. A musical version of Thornton Wilder's Pulitzer Prize–winning play, *Our Town* (1938), was presented on CBS-TV in the fall of 1955. Frank Sinatra took the role of the singing narrator. "Love and Marriage" was composed by Jimmy Van Heusen and Sammy Cahn.

8. Commandant of the Marine Corps, *Report on Progress of Women in the Marine Corps* (Washington, D.C.: Headquarters United States Marine Corps, 1988), pp. 3–3—3–5.

9. John Lewis Gaddis, "The Cold War, the Long Peace, and the Future," in Michael J. Hogan (ed), *The End of the Cold War: Its Meaning and Implications* (New York: Cambridge University Press, 1992), p. 28.

10. William H. Chafe, *The Unfinished Journey: America since World War II* (New York: Oxford University Press, 1986), pp. 146–176.

Chapter Seven

Of Time and Tides

In the wake of the Korean truce there were several tasks to be undertaken, among them the repatriation of prisoners of war and the consolidation of the DMZ.

Between August 5 and September 6, 1953 a final exchange of prisoners of war took place. Labeled "Operation Big Switch," it was the second and largest event of its kind. ("Operation Little Switch" occurred in April.) Of the 12,773 POWs turned over by the enemy, 3,597 were U.S. troops. Twenty-one Americans rejected the opportunity to come home, a development that stunned the American people and earned the men the descriptor "turncoat." It was a blow to our national pride. How could anyone not want to return to the "good old U.S. of A."?

The spotlight then shifted to the experiences of our POWs—38 percent of whom died in captivity—and questions, rumors, and allegations circulated throughout the nation for the next several years. We wondered: Is it possible that one of every three U.S. POWs collaborated with the enemy (as a massive Army study contended)? Why were our troops unprepared to withstand communist "brainwashing" techniques? Were our young men innately weak? Had society failed them? Is there such a thing as being tortured beyond one's capacity to remain loyal? Where is the fail-safe line that separates loyalty and treason? How could an American soldier betray his fellow POWs? Does the old rubric "name, rank, and serial number" make sense when men are subjected to starvation, solitary confinement, beatings, lies, and ideological indoctrination?

Military tribunals were convened to determine the guilt or innocence of men accused of collaboration. Very few were found culpable and the legal inquiries dribbled to an end by the late 1950s. The only concrete outcome, of dubious value at that, was President Eisenhower's "Code of Conduct for Members of the Armed Forces of the United States," promulgated on August 17, 1955.[1]

Always on the prowl for topics that might sell tickets, the motion picture industry thought it might have a new one in the "collaboration business." At least, MGM thought so. It released the first film of the POW genre in May, 1954. Titled *Prisoner of War* it attempts to tell the story of an Army officer (Ronald Reagan) who volunteers to parachute into North Korea so he can be captured and be sent to a communist camp. There, posing as a "Red" sympathizer, he is to find out how the "commies" do what they do to the minds and bodies of our men. The critics were not impressed. They described the movie as "largely uninspired," a "surface treatment" that was "strangely colorless and unconvincing." The dialogue was "cliché-ridden" they said, and the plot lacked credibility. MGM took a shot at the Soviets by making the camp commandant a Soviet general who recommended a Pavlovian approach to indoctrinating American soldiers. Two months before the film was distributed the U.S. Army withdrew its original endorsement on the grounds that the film was not accurate in its depiction of its troops' conduct as POWs.

In 1956 MGM tried again, but took a very different tack. On November 6 it released *The Rack*. Based on Rod Serling's teleplay of the same name, the film focused on whether or not mental persecution was a legitimate defense for apostasy. An Army captain (Paul Newman) is being court-martialed for collaboration. His attorney takes the position that Newman "cracked" as a result of extended, cruel, psychological maltreatment and, therefore, is not responsible for his actions. Nonetheless, Newman is convicted. The point of the film is that as stressful as imprisonment may be it is unacceptable as a rationale for traitorous conduct. Critics applauded Newman's acting but felt the movie was "dramatically thin" overall. It is unclear what conclusions viewers (of which I was one) were being asked to draw—other than, "Oh, isn't it a shame what happened to the captain. He was such a nice man and all."

A year later, United Artists released *Time Limit* (1957). It was based on a play produced by the Theater Guild. An Army major (Richard Basehart) is accused of making propaganda newsreels and radio broadcasts in November 1951 confirming UN employment of germ warfare. His co–POWs testify that Basehart appeared to have "gone over to the

Reds." The fact that he collaborated in order to save sixteen fellow
POWs from being executed for the murder of an informer surfaces after
the investigating officer (Richard Widmark) does a little digging. Sufficient extenuating circumstances are brought to light to persuade Widmark to defend the major at his upcoming trial. He believes that "every
man has his limit" and that it is "no crime to be human." Perhaps so,
but Widmark's superior disagrees. He believes that Basehart failed in
his duties as a military man and deserves to be held accountable for his
delinquencies. The audience is left with the distinct impression that
Basehart is going to be (perhaps ought to be) found guilty.

In his book, *The War Film* (1974), Norman Kagan makes the observation that:

> The harsh attitudes toward the breakdowns of soldiers in all these films,
> despite their sympathetic heroes, point up a new American emphasis on
> inner toughness even in a hopeless situation. Poor ability, sensitivity, and
> bad early experiences [during childhood] are no excuse: communists
> don't play by the rules. (p. 81)

Comparatively, the Marine Corps emerged from this phase of the Korean War in excellent shape. Only 221 Marines fell into enemy hands
and 172 were repatriated in the two "switch" operations. Twenty-two
others made it back to friendly lines by other means. A Congressional
report commended the Marines (and Turks and Colombians) for refusing
to "co-operate or collaborate with the enemy" despite the conditions
imposed upon them. Only one Marine succumbed to the inhumane treatment and signed a false "confession" acknowledging the use of germ
warfare by the U.N. forces.[2]

The second item to be dealt with after the 1953 armistice concerned
the DMZ. It slashed across the peninsula from south of the thirty-eighth
parallel in the west, cut north through Panmunjom, and slanted upward
in a northeasterly direction to the Sea of Japan. The process of making
its two sides impregnable began shortly after the cease fire. Over the
past forty-one years the forces that face each other have strengthened
their fortifications to a level of sophistication that surpasses the ill-fated
Maginot Line. It is common but, in this case, improper to describe the
DMZ as a "giant scar." Scarring suggests that a wound has healed,
which it has not. The DMZ is an open, oozing blemish that serves to
remind everyone that the Korean War is not over. It is a source of
constant aggravation to the North Koreans and a symbol of the frustration the ten million South Koreans who are separated from their families

experience every day. To Gwen Ifill of the *New York Times* (July 12, 1993) the DMZ is "one of the most menacing vestiges of the cold war."

In July 1993 President Bill Clinton made a special visit to the DMZ area. He paused in the middle of the Bridge of No Return about thirty yards from "enemy territory" and looked out over the expanse where human beings fear to tread. North Korean sentries were, as usual, impassive. The President had reason to be curious—and concerned. North Korea (officially, the Democratic Peoples Republic of Korea) has been fussy, inconsistent, provocative, and duplicitous for more than forty years and seems to enjoy the cat-and-mouse game it plays with the West. Throughout the decades since the armistice charges and counter-charges have been hurled across the DMZ and there have been a number of fatal clashes between the opposing security details. North Korea has been involved in assassination attempts and terrorist activities outside its borders. In 1968 it captured the *USS Pueblo* and held its crew incommunicado for nearly a year. Its highly regimented society supports a well-trained armed force of 1,200,000 men, twice the size of the South Korean military. When it feels threatened, or wants to unnerve the West, it moves its troops closer to the DMZ and commences its posturing about reunifying the peninsula by force (by 1995 at the latest). The West would like to believe that the death of Kim Il Sung on July 8, 1994 will result in an easing of tensions. That may be wishful thinking.

After it boycotted the 1988 Olympic Games in Seoul, North Korea teased the West into hoping that a thaw in North-South relations was evolving. In 1990 the prime ministers of the two countries met for preliminary talks and their national soccer teams played each other for the first time. That year also the United States agreed to reduce its force in South Korea by 7,000. In September 1991 the two Koreas were admitted to the United Nations as separate nations. In October the prime ministers met again and on December 12 they announced that a "comprehensive accord calling for reconciliation, nonaggression and cooperation" had been attained. Still, a pall was cast over these hopeful developments by North Korea's enigmatic behavior on two issues of major concern to both the West and to North Korea's far eastern neighbors: persons missing in action and nuclear capability.

In August 1993, the North consented to aid the United States and its allies in their efforts to account for the thousands of men classified as missing during the war. It even handed over seventeen sets of remains in July as a goodwill gesture. A few of the remains were verified as human. Since that cynical offering the North Koreans have returned over thirty more remains. When asked if it was building a nuclear facility,

North Korea reverted to its typical, paranoidal attitude regarding its internal affairs. Early in 1993 it said it would permit an international inspection of its program, and then refused to grant the International Atomic Energy Agency the supervisory powers it requested. What *does* North Korea want? Diplomatic recognition from the United States? Cancellation of United States–South Korean joint military maneuvers? The withdrawal of American troops from the South? An admission by the West that North Korea did not start the war in 1950? All of the above— and more? And if the North does *not* get what it wants, what then? To borrow a question raised by the *Washington Post* (October 23, 1993): "Will North Korea Start an Asian Nuke Race?" What can be done about the impasse on the "Peninsula of Fear"? During his visit to Seoul in November 1993 U.S. Secretary of Defense Les Aspin hinted that the levying of economic sanctions against the North might be a feasible course of action. That notion brought snarls from Pyongyang and caused palpitations in Seoul and Tokyo. In November also the South's first democratically elected president, Kim Young Sam, flew to Washington for talks with Mr. Clinton. At this writing the situation is perilous. Korea is a tinderbox. In March 1994 North Korea put its armed forces on high alert, banned all domestic travel, and told its people that war appeared inevitable. The South Koreans responded with their own alert. No one in the West doubts that the North Koreans are capable of doing something reckless. If they do, the United States will be obliged to respond. That could be the beginning of what twenty-first century historians may call: The Second Korean War.[3]

Politicians and appointees of our major political parties have had to deal with the "Korean problem" through the administration of ten U.S. presidents. Veterans of the 1950–1953 war, however, are less concerned with geopolitics than with the place "their war" has in the public mind and, eventually, occupies in their nation's annals. Veterans of World War II have not had to fret about their standing, and the men and women who served in Vietnam may be satisfied at last that their country respects their sacrifices. Since the Korean War has not been settled—there is no peace treaty or political document, only a cease fire agreement— it has not been assigned a permanent niche in history texts, on film, in contemporary literature, onstage, or in public memorials. For the past nine years or so the common sobriquet applied to the Korean "conflict" has been "the forgotten war." In 1986 William C. O'Neill wrote:

This is America's forgotten war. Few national adventures are so green in the memory as World War II, about which an endless flood of books,

films, and television programs gush forth annually. Few are so neglected
as Korea, which is remembered only by scholars and veterans of it. Even
most veterans are quiet, honoring it, if at all, in the privacy of their hearts
. . . As a rule, surveys of American history pass over the fighting in
Korea quickly, reaching conclusions and moving on as if suffering from
embarrassment. (p. 110)

Two years later Drew Middleton of the *New York Times* (February
28, 1988), in his perceptive review of Clay Blair's huge history of the
war, observed: "For the majority of Americans Korea is a forgotten war.
It has none of the political emotion that still clings to Vietnam, nor any
of the gut-wrenching anxiety that is a legacy of World War II." In his
excellent study, *The Korean War* (1987), Max Hastings points out that:

It is a source of widespread bitterness among Korean veterans . . . that
their memories and sacrifices seem so much less worthy of attention than
those of Vietnam veterans. It was their misfortune to endure a war that
aroused less public emotion, because in those early days of television it
was infinitely less vividly projected, less impressed upon the consciousness of Americans. Even at the height of the Korean War, that Asian
peninsula seemed an infinitely remote place, far less real than Vietnam
became. (p. 331)

Each of the foregoing citations is more than six years old. Is the war
any *less* forgotten in 1994 than it was then? There is some reason for
thinking so (although veterans may not feel any better about it). For
example, there are ten items in the "Korean War Era" section of the
bibliography at the rear of this volume that have been published since
1988, a clear sign that writers have finally "discovered" the war. Glenn
Steven Cook, director for Archives and Library at the George C. Marshall Foundation in Lexington, Virginia, makes the point that "Korea is
no longer the forgotten war" in his review essay in *The Journal of Military History* for July 1992 (pp. 489–494) and cites eighteen literary publications as evidence that the level of recognition is rising steadily. There
are four video documentaries available for purchase by citizens who are
impelled to learn something about "one of the least known wars of our
time": *This Is Korea,* made during the war and directed by John Ford;
Korea: War at the Thirty-Eighth Parallel (1987), presented by Kirk
Douglas; *Korea: The Forgotten War* (1987), narrated by actor Robert
Stack; and *The Korean War Set* (1992), a five-volume package narrated
by former Marine James Whitmore. They are informed, relatively dis-
passionate presentations of one of the most fascinating—and one of the

deadliest wars we ever fought. It is encouraging to find the war included in popular compendiums such as *What Every American Should Know About American History: 200 Events That Shaped the Nation* (1992) by Alan Axelrod and Charles Phillips (pp. 302–304). Outlets with a military bent such as *Leatherneck* and *American Legion Magazine* did commemorative series and special editions on the war in the early 1990s.

Ever since the Civil War it has been traditional to validate our armies' efforts in two tangible ways: parades and war memorials. As James Barron of the *New York Times* (June 24, 1991) said of Korean veterans, "The troops who fought in Chosin and Panmunjom came home to silence—no peppy marching bands, no patriotic speeches, no one asking them to autograph their T-shirts." Finally, on June 25, 1991, four decades later, the veterans got a parade in New York City. About 9,000 of them marched down Broadway to Battery Park to attend the dedication of a war memorial. Only 250,000 onlookers turned out. Millions lined the street when the troops returned from the Gulf War but, as one veteran of Korea remarked, "It's been forty years, but this is like a dream." "We're finally being recognized," another said. Still another veteran noted, "We're here not for us but for the guys we left in Korea."

The issue of an appropriate memorial of national significance has not yet reached closure. There are memorials scattered around the United States in communities that decided to erect their own in memory of their veterans. A Korea "unknown" has lain in his crypt at Arlington National Cemetery since May 1958. "Korea 1950" is inscribed on the foundation of the Marine Corps War Memorial nearby. Korean War dead and missing have been honored handsomely in the Honolulu Memorial National Cemetery of the Pacific in Hawaii. (The Republic of Korea established memorials to American and Allied forces at Paju and Pusan in the 1970s.) In Milwaukee, Wisconsin, a county memorial to veterans of World War II and Korea was dedicated twenty-five years ago.

These fragments—in honor of a war that remains fragmented in the public imagination—are gratifying but, in this country, the ultimate compliment comes when a memorial is erected in the Washington, D.C. area. The Vietnam memorial complex was completed on November 11, 1993 when a bronze statuary grouping of nurses was unveiled—but, to date, the Korean War has no equivalent remembrance in the nation's capital. Construction of such a memorial began in April 1993 and dedicatory ceremonies are scheduled for July 27, 1995—forty-two years after the armistice. Will that memorial be meaningful by then? To combat veterans of the war, the youngest of whom will be in their sixties, it will be. To the American people in general, who have mixed feelings about a war that is not over, perhaps. And, if and when the memorial is completed, Professor James M. Mayo believes "the Korean War will continue to be overshadowed by other wars in recent American history."[4]

Over the years some historians have put forth both negative and revisionist views of the war which must be recognized. In his brilliant synthesis, *Modern Times* (1991), Paul Johnson expressed the opinion that:

> The Korean War was a characteristic 20th century tragedy. It was launched for ideological reasons, without a scintilla of moral justification or any evidence of popular support. It killed 34,000 Americans, a million Koreans, a quarter of a million Chinese. It achieved no purpose. All its consequences were unintended. Its course was a succession of blunders. (p. 450)

John Toland, in *In Mortal Combat: Korea 1950–1953,* raises the question "Was the Korean War Worth Fighting?" and then answers it thus:

> It was a war of cruelty, stupidity, error, misjudgment, racism, prejudice, and atrocities on both sides . . . Yet recent events in both Asia and Europe call a negative view of the Korean War into question. The forgotten war may eventually turn out to have been the decisive conflict that started the collapse of communism. In any case, those who fought and died in the war did not fight and die in vain. (p. 596)

The revisionist school's leading personality is Professor Bruce Cumings. A persuasive, incisive writer, Cumings has invested a great deal of time in maintaining that the North Koreans did not actually start the war or, to be more precise, that the American version of who did what to whom is an oversimplified, self-serving distortion of the facts. This indictment was first put forth during the war by Isidor Feinstein "I.F." Stone, and Cumings has elaborated upon it in four major scholarly works since 1981. Stone was an articulate iconoclast of the Socialist persuasion who harpooned bureaucrats and governments with his own special brand of sarcasm. He was a first-rate satirist who, unlike most writers of his ilk, never lost his sense of humor. In his daring book, *The Hidden History of the Korean War, 1950–1951* (1952), Stone cast doubt on the prevailing consensus that the North Korean assault on June 25, 1950 was "a surprise." He posited that South Korea's President, Syngman Rhee, either started the war or "deliberately provoked a massive attack" in order to shore up his sagging regime. Needless to say, Stone's nonconformist interpretation was not received with enthusiasm and it was allowed to go out of print by the *Monthly Review Press.* In 1988 it was exhumed by Little, Brown and Company. A laudatory preface was provided by Bruce Cumings, who saw Stone's work as a "truthful book" and a "model of honest inquiry" deserving of another look.

Stone died in 1989 at age eighty-two. He may have lived long enough to know that North Korea had taken up a hardened view very similar to his own. Kim Il Sung and his minions have their 21,000,000 countrymen and women believing that the United States started the war and is responsible for keeping the two Koreas divided. History, as taught and studied in the North, is less of an academic discipline than a propaganda tool. "Who started the war, and who poses a military threat, is never debated by North Korean scholars whose official textbooks are used by schools all over the country," Sheryl Wu Dunn reported in the *New York Times* (August 12, 1989) following her visit to Panmunjom and Pyongyang. North Korean authorities are dedicated to the proposition that the United States "launched the attacks from behind the scenes." Interestingly, a year after Ms. Dunn's visit, a former North Korean ambassador to Moscow, Li San Cho, who was deputy chief of staff of the North's military forces during the war, confessed that Kim Il Sung "invented a border incident"—echoing Adolf Hitler's excuse for invading Poland in 1939—to start the war with the South in 1950. "My conscience does not allow me to keep silent on a deception on this scale," Mr. Li told reporters from the *Moscow News* in July 1990. "It was a carefully prepared invasion," he said, carried out after Kim Il Sung discussed his plans with Josef Stalin (*New York Times,* July 6, 1990).

*   *   *

In his sweeping history of the U.S. Marine Corps J. Robert Moskin describes the twelve years following the Korean War as "tumultuous times," perhaps because the Corps was engaged in a centripetal-centrifugal tug of war that was potentially injurious to its reputation. Its performance in Korea was a booster shot to be sure, but by 1955 the Corps was once more in a struggle with a Presidential administration for control of its mission, size, and budget. Dwight Eisenhower believed that the armed services were fertile areas for cutbacks. A sympathetic U.S. Congress did what it could to keep the reductions from crippling the Corps completely but it was not inclined to argue too vociferously against the need to be fiscally responsible. The President's reelection in 1956 meant four more years of web belt tightening for the Corps. Between 1955 and 1960 Marine Corps active duty strength was reduced from 248,000 to 170,621 (just 7,000 less than it will be in 1994–1995). During that decade the Corps' budgetary allocation slipped under $1,000,000,000 to $920,000,000. In a parallel channel the Corps was called upon to represent the United States and its interests in foreign arenas. Throughout the 1950s and early 1960s Marines were dispatched on protective and humanitarian missions to locations such as Lebanon, Greece, Guatemala, Taiwan, Mexico, Israel, Morocco, Egypt, Cuba, and Japan. Marines were put on alert during the 1962 Cuban missile crisis, and in 1965, 6,000 Marines were sent to the Dominican Republic to "prevent a Communist takeover." Nine Marines were killed and thirty were wounded there.

In addition to the external influences exerted upon it, the Corps had internal problems to resolve. For example, despite budgetary and manpower constraints, the FMF (and the Reserve) had to be reorganized and strengthened. There were concerns over the quality of leadership at the lower ranks and the always "sticky" issue of how to expunge officers and NCOs who were no longer needed. On top of this mountain of arduous tasks fell a calamity so heavy that is almost pulverized the credits the Corps had amassed in the Korean War: the Ribbon Creek debacle.

Staff Sergeant Matthew C. McKeon, a veteran of World War II and Korea, ordered a recalcitrant platoon of Parris Island boots to march into a tidal stream on April 8, 1956. Six recruits drowned in the process, "setting off a furor among both defenders and detractors of Marine Corps training methods," Keith Fleming observed. McKeon's sentence—a bad conduct discharge, forfeiture of $270.00 pay, nine months confinement at hard labor, and a "bust" in rank to private—was lessened by Secretary of the Navy Charles S. Thomas. McKeon spent twelve days in the brig and was transferred to MCAS Cherry Point, as a private. In 1958 he was promoted to corporal. A year later he was discharged for medical reasons.[5]

Fleming does not exaggerate when he states that although McKeon's official connection with the Corps was severed, his "legacy of upheaval within the Marine Corps continued" (p. 86). Anyone who was affiliated with the Corps in the late 1950s remembers the turmoil surrounding the case. Former WM Edna Mae Cogswell's recollection of that discomfiting incident and its aftermath is tinged with both regret and reproof:

I was stationed at Parris Island in 1956 when Sergeant McKeon drowned six young boots during a training accident. I remember seeing him at

Catholic Mass before that—and after. He deteriorated so much. It must have been very hard for him to go into Beaufort [S.C.] and be called so many bad names. Later I heard he got out of the Marines on a disability [a ruptured disk]. The real tragedy to me was that he marched them into the water in the first place and, in the second place, that the recruits didn't listen to orders.

This writer remembers the Ribbon Creek disaster, too. In 1956 I was in charge of the Officer Procurement team in Boston, Massachusetts. Our mission was to visit colleges and universities in a five-state New England region and persuade qualified undergraduates to enroll in the Platoon Leaders Class (PLC) program. When schools were in session we were on the road five days a week. Saturday mornings were reserved for paperwork at the office. Monday we were back on the trail to another set of colleges. We had quotas to meet and enough pride in our product, a commission as a second lieutenant in the Marine Corps, to want to achieve our annual goals. We were on a college campus displaying our wares when the news of the drownings was broadcast. There was an immediate decline in student interest in our program. For several months we were greeted with silence, sullen looks, passing remarks about Marines being "murderers," and dismissive comments such as "why don't you guys pack up and go somewhere else to find suckers?" The icy receptions continued for nearly a year. It taxed our patience and our diplomatic skills, stuck as we were out there on a public relations outpost with little guidance from HQMC, but we did not crumble under the pressure or make alibis. What we did make was—our quota. (Fortunately, the young men we were recruiting were being sent to Quantico, not Parris Island, for their basic training.)

Before we move too far away from the 1950s it would be useful to take an over-the-shoulder glance at that generation of WMs through the eyes of a woman who was there, and went on to rise to the top of her chosen profession. Margaret A. Brewer entered the Corps as a second lieutenant in 1952 following her graduation from the University of Michigan. Twenty-one years to the month after that commencement she was appointed the seventh director of WMs. Colonel Brewer was the last person to fill that post prior to its disestablishment in June 1977. On May 11, 1978 she was appointed Director of Information and promoted to the next highest rank, brigadier general. Thereby, she "became the first woman general officer in the history of the Marine Corps." Brigadier General Brewer retired in July 1980. In September 1993 I asked her to look back four decades and share her recollections, which she was kind enough to do. Among her comments I found this insightful paragraph:

> As I reflect on those years of service from today's perspective, my impression is that the decade of the 1950s could be described as a time of "status quo transition" for military women. Although this might seem like a paradox, it does reflect the attitudes and policies of the era as well as the institutional uncertainties regarding the role of military women after the enactment of the Women's Armed Services Integration Act of 1948. For example, many of the "separate" policies and regulations established during World War II were maintained; at the same time, however, some of the very restrictive assignment and classification policies established after World War II were modified. As a result, the 1950/1960 era provided a foundation for the evolutionary change in the role of military women from the "Free a Man to Fight" role during World War II to the more integrated role resulting from the implementation of the "All Volunteer Force" during the 1970s.

It is not within the province of this volume to chronicle all the changes in policy and direction that affected the female side of the Corps' personality after the 1950s. There were many major developments, most of them resulting in improvements in the quality of the women's lives. The crucial regulatory reforms have been fully covered elsewhere, notably in Mary Stremlow's history of Women Marines. It may be useful, however, to examine briefly where Women Marines stand in the Corps of the 1990s. That will tell us just how far they have come since the Korean War—and what yet remains to be decided.

One index of both visibility and acceptance is how often WMs are mentioned in contemporary Corps-related literature, and what is said about them therein. Over the past eight years WMs have emerged from obscurity and received pretty fair coverage in commercial pictorial histories. Kathleen Jaeger's *The United States Marines Today* (1986) gives WMs a sub-chapter all their own (pp. 38–45) and sixteen color photographs in and around that section. In his 1988 work, *Warriors: The United States Marines,* Agostino Von Hassell stresses the Corps' combat readiness and its historic achievements. There is no reference to WMs in the text but he includes three small pictures of individuals (pp. 41, 54, 79). The most complimentary depiction of WMs lies between the 9"x12" covers of John de St. Jorre's *The Marines* (1989). In addition to several pictures on pages 38 and 44, de Jorre presents eighteen color photographs between pages 238 and 245 of WMs in their various uniforms. On the other hand, Jack Murphy's 225–page, lavishly illustrated *History of the U.S. Marines* contains but one picture of a WM at work and a single paragraph about women "rising in the ranks" (p. 201). The 1992 revised edition of Chuck Lawliss's *The Marine Book* has seven black and white photos of WMs, a solid narrative about their history (pp. 155–163) and a listing of WM directors (p. 196). Present-day WMs will enjoy revisiting their pioneering antecedents in Jim Moran's *U.S. Marine Corps Uniforms & Equipment in World War 2* (1992). He devotes an entire chapter to "Beautiful American Marines" (pp. 127–138) and shows them in their 1943–1945 garb in twenty-nine photographs.

In works of a more historiographic nature Women Marines fare reasonably well. Their history, duties, and assignments are treated with a straightforward brevity in the third edition (1988) of the late Robert Debs Heinl, Jr.'s *Handbook for Marine NCOs* (pp. 38–39, 101, 106–107, 113). Allan R. Millett revised and expanded his *Semper Fidelis: The History of the United States Marine Corps* for publication in 1991 and takes note of WMs as he proceeds down through the Persian Gulf War on pages 307, 374, 468, 508, 615–616, and 643. The revised, paperback edition of Victor R. Krulak's *First to Fight: An Inside View of the U.S. Marine Corps* (1991) gives WMs eight words of a footnote at the bottom of page 179, which is all they got in his 1984 edition (p. 171). WMs are afforded the most human, caring treatment in J. Robert Moskin's third revised edition of his *The U.S. Marine Corps Story* (1992). Moskin devotes a chapter (pp. 810–817) to the women's progress (and lack of same) as Marines since World War I, ending their story on an optimistic note. There is something haunting about a sentence I found in Allan Millett's award-winning biography, *In Many a Strife: General Gerald C. Thomas and the U.S. Marine Corps, 1917–1956* (1993). On page 236 Millett states (and supports in a chapter footnote) that Thomas was not very enthusiastic about females in the Corps. Millett observes that Thomas "favored the use of women Marines for administrative duties at Headquarters but pictured their service as only a wartime expedient." That is a disturbing echo to hear in 1994, but apparently it represents an attitude that has not entirely vanished within the Corps.

There were twenty women among the Marines who were put ashore at Mogadishu, Somalia, in 1992 as a part of Operation Restore Hope. Reporter Judy Keen visited the camp set up at the port and made some telling observations for *USA Today* (December 14, 1992). "It doesn't take much to provoke a flare-up of resentment between the sexes," she wrote, "and at least so far, this humanitarian military exercise provides little hope for detente." She interviewed three WMs and two male Marines. The results were neither surprising nor encouraging. From the men Keen elicited comments such as: "A WM isn't really a woman. She lost a little of that once she's been in boot camp"; "They should stay in the office. I don't think they're physically capable of keeping up with us grunts," and "You stay the hell away from them. They can take the smallest thing and use it against you." Obviously, the poltergeist of the Tailhook sexual harassment scandal has not been exorcised yet.

And the women? How did they react to what the men were projecting? A WM corporal had some things to say: "You're a woman in a man's world. . . . Sometimes you have to prove to these guys that although you're a woman you can do the job. . . . But sometimes people don't even want to deal with you because you're a woman. There's some resentment." As minuscule as it may seem, the "flashpoint" between the Marines was the "inevitable debate" over the use of the head. Ms. Keen noticed that the men were annoyed because the women "wander by while they're using the facilities," thus violating what little privacy there was to be had in the field.

Accompanying Keen's article is a (posed) photograph of a WM in camouflage gear. She is carrying a rifle and has assumed a ready-for-action stance, which brings to mind the heated debate over women in combat. In the Corps there is no middle ground on that subject. One is either for it or against it. The "against" group is vehement in its opposition and probably outnumbers the "fors" by a wide margin. A few samples will illustrate just how strongly Marines of both genders feel about retaining the ban (which the Corps' leaders support). First, it should be said that women constitute 4.5 percent of the regular Marine Corps establishment and, at this writing, all combat-related jobs remain closed to them. Even now, after decades of urging the Corps to relax its restrictions on the deployment of women, over one-half of its women officers are placed in traditional positions such as personnel, administration, and finance. Nearly 48 percent of enlisted WMs occupy those billets also (plus motor transport and communications). The Corps has not been totally inflexible, however. It allows women to be assigned to security guard duties, has integrated Basic School platoons, and permits female recruits to participate in (dummy) grenade-tossing exercises and bayonet drills. But actual combat?

The cover of the May 10, 1993 edition of the *Navy Times* asked: "Women Marines; When Will They Fly? Will They Join Ground Combat Units? Will the Corps Resist?" The answer to the first question is: sooner than we think. Marine Second Lieutenant Sara M. Deal received authorization in July 1993 to stand by for aviation training. Perhaps, before the end of this decade, women will be piloting aircraft that might be used under combat conditions. If Lieutenant Deal succeeds, it could be the first inroad in the Corps policy. If women become "airdales," can female "grunts" be far behind? *Very* far behind, if the rank and file, Marine alumni, and a few outspoken "brass" carry the day.

Former Commandant of the Marine Corps (1979–1983), General Robert H. Barrow USMC (Ret.), has said:

> Clearly we are moving toward women on the battlefield. As a combat commander in three wars, I can tell you that would be a serious mistake. Strangely, the women who advocate sending their younger sisters into the bloody hell of combat have never seen combat themselves, nor will they ever see it. The rest of us have either been duped or intimidated.[6]

Major General Gene Deegan, then the commanding general of MCRD Parris Island, was quoted in the New Orleans *Times-Picayune* (October 10, 1992) as saying that it would be "pure lunacy" to allow women to be involved in combat operations. "The most important ingredient is the heart and gut of Marines to kill the enemy," he said. "There's no doubt in my mind that [by putting females into combat] we are planting the seeds for future failure on the battlefield." In the *Naval Institute Proceedings* for November 1992 former Marine John Luddy insisted that women will "jeopardize the lives of others by disturbing the essential cohesiveness of a fighting unit." A former WM named Colleen M. McHale was quite firm in her conviction that "women do not belong in combat," or so she said in the November 1993 issue of *Military* magazine. "Women today must be limited to the support roles we manage so well, out of harm's way." It seems likely that this controversy will continue unabated into the mid-1990s. The women are divided on the issue. To quote Judy Keen again, some "think they should have a shot at every military assignment; others worry they'd hinder a combat operation and don't mind keeping their distance."

Inside the Corps the gender friction manifested in a childish argument over physical fitness. Over fifty WM volunteers participated in a study "to determine if, with proper training, they can perform the same fitness tests required of male Marines." The study was conducted between February and May 1993. Evidently it was initiated, in part, because of perceptions men had, viz., that females were not worthy to claim the title of United States Marine if they were unable to do what men do in the realm of physical prowess. Complaints (by males) that dual standards were discriminatory stretched back to 1975. The 1993 experiment was intended to see if the differentiated standards then in effect might be validated or upgraded. A woman staff sergeant saw all the hoopla for the sham that it was. She said: "A lot of men who complain that we're treated differently just refuse to [acknowledge] that there is a distinct difference. They never will, and they'll always whine about it." Most of the women participants had no desire to prove they were able to do everything a man could do, even if, in so doing, they would cease to be "second class citizens." They wanted to be respected for who they were and for their contributions to the well-being of the Corps.

In any event, after the three-month study was completed, the Marine Corps announced that "the current standards set for the female fitness test meet the Corps' requirements." In fact, it was a Catch-22 for the Corps even before the study began. If the women could not meet the male standards (which all parties knew they could not) then the only alternative was to lower the men's standards in order to achieve parity (which all parties knew would never happen). The findings? Women can do sit-ups almost as well as men; women are slower runners than men; and women do poorly on pull-ups because they "do not possess the upper-body strength of men." After all these revelations, the *Navy Times* (August 23, 1993) reported, the Corps "is reaffirming its commitment to separate standards for the sexes."

While the fitness study was in progress *Leatherneck* magazine was interviewing six WMs in an attempt to determine how they felt about themselves as members of the Corps. The outcome was written up by R. R. Keene in a piece entitled "A Blueprint for Success" and published in the May 1993 issue (pp. 52–54). Keene talked to a lieutenant colonel, a captain, and four sergeants of varying ranks. Their remarks are very enlightening and may be distilled as follows:

A. The Marine Corps is still a haven for macho thinking and behavior, or, to quote one of the women, it's the " 'malest' of all the armed forces." One's "comfort level" with profanity had better be "fairly high."

B. It is wise to "show a lot of physical endurance." Male Marines equate physical weakness with mental weakness. To gain their respect a woman has to "hang in there with the best of them, work hard and apply [herself]."

C. Sexual harassment still occurs. Whether or not it becomes problematic depends on how a woman handles it. Firmness tempered by a sense of humor may be the most effective strategy. "A lot of men don't realize they are doing it," one WM believes. "Both men and women need to be educated."

D. A WM best be prepared to be watched by potential critics. "Marines are very critical and won't let you get away with anything," a staff sergeant states. They look for "screw-ups." If a woman makes a mistake, another senior sergeant says, "it may be blown out of proportion simply because she's a female. We definitely work twice as hard to be recognized" . . . and,

E. Above all, it is important to be a true professional in both attitude and performance. A WM needs to develop the moral strength, confidence, emotional self-discipline, and flexibility to stand tall in the ranks with all Marines she encounters.

This "blueprint" could easily have been drafted in 1944. It sounds very much like what smart WRs were inclined to do during World War II once they understood what it took to get along in an all-male fraternity that was not eager to be integrated.

As the French say, *plus ça change, plus c'est la même chose.* The more things change, the more they seem to remain the same. As it was in 1954, so it was in 1993—at least in some ways. For example, in the November 1993 *Leatherneck* there was a cartoon that was a throwback to the 1950s. A decidedly uncomely, knobby-kneed woman Marine sergeant is standing in front of a barber's chair—in which her friend, a female gunnery sergeant, is sitting, upright and tense. The male civilian barber—perhaps accustomed to mowing recruits' heads, or, perhaps mistaking the iron-jawed gunny for a man—has just shaved her head down to a stubble. The gunny, feeling her dome, is in shock. The barber is appalled at what he has done. But the caption has the gunny's friend saying, "A crew-cut, Maggie. How daring!" Amusing? Maybe. Insulting? A little.

It is time now to return to the former WMs who made this story possible. As we do, it is useful to remember that there is a gap between what was happening to WMs *as a component of the Corps* during the Korean War era—and what women veterans recall about their tours on active duty. Generally, women who served brief "hitches" tend to view the Corps and how it treated its women through the narrow lens of their own experiences. Career WMs have a keener sense of history, broader perspectives on where their organization was heading, and a surplus of considered opinions about "then and now." The fascinating aspect of all this is that both the "short-timers" and the "lifers" share an abiding love for the U.S. Marine Corps that has not eroded. If anything, the passage of time has magnified the pride they feel for having been real Marines. It is not merely nostalgia, which, Robert Nisbet wrote, is the "rust of memory." Perhaps it is an inexplicable factor, best left undissected. Perhaps baseball legend Ted Williams, a former Marine aviator who saw combat in Korea, has said it for all of us: "It's a funny thing, but, as the years go by, I think you appreciate more and more what a great thing it was to be a U.S. Marine."

The twelve women whose afterthoughts are expressed below range in age from their early sixties to their early eighties. They are a mixture of former officers and enlisted personnel. Some married, some did not. They are a blend of World War II, Korea, and Vietnam veterans. Today, they live in California, Connecticut, Florida, Minnesota, Nevada, and Texas. As disparate as they may seem, they have in common the bond embodied in the motto, "Once a Marine Always a Marine." I think of them as a squad that represents *all* women who wore a Marine uniform. A "Mod Squad"? "The Dedicated Dozen"? "The Gung-Ho Girls"? No matter, we need only listen. The message is "loud and clear." Attention, all hands:

(Major) Marie Anderson: I have never regretted a moment of the years I spent in the Marine Corps. . . . As women we contributed what we had to offer and worked hard at our jobs. Many of the opportunities available to women in the service now were not available to us during the two wars, but we had to convince the Commandant, Generals, and other ranking officers that women were an asset to the Corps—and I think we succeeded admirably. I will be eternally grateful to the Corps. It gave me the opportunity to show leadership ability and instilled in me a sense of bonding with all other Marines. The Corps is unique and so are all its members, male and female.

(CWO 2) Ethel Barker: It was my privilege to have served in the Marine Corps. Although it was a serious career move it had its moments. All in all, I wouldn't have changed a thing. Saw a lot, did a lot, made lifelong friends, and am now in my twilight years, reminiscing a lot. Boy, what a life I've had!

(T/Sgt.) Gladys DeKlotz: I think being in the Marine Corps was the most rewarding experience any girl could have. The Marine Corps was brother, mother, and father to me. I went from an immature individual to a mature, self-disciplined, goal-minded woman.

(1st Sgt.) Delphine Biaggi: My 22–year career as a Woman Marine was an enjoyable and memorable period in my life. I made many long and lasting friendships. . . . I believe that women who served in the military during my era paved the way for the present career opportunities and equality available to women in the current armed forces.

(S/Sgt.) Mary Boyd: In retrospect, everything was wonderful and I get hysterical thinking about some of the situations, and—although there were things I hated, like 4 A.M. fire drills in the middle of winter—I have nothing but fond memories now. I still admire the gentleness of the "warriors" who went through the hell of Korea in the winter. I didn't realize it at the time, but the experience gave me the self-confidence and fortitude to handle the rough years ahead.

(Sgt.) Betty Moore: Looking back on my WM experience, it taught me a great deal. First and foremost, it taught me independence and responsibility, and how to get along with other people. It made me very proud to have served my country twice. I'm still thrilled about it at age 70. I would not take a million for my Marine Corps days. I've traveled, seen things, met numerous friends, and had great experiences not possible if I hadn't been a Marine.

(Sgt.) Clare Bullitt: It's an experience I wouldn't trade for the world. It's shown me how short life really is—when I saw so many men go to Korea and not return. Also, knowing so many people from poor and/or unfortunate life circumstances, I've learned how fragile life can be. Most of all, my WM experience has taught me independence, how to take care of myself, and that I can accomplish whatever I decided I wanted to do. It has also taught me the value of friendship.

(Gy Sgt.) Ellen Juhre: Being a WM was the most *important* part of my life. At 63 years old, I'm still trying to adjust to the civilian world. The Marine Corps made me a better person, gave me confidence, taught me the importance of compassion, leadership, and teamwork and truly instilled in me a love of God, Country, and Corps.

(Major) Joan Collins: Until I joined the Marine Corps in 1953, I was an insecure young woman who did what society expected of me. I worked for the local telephone company, got engaged, planned on marriage, etc. I was not my own person. The Marine Corps is the most important thing that ever happened in my life. It gave me a belief in myself and a stronger love of my country. It taught me that hard work, dedication, and loyalty pay off. My identity today is still that of a Marine. All else is secondary.

(Lt. Col.) Bobbie Lee: I am proud to have been a woman Marine because, as any Marine will tell you, the Marine Corps is the best! I would not like to be in now because it is definitely not the Corps that I knew, particularly as far as women are concerned. True, they have gained a lot I suppose by becoming completely integrated with the men—but they have lost a lot, too . . . The thing I think I would miss the most is that there are no longer any woman Marine units with their own commanding officers and first sergeants. After all, 18- and 19-year-olds are still teenagers and really could use the firm, but more gentle, leadership of a woman officer or staff NCO.

(Pfc.) Betty Patterson: It made me self-confident, proud, neat, structured, organized, and well-groomed. It prepared me to handle winning and losing. I have remained "gung ho" about the Corps, my country, and the men and women who have paid such a high price for the freedom and the "rights" that are being made such a mockery of in this time period. I still do not believe women should be in combat, except for nurses who volunteer for that duty.

(1st Lt.) Lenore Sandager: Oh, there are so many, many little things over the years that have influenced me and my decisions. "Hitching your bootstraps a little higher"—the advice given me by the first Major I worked for at Lejeune, after I lost a loved one. . . . Maybe it is true that the Marines build men, but I suspect they build a few women, too. . . . I think I was a better mother because I was a Marine. My two sons claim that I preached the idea that you owe it to yourself to be the best that you can be. Pride in yourself, in what you do, in what you believe, are an integral part of Marine Corps training. . . . I still polish my shoes, I still hang my clothes with the hangers all facing the wall. I'm a NEATNIK! My home can usually pass inspection.

I feel compelled to convert the foregoing squad of heroines into a "Baker's Dozen" by adding one final testimony from a woman who was a WM during the Korean War era—and who has a special way of preserving what she calls her "days of innocence."

Anna Orlando served in the Corps from May 1949 through June 1952. In the southeast corner of her bedroom on the second floor of her California home there stands a headless, legless "dress form." "She" (the form) is wearing a two-piece, seersucker, WM summer uniform. There are Marine Corps emblems on her lapels and staff sergeant stripes on her short sleeves. A regulation, green-covered purse hangs from her left (*not* her right) shoulder and a green overseas cap is draped over the top of her torso. Anna glances at her motionless alter ego frequently. "Looking at it every day is a wonderful reminder of those wonderful days in the United States Marine Corps," she says. I am not convinced that Anna's "days of innocence" are forever gone, as she seems to think. I *am* certain that those of us who belong to her generation have undergone some physical changes. Anna's dress form display inspires her to exercise regularly in hopes that she will return to the 113 pounds which used to fit into that uniform. I have no doubt she will achieve her goal. For some of us who wore military gear forty years ago that would be less of an inspired act than an exercise in masochism—but to Anna it is a meaningful, symbolic, and practical tribute to her Marine Corps experiences. If anyone truly lived up to the slogan "Once a Marine Always a Marine," it is Anna—and there is an endearing sort of innocence about how she has chosen to remember what it all meant.

In his moving volume, *The Korean War* (1987), Max Hastings makes the point that "Almost all men are marked in some way by the experience of taking part in any war. Those who fought in Korea are no more and no less deserving of respect—and of a memorial—than those who fought in Vietnam, World War II, World War I." Women, too, have been "marked" by their wartime experiences, albeit in different ways.

Let this modest book be one mark of our respect for, and a memorial to, the women who willingly gave the irretrievable years of their youth to the cause of preserving freedom in that "infinitely remote place," Korea.

Semper Fidelis, Marines.

NOTES

1. A copy of the Code is included in Eugene Kinkead, *In Every War but One* (New York: W.W. Norton and Co., 1959), pp. 20–21.

2. The Marine in question was Colonel Frank H. Schwable. A sufficient review of his case is rendered in Allan R. Millett, *In Many a Strife: General Gerald C. Thomas and the U.S. Marine Corps, 1917–1956* (Annapolis, Md.: Naval Institute Press, 1993), pp. 325–326.

3. I am indebted to John C.F. Tillson IV, senior researcher at the Institute for Defense Analysis in Alexandria, Va., for the perspectives he shared with me during a telephone conversation on November 16, 1993. He assured me that there are persons "in high places in the intelligence community who are seriously concerned about the Korean situation." Tillson knows also that the U.S. military leaders on the ground in South Korea are well aware of the threat posed by North Korean forces and have planned how they may respond if an attack across the DMZ is launched.

4. James M. Mayo, *War Memorials as Political Landscape: The American Experience and Beyond* (New York: Praeger Publishers, 1988), p. 198.

5. This subject is covered in scholarly, informative fashion in Keith Fleming, *The U.S. Marine Corps in Crisis: Ribbon Creek and Recruit Training* (Columbia, S.C.: University of South Carolina Press, 1990). A less objective presentation, written at the height of the Vietnam era's antiestablishment protest, may be found in H. Paul Jeffers and Dick Levitan, *See Parris and Die: Brutality in the U.S. Marines* (New York: Hawthorn Books, Inc., 1971).

6. General Barrow's comment appears on the dust jacket of Brian Mitchell, *Weak Link: The Feminization of the American Military* (Washington, D.C.: Regnery Gateway, 1989).

Chapter Eight

L'Envoi

Recently a good friend told me that her teenage son asked, "How did Dr. Soderbergh get to know so much about Women Marines?" She replied, "Well, I presume the same way you get to learn a lot about any subject: research." In part, that is true. But there is much more to it than that, as we shall see.

A more common question—seldom asked aloud—is, "Why is Soderbergh investing his time and energy writing about Women Marines? Let the women themselves do that." Up to this point it has been exactly that, women's territory. I know of no works about women in the military that were done by men—excepting the scores of articles and a few books by males who mourn the loss of military starch and attribute that limpness to the presence of women in the ranks. An example of such pettifoggery is Brian Mitchell's 1989 study, *Weak Link: The Feminization of the American Military,* in which he maintains that "women have had a profoundly disruptive and negative effect on the fighting capabilities of the American armed forces."

I do not believe any subject is out of bounds or that any topic is the exclusive preserve of one gender. On the other hand, I do not expect my books about WMs to evoke much interest among male Marines, past or present. The subtle and overt answers to the questions, "Oh? Why not?" and "Really? How come?" may be found in chapters previous to this one. In a clinical sense, telling the Women Marines' story is as legitimate a scholarly endeavor as any other. In the Corps, however, it does not "cut much ice" unless it is an official, authorized study and, even then, a single work (such as Mary Stremlow's definitive history) is sufficient. So, why bother? And what would impel a former Marine of the masculine persuasion to take up the topic? I have what I feel are sound reasons but I have to go back in time forty-four years if I am to explain my motives properly. This story concerns two Women Marines—one is still living, the other has been in her grave for fifty years.

If I was conscious of the existence of WRs during World War II it was a vague perception. As I think about it, our valiant nurses, WAVES, and WACs received much more publicity in the press and on film than WRs did. I did not see a WM until after I graduated from boot camp at Parris Island in November 1950, and that was not by choice. My dreams of combat—greatly intensified by the Marines' heroic escape from the Chosin Reservoir—were dashed. To my chagrin, I was ordered to stay at Parris Island as a schools instructor in the battalion in which I was a recruit only a week before. I was sure that my American Spirit Honor Medal and my Private First Class stripe guaranteed me a place as a "snuffy" in the First Marine Division. Spending the Christmas season in the slopchute at Parris Island was not my idea of Marinehood.

During my six months at Parris Island I did see, meet, and manage to talk with WMs, all of whom were enlisted personnel. I found them to be attractive, smart, socially savvy young women who knew how to have a good time without tainting their reputations. At twenty-two, and full of myself, I was very anxious to establish a relationship with one of them, at least. Nothing developed. I am pretty sure it was my fault. I was older and poorer than most privates first class, a "college man," tongue-tied, and too smug to appeal to healthy young ladies who saw neither fun nor security in a liaison with me. They were absolutely right. My WM *was* at Parris Island when I was but we never met, fortunately for her. I had things to do, and so did she.

In April 1951 I was transferred to Quantico to attend an officer candidate screening course. I did not see a WM until the summer of 1952 and none of them knocked my brown socks off. I was a second lieutenant just back from Korea assigned to teach tactics to new officers and, it seemed, spending all my time either conducting classes or monitoring field problems in the boondocks. My social life was in reverse. I do not recall doing anything but fantasizing—until November 10, 1952, the Marine Corps' 177th birthday. A senior officer directed me to organize a small detail, prepare an emotional speech, and deliver same at three locations on the tenth: the enlisted club (Daly Hall), the Quantico air station, and the officers' club. During a rehearsal at Daly Hall I noticed a WM sergeant. She noticed me, too—but not in the same way. She was totally turned off by what she perceived to be my supercilious, cold, officious mannerisms. Perhaps I was a tad arrogant and abrupt but, then, my awesome responsibilities that evening—which I could ill-afford to bungle—made me less personable than usual. Or perhaps I was just being my real self. In any event, I forgot that 5'4", 110 lb., blue-eyed blond sergeant after November 10. There she was, the personification of *Leatherneck* magazine's stereotypic WM, and then she was gone. I consoled myself with the knowledge that the Corps frowned upon officers getting too chummy with enlisted women. I filed it all away as "just one of those things" that was doomed from the start. Did I not? Well, I thought I did.

In January 1953 I was selected to train and direct the chorus—and play the role of Andrew Carnes—in the Quantico Players' production of *Oklahoma.* To my surprise, one of the women who auditioned for the chorus was the WM sergeant whom I had banished from my mind. She had a fine, clear voice and no little stage presence. I like to think that was the reason I admitted her to the talented group of singers. I am sure it was, given my scrupulous adherence to the standards we set. I like to think that I would have blackballed my saintly mother if her tryouts were below par. I like to think that. At that point, I was still dominated by my intellect—but my heart was closing the gap, fast.

For two months we rehearsed every night after working hours and sometimes, as the March debut of the musical drew nigh, we rehearsed twice a day. In previous years I found that preparatory regimen very tedious. Suddenly, I looked forward to spending my evenings at the base theater. The sergeant and I began seeing each other "on the side," so to speak. I was so smitten I convinced myself that no one noticed. Of course, everyone in the cast knew full well that she and I were an "item." And if a cast of ninety knows, so do a host of other people— including, I discovered, my CO at Basic School headquarters. One morning he sent for me, told me to stand "at ease," and asked me if I was "seeing" an enlisted WM. I knew he knew so I replied, "Yes, Colonel, I am." He then proceeded to inform me that (a) in the Corps that was not kosher, (b) I was endangering a promising career by doing so, and (c) it was evidence of poor judgment on my part. Did I understand? Yes, I said. "Fine," he said, "then we'll consider this a closed issue. In the future I suggest you adjust your sights accordingly. That is all."

I did not say I would, and I did not. I was too far gone to imagine saying to her: "Look, sweet-, er, Sergeant, we have to terminate our friendship as of 0600 hours tomorrow. I want to thank you sincerely for an interesting three months. You have been a good sport. About face.

Dis-missed." Indeed, the colonel's intervention, even though well-intentioned, got my dander up fairly high. The stubborn Swede in me was saying: no one is going to tell me whom I can or cannot love—not even the U.S. Marine Corps.

My WM and I carried on (in the military sense) as if nothing had been said. The situation was getting so serious that her closest WM friend advised her to drop me while the dropping was good, contending that I would drop her eventually anyway. "You know how these Marine officers are. They're just in it until they get what they want and then it's *sayonara,* baby." The only things we dropped were a few dollars when we went to D.C. (in civilian clothes) on a date, ate peaches and ice cream at a diner near Quantico, and put gas in my 1952 Dodge. We did a lot of walking and talking. We parked on the base at night in locations where MPs were scarce. "Our song" was Percy Faith's "Song from Moulin Rouge," also known as "Where is your heart?" By April my heart was in her hands. It was obvious to my peers at the BOQ (bachelor officers quarters) that I was eager to put on "the old ball and chain." One of them said to me, "Well, I *guess* you know what you're doing. I will say that if you have to get involved with a WM, you've got a really great girl." How right he was.

When she and I got married in May 1953 in Manassas, Virginia—an event we later referred to as the Third Battle of Bull Run—she was still on active duty. We drove to Washington for our one night "honeymoon" at the Carroll Arms Hotel. I went out to a local deli for ham and cheese sandwiches and set the alarm for 4:30 A.M. so she could get back to Quantico for morning muster. We were nearly late. When we drove up, the WM detachment was forming ranks—and the women were looking at us out of the corner of their eyes, knowing grins on their sleepy faces. My sergeant jumped out of the car—no goodbye kiss that morning— and ran to her appointed slot in the assembled company. It was sort of awkward, for her. I just turned the car around and took off. I remember thinking how lucky we were that Colonel Hamblett had departed the Quantico detachment less than two weeks earlier. She would not have been pleased with such a tasteless flaunting of the prohibitions against fraternization. Shortly afterwards I was transferred from the Basic School staff to the so-called "charm school," officially known as the Instructor Training Section, where we taught incoming officers how to teach. Perhaps my Basic School CO decided I had more charm than wisdom. My bride was discharged honorably in June and we set up housekeeping in an Arlington, Virginia, apartment (that had no kitchen sink). At eighty-five dollars a month it was a bargain, even if we had to wash dishes in the bathtub.

Nearly thirty years and six children later my WM and I were divorced, to the day, almost, that we began rehearsing *Oklahoma* at the Quantico theater. Her presence in my life is one half of my reason for writing about Women Marines. We were Korean War era Marines, both of us—brought together, as so many were, by wartime conditions. Whatever else happened to us, that period of my life remains unsullied. She will always be that slim, pretty, talented sergeant who represented everything that was good about WMs in those far-off years of my youth.

My other motive for pursuing the history of Women Marines is rooted in the life and premature death of a young woman who served as a WR in World War II.

Not until I had been at Louisiana State University for a number of years did I realize that a campus building was named for a deceased WR. It may be the only structure in the nation so designated. I had heard something about her but it did not really register in my mind, just as vaccinations do not always "take." Finally, in 1987, on an impulse, I walked over to the women's dormitory that bore her name to see if, as someone said, there was a picture of her in the foyer. There, prominently displayed, was a framed photograph of Corporal Germaine C. Laville, USMCWR, LSU '42, in her summer "whites," looking down at me. She was very lovely and very young—barely twenty-two.

A flood of questions raced through my brain. How did she die? Where, when, and how did it happen? Why did she join the Marines? Where was she from? What did she do to warrant the distinction of having a building christened in her name? Where was she buried? What had been written about her since her death in 1944?

None of the resident students seemed to know anything about her. The more people on campus who confessed ignorance the more intrigued I became. How could it be that the name Laville had evoked so little curiosity over the years? At that moment I was, as they say, "hooked." I embarked on a year-long journey into the past to find an answer to the question, "Who was Germaine Catherine Laville?" In addition to her being an alumna of the university in which I served, I felt another sort of kinship with her. Marines have a standing agreement among them. They say: "We always bring out our dead and wounded, whatever the cost. Marines do not leave their buddies behind." In a sense, I began to feel that Corporal Laville had been left behind, abandoned on the field of history, her memory overwhelmed by forty years of earthshaking occurrences. She was like an MIA insofar as the university community was concerned. She had no champions, no rescuers—only her immediate family and a few close friends to sustain her memory. Who else should reach out and bring her home, if not a fellow Marine? I found the issue compelling, the challenge irresistible. And, in time, all my questions were resolved.

Germaine was born on May 16, 1922 in Plaquemine, Louisiana, a small community on the west side of the Mississippi River near Baton Rouge. She was the eldest of seven children in a Roman Catholic household. Following her graduation from the local high school she matriculated at LSU in the class of 1942 and declared a major in elementary education. At twenty she was a petite brunette, standing very close to 5'0" and weighing one hundred pounds. She taught in the public schools for one year (1942–1943). Sometime during her first year as a fifth-grade teacher Germaine decided she wanted to contribute to her country's war effort in a direct way. Since her brothers were too young to be drafted she felt a strong obligation to represent her family in the armed forces. In July 1943 she enlisted in the USMCWR as a private. Although she was eligible for a commission by virtue of her university diploma, Germaine did not want to wade through a lot of red tape. She wanted to be a WR as soon as possible. In October she went to boot camp at Lejeune and was ordered thereafter to MCAS Cherry Point. That was in December 1943. She had only six months to live.

Germaine's primary assignment at Cherry Point was as an aerial gunnery instructor. Consequently, she spent her working hours in a large, two-story structure called the Synthetic Training Building (STB). Every day hundreds of student pilots moved through the corridors on their way to classes. It was a relatively new structure first opened to human traffic in June 1943, and during the week it was a very busy facility. On Saturday there were no classes, so the STB was occupied by permanent personnel who had "the duty" (worse luck, they would say). Germaine was on duty in the STB on Saturday, June 3, 1944 when a fire broke out on the first floor at 2:55 P.M. The deflagration spread so quickly that the thirty-odd Marines in the STB had much difficulty keeping one step ahead of the flames and the thick, black smoke. Five Marines died in that holocaust, all of them near their duty stations on the second floor. Two of the five were WRs: Lieutenant Mary Rita Palowitch 034236 of Johnstown, Pennsylvania, and—Germaine. A week later, her remains were returned to Plaquemine for interment in St. John's Cemetery, where she still rests. Germaine and Rita were the only WRs—out of the 20,000 who wore Marine uniforms—to perish while performing their official duties during World War II. Germaine is the only alumna of LSU to lose her life while on active duty in the U.S. military. In commemoration of her unselfish patriotic sacrifice, the LSU Board of Supervisors voted on May 29, 1950 to name a new dormitory Laville Hall.

In December 1988 my biography of Germaine was published under the title *Years of Grace, Days of Glory: The Legacy of Germaine Laville*. In it, I present the details of her beautiful life and tragic death. In the process of preparing that manuscript I established contact with a number of former WRs, including six of the women who were inside the STB when it caught fire. I came away from the Laville story with new impressions of the women who joined the Marines in the 1940s. As I wrote in *Women Marines: The World War II Era*:

> As a former Marine I was deeply moved not only by Germaine's dedication to the Corps but also by the strength of character her female peers displayed during "the good war." The women of Germaine's generation who joined the MCWR were patriotic, courageous, and eager to . . . "free a Marine to fight." Over the often vociferous objections from family and friends, in the face of scurrilous allegations directed their way by certain segments of society, and despite the crude reception from the men they were attempting to help, those 20,000 young women barged into uncharted, all-male territory and distinguished themselves. (p. xvi)

What was it that teenager asked his mother?—"Ma, how did Dr. Soderbergh get to know so much about Women Marines?" His mother was right to say, "Research, son," but that was only a partial explanation. Had he asked me, what would I have told him? Probably more than he wanted to know. Adults are like that. Nevertheless, I would have said: First, I married a Woman Marine—and I never forgot what she and her comrades were like. They were a special breed: stable, snappy, sunny, and shyly sensual. Above all, they were (and remain) faithful to the principles the Corps has espoused for 218 years. Second, I "met" Germaine Laville in the late 1980s and she introduced me to her generation of WRs. They set the forces in motion that resonate within the Corps to this day. Third, they inspired me to tell their story in book form, and that exercise was the impetus for this new study. How could I not honor their successors who wore Marine uniforms during "my war"?

With each volume my appreciation for these women grows. I realize that the Globe and Anchor emblem means as much to them as it does to me. All told, I have come to know nearly 200 women who served with pride in the Marine Corps between 1943 and 1955, and they are a part of me now.

I have no doubt that many men who were in the Corps can claim that they, too, know a great deal about Women Marines. The difference, if any, is that I chose to commit their histories to the printed page so their unique achievements might be remembered by persons as yet unborn. It is that simple, actually. I do not want them to slip into the backwaters of the twentieth century.

Now, perhaps, they will live on in libraries and private collections into the next millennium. Someday, certainly, a young bibliophile will take a book from a shelf, blow the dust from its cover, leaf through its chapters and exclaim: "Ma, I didn't know your grandmother was a *Marine*. Why did she do that? I had no idea there were women in the Marine Corps way back then. What must it have been like?"

And "Ma" will say: "Read on, dear, read on. It's quite a story."

References

PRIMARY SOURCES

Unpublished Letters, Memoirs, and Studies

Brewer, Margaret A. Oral History Transcript. Washington, D.C.: History and Museums Division, Headquarters, U.S. Marine Corps, 1983, 222 pp.

Cugini, Mary F. 54 personal letters to family. January 18, 1945–May 23, 1946.

Hamblet, Julia E. "Enlisted Jobs in the Marine Corps Which Can Be Performed by Women in the Event of Mobilization." Unpublished M.S. thesis, The Ohio State University, Columbus, 1951.

Shaw, Wilma M. 203 letters and cards to family. October 22, 1952–October 15, 1955.

Soderbergh, Peter A. 23 letters and 8 essays to parents from Korea. November 1951–June 1952.

Streeter, Ruth Cheney. "History of the Marine Corps Women's Reserve: A Critical Analysis of Its Development and Operation, 1943–1945." Typescript, 1945.

Towle, Katherine A. "Administration and Leadership." Los Angeles, Calif.: Regional Oral History Office, Bancroft Library, University of California at Los Angeles, 1970, 309 pp.

SECONDARY SOURCES

Books, Pamphlets, and Articles
General

Adair, Gilbert. *Hollywood's Vietnam*. London: William Heinemann, Ltd., 1989.

Andrews, Maxene and Bill Gilbert. *Over Here, Over There: The Andrews Sis-*

ters and The USO Stars in World War II. New York: Kensington Publishing Corp., 1993.

Axelrod, Alan and Charles Phillips. *What Every American Should Know about American History*. Holbrook, Mass.: Bob Adams, Inc., 1992.

Baritz, Loren. *The Good Life: The Meaning of Success for the American Middle Class*. New York: Alfred A. Knopf, 1989.

Blum, John M. *V Was for Victory: Politics and American Culture During World War II*. New York: Harcourt Brace Jovanovich, 1976.

Boettcher, Thomas D. *First Call: The Making of the Modern U.S. Military, 1945–1953*. Boston: Little, Brown and Company, 1992.

Branch, Taylor. *Parting the Waters: America in the King Years, 1954–63*. New York: Simon and Schuster, Inc., 1989.

Butler, Ivan. *The War Film*. Cranbury, N.J.: A. S. Barnes and Co., 1974.

Cardozier, V. R. *Colleges and Universities in World War II*. Westport, Conn.: Praeger, 1993.

Chafe, William H. *The Unfinished Journey: America since World War II*. New York: Oxford University Press, 1986.

Coffey, Frank. *Always Home: 50 Years of the USO*. Washington, D.C.: Brassey's (U.S.), Inc., 1991.

Cumings, Bruce. *War and Television*. London: Verso, 1992.

Dalfiume, Richard M. *Desegregation of the U.S. Armed Forces: Fighting on Two Fronts, 1939–1953*. Columbia, Mo.: University of Missouri Press, 1975. (Original ed. 1969.)

Dammann, Nancy. *A WAC's Story*. Sun City, Ariz.: Social Change Press, 1992.

Gordon, Lois and Alan Gordon. *American Chronicle, 1920–1980*. New York: Atheneum, 1987.

Goulden, Joseph C. *The Best Years: 1945–1950*. New York: Atheneum, 1976.

Halberstam, David. *The Fifties*. New York: Villard Books, 1993.

Harvey, Brett. *The Fifties: A Women's Oral History*. New York: HarperCollins, 1993.

Hogan, Michael J. (ed.). *The End of the Cold War: Its Meanings and Implications*. New York: Cambridge University Press, 1992.

Hoopes, Townsend and Douglas Brinkley. *Driven Patriot: The Life and Times of James Forrestal*. New York: Alfred A. Knopf, 1992.

Johnson, Paul. *Modern Times: The World from the Twenties to the Nineties*. New York: HarperCollins, 1991. (Rev. ed.)

Judd IV, Gerrit P. *Hawaii: An Informal History*. New York: Collier Books, 1961.

Kagan, Norman. *The War Film*. New York: Pyramid Publications, 1974.

Klein, Michael (ed.). *The Vietnam Era: Media and Popular Culture in the United States and Vietnam*. London: Pluto Press, 1990.

MacGregor, Morris J., Jr. *Integration of the Armed Forces, 1940–1965*. Washington, D.C.: Center of Military History, United States Army, 1981.

May, Elaine T. *Homeward Bound: American Families in the Cold War Era.* New York: Basic Books, 1988.

Mayo, James M. *War Memorials as Political Landscape: The American Experience and Beyond.* New York: Praeger Publishers, 1988.

Michener, James A. *The Bridges at Toko–Ri.* New York: Ballantine Books, 1984. (Original ed. 1953.)

Mitchell, Brian. *Weak Link: The Feminization of the American Military.* Washington, D.C.: Regnery Gateway, Inc., 1989.

Nalty, Bernard C. *Strength for the Fight: A History of Black Americans in the Military.* New York: The Free Press, 1989. (Original ed. 1986.)

Oakley, J. Ronald. *God's Country: America in the Fifties.* New York: Dembner Books, 1986.

Olian, JoAnne (ed.). *Everyday Fashions of the Forties as Pictured in Sears Catalogs.* New York: Dover Publications, Inc., 1992.

O'Neill, William L. *American High: The Years of Confidence, 1945–1960.* New York: The Free Press, 1986.

Parrish, James R. *The Great Combat Pictures: Twentieth-Century Warfare on the Screen.* Metuchen, N.J.: The Scarecrow Press, 1990.

Ray, Ronald D. *Military Necessity and Homosexuality.* Louisville, Ky.: First Principles, Inc., 1993.

Severo, Richard and Lewis Milford. *The Wages of War: When American Soldiers Came Home—From Valley Forge to Vietnam.* New York: Simon and Schuster, 1989.

Shilts, Randy. *Conduct Unbecoming: Gays and Lesbians in the U.S. Military.* New York: St. Martin's Press, 1993.

Suid, Lawrence H. *Guts and Glory: Great American War Movies.* Reading, Mass.: Addison-Wesley Publishing Co., 1978.

Terkel, Studs. *"The Good War": An Oral History of World War Two.* New York: Pantheon Books, 1984.

Wells-Petry, Melissa. *Exclusion: Homosexuals and the Right to Serve.* Washington, D.C.: Regnery Gateway, 1993.

Winokur, Jon (ed.). *Writers on Writing.* Philadelphia: Running Press, 1987.

Korean War Era

Alexander, Bevin. *Korea: The First War We Lost.* New York: Hippocrene Books, 1986.

Blair, Clay. *The Forgotten War: America in Korea, 1950–1953.* New York: Times Books, 1987.

Cagle, Malcolm W. and Frank A. Manson. *The Sea War in Korea.* Annapolis, Md.: U.S. Naval Institute, 1957.

Clark, Mark W. *From the Danube to the Yalu.* London: George C. Harrap and Co., Ltd., 1954.

Clough, Ralph N. "The Two Koreas and Washington," *The Wilson Quarterly* 2 (Summer 1978): 142–150.

Collins, J. Lawton. *War in Peacetime: The History and Lessons of Korea.* Boston: Houghton Mifflin Co., 1969.

Cook, Glenn S. "Korea: No Longer the Forgotten War," *The Journal of Military History* 56 (July 1992): 489–494.

Cumings, Bruce. *The Origins of the Korean War.* Princeton, N.J.: Princeton University Press, 1990. Volume II: The Roaring of the Cataract, 1947–1950.

Duncan, David Douglas. *This Is War! A Photo-Narrative of the Korean War.* Philadelphia: Temple University Press, 1986.

Dvorchak, Robert J., *et al. Battle For Korea.* Conshohocken, Pa.: Combined Books, Inc., 1993.

Fehrenbach, T. R. *This Kind of War: A Study in Unpreparedness.* New York: Bantam Books, 1991. (Original ed. 1963).

Frank, Pat. *Hold Back the Night.* New York: Lippincott. 1952.

Geer, Andrew C. *The New Breed: The Story of the U.S. Marines in Korea.* New York: Harper, 1952.

Giangreco, D. M. *War in Korea, 1950–1953.* Novato, Calif.: Presidio Press, 1990.

Goulden, Joseph C. *Korea: The Untold Story of the War.* New York: McGraw-Hill Book Company, 1983.

Halliday, Jon and Bruce Cumings. *Korea: The Unknown War.* New York: Pantheon Books, 1988.

Hamby, Alonzo L. "Public Opinion: Korea and Vietnam," *The Wilson Quarterly* 2 (Summer 1978): 137–141.

Hastings, Max. *The Korean War.* New York: Simon and Schuster, 1987.

Heinl, Robert D., Jr. *Victory at High Tide: The Inchon-Seoul Campaign.* Annapolis, Md.: The Nautical and Aviation Publishing Company of America, 1979.

Higgins, Marguerite. *War in Korea.* New York: Doubleday and Co., 1951.

Hoyt, Edwin P. *The Pusan Perimeter.* New York: Military Heritage Press, 1984.

———. *The Bloody Road to Panmunjom.* New York: Stein and Day, 1985.

James, D. Clayton and Anne S. Wells. *Refighting the Last War: Command and Crisis in Korea, 1950–1953.* New York: The Free Press, 1993.

Kaufman, Burton I. *The Korean War.* Philadelphia: Temple University Press, 1986.

Kinkead, Eugene. *In Every War but One.* New York: W.W. Norton and Co. Inc., 1959.

Knox, Donald. *The Korean War: Uncertain Victory.* San Diego: Harcourt Brace Jovanovich, 1991.

MacDonald, Callum A. *Korea: The War before Vietnam.* New York: The Free Press, 1986.

Marshall, S. L. A. *The Military History of the Korean War.* New York: Franklin Watts, Inc., 1963.

Ridgway, Matthew B. *The Korean War.* New York: DaCapo Press, 1967.

Soderbergh, Peter A. "Remembering Korea—Thirty-five Years Later," *Congressional Record* (June 25, 1985): S8713–8714.

Stokesbury, James L. *A Short History of the Korean War.* New York: William Morrow and Co., 1988.

Stone, I. F. *The Hidden History of the Korean War, 1950–1951.* Boston: Little, Brown and Co., 1988. (Original ed. 1952.)

Summers, Harry G., Jr. *Korean War Almanac.* New York: Facts on File, 1990.

The History of the United Nations Forces in the Korean War. Seoul: The Ministry of National Defense, 1977, Volume VI.

Toland, John. *In Mortal Combat: Korea, 1950–1953.* William Morrow and Company, Inc., 1991.

Tomedi, Rudy. *No Bugles, No Drums: An Oral History of the Korean War.* New York: John Wiley and Sons, Inc., 1993.

Vatcher, William H., Jr. *Panmunjom: The Story of the Korean Military Armistice Negotiations.* New York: Frederick A. Praeger, Inc., 1958.

Wells, Samuel F., Jr. "The Lessons of the War," *The Wilson Quarterly* 2 (Summer 1978): 119–127.

Whelan, Richard. *Drawing the Line: The Korean War, 1950–1953.* Boston: Little Brown and Co., 1990.

Wiltz, John E. "The Korean War and American Society," *The Wilson Quarterly* 2 (Summer 1978): 127–134.

U.S. Marine Corps

Alvarez, Eugene. *Where It All Begins: A History of the United States Marine Corps Recruit Depot, Parris Island, South Carolina.* Byron, Ga.: Privately printed, 1984.

Applebome, Peter. "The Few, the Proud, the Loved," *New York Times* (September 2, 1993), B1, B4.

Berry, Henry. *Hey, Mac, Where Ya Been? Living Memories of the U.S. Marines in the Korean War.* New York: St. Martin's Press, 1988.

Brady, James. *The Coldest War: A Memoir of Korea.* New York: Orion Books, 1990.

Brainard, Morgan. *Then They Called for the Marines: A Marine Rifle Company in Korea, 1950–1951.* Rutland, Vt.: Academy Books, 1989. (Original ed. 1986.)

Carpenter, Dennis and Frank Bisogno. *Anyone Here a Marine?* Great Neck, N.Y.: Brightlights Publications, 1992.

Cohen, Bernard H. *The Proud: Inside the Marine Corps.* New York: William Morrow and Co., 1992.

Commandant of the Marine Corps (Gen. Alfred M. Gray). *Report on Progress of Women in the Marine Corps.* Washington, D.C.: Headquarters, United States Marine Corps, 1988.

daCruz, Daniel. *Boot.* New York: St. Martin's Press, 1987.

De St. Jorre, John. *The Marines.* London: Sidgwick & Johnson Ltd., 1989.

Donovan, James A., Jr. *The United States Marine Corps.* New York: Frederick A. Praeger Publishers, 1967.

Fleming, Charles A., *et al. Quantico: Crossroads of the Marine Corps.* Washington, D.C.: History and Museums Division, Headquarters, U.S. Marine Corps, 1978.

Fleming, Keith. *The U.S. Marine Corps in Crisis: Ribbon Creek and Recruit Training.* Columbia, S.C.: University of South Carolina Press, 1990.

Heinl, Robert Debs, Jr. *Handbook for Marine NCOs.* Annapolis, Md.: Naval Institute Press, 1988.

Isely, Jeter A. and Philip A. Crowl. *The U.S. Marines and Amphibious War.* Princeton, N.J.: Princeton University Press, 1951.

Jaeger, Kathleen. *The United States Marines Today.* Greenwich, Conn.: Bison Books, 1986.

Jeffers, H. Paul and Dick Levitan. *See Parris and Die: Brutality in the U.S. Marines.* New York: Hawthorn Books, 1971.

Kaljot, Lena. "Forty Years Later, Women Play a Vital Part of the Corps' Team," *Marines,* January 1989, 25–27.

Keiser, Gordon W. *The U.S. Marine Corps and Defense Unification 1944–47: The Politics of Survival.* Washington, D.C.: National Defense University Press, 1982.

Krulak, Victor H. *First to Fight: An Inside View of the U.S. Marine Corps.* New York: Pocket Books, 1991. (Original ed. 1984.)

Lawliss, Chuck. *The Marine Book: A Portrait of America's Military Elite.* New York: Thames and Hudson, Inc., 1992.

Meid, Pat. *Marine Corps Women's Reserve in World War II.* Washington, D.C.: Historical Branch, G–3 Division, Headquarters, U.S. Marine Corps, 1968.

Meid, Pat and James M. Yingling. *Operations in West Korea.* Washington, D.C.: Historical Division, Headquarters, U.S. Marine Corps, 1972. (Reprinted Brandy Able 1, Austin, Tex., 1987.)

Melson, Charles D., *et al. U.S. Marines in the Persian Gulf, 1990–1991: Anthology and Annotated Bibliography.* Washington, D.C.: History and Museums Division, Headquarters, U.S. Marine Corps, 1992.

Mersky, Peter B. *U.S. Marine Corps Aviation: 1912 to the Present.* Baltimore: The Nautical and Aviation Publishing Co., 1990. (Original ed. 1983.)

Miller, Marjorie, *et al. WMA: The First Twenty-Five Years, 1960–1985.* (No location), Women Marines Association, 1985.

Millett, Allan R. *Semper Fidelis: The History of the United States Marine Corps.* New York: The Free Press, 1991. (Original ed. 1980.)

————. *In Many a Strife: General Gerald C. Thomas and the U.S. Marine Corps, 1917–1956.* Annapolis, Md.: Naval Institute Press, 1993.

Montross, Lynn and Nicholas A. Canzona. *The Pusan Perimeter.* Washington, D.C.: Historical Branch G–3, Headquarters, U.S. Marine Corps, 1954. (Reprint ed. 1992.)

Montross, Lynn, *et al. The East-Central Front.* Washington, D.C.: Historical Branch, G-3, Headquarters, U.S. Marine Corps, 1962. (Reprint ed. 1957.)

Moore, Molly. *A Woman at War: Storming Kuwait with the U.S. Marines.* New York: Charles Scribner's Sons, 1993.

Moran, Jim. *U.S. Marine Corps Uniforms and Equipment in World War II.* London: Windrow and Green, Ltd., 1992.

Moskin, J. Robert. *The U.S. Marine Corps Story.* Boston: Little, Brown and Company, 1992. (Third revised ed.)

Murphy, Jack. *History of the U.S. Marines.* Greenwich, Conn.: Brompton Books Corp., 1990. (Original ed. 1984.)

Pierce, Philip N. and Frank O. Hough. *The Compact History of the United States Marine Corps.* New York: Hawthorn Books, Inc., 1965. (Rev. ed.)

Quilter, Charles J., II. *U.S. Marines in the Persian Gulf, 1990–1991: With the I Marine Expeditionary Force in Desert Shield and Desert Storm.* Washington, D.C.: History and Museums Division, Headquarters, U.S. Marine Corps, 1993.

Saluzzi, Joseph A. *Red Blood . . . Purple Hearts: The Marines in the Korean War.* Brooklyn, N.Y.: Eagle Publications, 1993. (Original ed. 1990.)

Schuon, Karl. *U.S. Marine Corps Biographical Dictionary.* New York: Franklin Watts, Inc., 1963.

Shaw, Henry I., Jr. and Ralph W. Donnelly. *Blacks in the Marine Corps.* Washington, D.C.: History and Museums Division, Headquarters, U.S. Marine Corps, 1975.

Skelly, Anne. "Women Marines—the First 50 Years." *Marine Corps League* 49 (Autumn 1993): 38–46.

Soderbergh, Peter A. *Women Marines: The World War II Era.* Westport, Conn.: Praeger Publishers, 1992.

Stremlow, Mary V. *A History of the Women Marines, 1946–1977.* Washington, D.C.: History and Museums Division, Headquarters, U.S. Marine Corps, 1986.

————. *Free a Marine to Fight: Women Marines in World War II.* Washington, D. C.: History and Museums Division, Headquarters, U. S. Marine Corps, 1994.

Vandegrift, A. A. *Once a Marine.* New York: Ballantine Books, Inc., 1982. (Original ed. 1966.)

Von Hassell, Agostino and Keith Crossley. *Warriors: The United States Marines.* Charlottesville, Va.: Howell Press, Inc., 1988.

Women Marines Association. Paducah, Ky.: Turner Publishing Company, 1992.

Women Marines in the 1980s. Washington, D.C.: Division of Public Affairs, Headquarters, U.S. Marine Corps, 1983.

Women's Studies

Alsmeyer, Marie B. *The Way of the WAVES.* Conway, Alaska: Hamba Books, 1981.

Campbell, D'Ann. *Women at War with America.* Cambridge: Harvard University Press, 1984.

————. "Women in Combat: The World War II Experience in the United States, Great Britain, Germany, and the Soviet Union," *The Journal of Military History* 57 (April 1993): 301–323.

Earley, Charity A. *One Woman's Army: A Black Officer Remembers the WAC.* College Station, Tex.: Texas A&M University Press, 1989.

Ebbert, Jean and Marie-Beth Hall. *Crossed Currents: Navy Women from WW I to Tailhook.* Washington, D.C.: Brassey's (U.S.), 1993.

Evans, Sara M. *Born for Liberty: A History of Women in America.* New York: The Free Press, 1989.

Granger, Byrd H. *On Final Approach: The Women Airforce Service Pilots of WW II.* Scottsdale, Ariz.: Falconer Publishing Co., 1991.

Gunter, Helen C. *Navy WAVE: Memories of World War II.* Fort Bragg, Calif.: Cypress House Press, 1992.

Hancock, Joy B. *Lady in the Navy: A Personal Reminiscence.* Annapolis, Md.: U.S. Naval Institute, 1984. (Original ed. 1972.)

Hartmann, Susan M. *The Home Front and Beyond: American Women in the 1940s.* Boston: Twayne Publishers, 1982.

Holm, Jeanne. *Women in the Military: An Unfinished Revolution.* Novato, Calif.: Presidio Press, 1992. (Rev. ed.)

Jacobs, Helen H. *"By Your Leave, Sir": The Story of a WAVE.* New York: Dodd, Mead and Co., 1943.

Lyne, Mary C. and Kay Arthur. *Three Years Behind the Mast: The Story of the United States Coast Guard SPARS.* No publisher. 1946.

Morden, Bettie J. *The Women's Army Corps, 1945–1978.* Washington, D.C.: Center of Military History, 1990.

Stiehm, Judith H. *Arms and the Enlisted Woman.* Philadelphia, Pa.: Temple University Press, 1989.

Stremlow, Mary V. *Coping with Sexism in the Military.* New York: The Rosen Publishing Group, 1990.

Treadwell, Mattie E. *The Women's Army Corps.* Washington, D.C.: Office of the Chief of Military History, Department of the Army, 1954.

Verges, Marianne. *On Silver Wings: The Women Airforce Service Pilots of World War II, 1942–1944.* New York: Ballantine Books, 1991.

Weatherford, Doris. *American Women and World War II.* New York: Facts on File, 1990.

Weirick, Dorothy M. *WAC Days of WWII.* Laguna Niguel, Calif.: Royal Literary Publications, 1992.

Wekesser, Carol, *et al.* (eds.) *Women in the Military.* San Diego: Greenhaven Press, 1991.

Willenz, June A. *Women Veterans: America's Forgotten Heroines.* New York: Continuum Publishing, 1983.

Women in the Military: A Selective Bibliography. Washington, D.C.: Pentagon Library RM 1A518, 1987.

Newspapers, Magazines, Periodicals

American Legion Magazine
Atlanta Constitution
Baton Rouge (La.) *Advocate*
Fortitudine
Leatherneck
Life
Marine Corps *Gazette*
Marine Corps Recruit Depot, Parris Island *Boot*
Marine Corps Schools, Quantico *Sentry*
Marines
MCAS Cherry Point *Windsock*
Naval History
Naval Institute *Proceedings*
Navy Times
New York Times
Parade Magazine
Time Capsule/1950
US News and World Report
USA Today
Variety
WMA *'Nouncements*
The Word

Index

ABOUT THE AUTHOR

PETER A. SODERBERGH is a Professor of Education at Louisiana State University at Baton Rouge. He served as a platoon commander in Korea and resigned from the U.S. Marine Corps as a captain in 1958. He has published nine books and numerous articles in a variety of professional journals and magazines. His most recent work is *Women Marines: The World War II Era* (1992). He is on the Board of Directors of the Marine Corps Historical Center in Washington, D.C.

ISBN 0-275-94827-7

EAN

9 780275 948276

HARDCOVER BAR CODE